# A PASTORAL HANDBOOK FOR ANGLICANS

*Guidelines and resources for pastoral ministry*

The Anglican Church of Australia

Revised and edited by Bradly S Billings

A Pastoral Handbook for Anglicans: guidelines
and resources for pastoral ministry

Copyright © The Anglican Diocese of Melbourne 2018

First published 1988   Published by Acorn Press
                      Based on material supplied by
                      The Anglican Diocese of Melbourne
                      Edited by the Revd Dr Charles Sherlock

Second edition 2001   Updated and edited by
                      the Revd Dr Charles Sherlock

Third edition 2018    Published by Broughton Publishing Pty Ltd
                      Revised, updated, expanded and edited by
                      the Rt Revd Dr Bradly S Billings

All rights reserved. No part of this publication may be reproduced, stored in a retrieval system or transmitted, in any form or by any means electronic, photocopying, recording or otherwise, without the prior written permission of the publisher.

Broughton Publishing Pty Ltd
32 Glenvale Crescent
Mulgrave VIC 3170

ISBN 978 0 9870458 8 1 (pbk)
ISBN 978 0-9870458 9 8 (eBook)

# Contents

| | |
|---|---|
| Foreword | 1 |
| Preface to the 2018 edition | 3 |
|    Changing contexts | 3 |
|    The pastoral services and mission | 6 |
|    Abbreviations | 8 |
|    Definitions | 8 |
| Introduction | 11 |
|    The Ordinal | 11 |
|    Faithfulness in Service | 12 |
|    Pastoral ministry in today's world | 13 |
|    Authorised pastoral ministry | 15 |
|    Pastoral relationships | 15 |
|    Dress for pastoral ministry | 17 |
|    Care of the carers | 20 |
|    The limits of ministry | 22 |
|    A pastoral services policy | 23 |
|    Fees for pastoral ministry | 24 |
| **Chapter One—Pastoral Ministry Today** | 25 |
| Reaching Out Through Pastoral Services | 29 |
|    Reaching Out Through Cross-cultural Community-building | 35 |
|    Reaching Out Through Fresh Expressions | 41 |
|    Conclusion: making connections | 48 |
|    Selected further reading | 50 |
| **Chapter Two—Christian Initiation** | 51 |
| Christian initiation in today's world | 52 |
|    Christian initiation in today's Church | 54 |
|    Renewed practice in initiation | 55 |
|    B1 Baptism in Scripture, theology and Anglican formularies | 57 |
|    B2 The sacrament of Holy Baptism | 60 |
|       B2.1 Word and sacrament | 61 |
|       B2.2 Baptism and faith | 61 |
|       B2.3 Speaking about baptism | 63 |

| | | |
|---|---|---|
| B3 | Who may be baptised? | 65 |
| | B3.1 Some pastoral guidelines | 65 |
| | B3.2 The baptism of infants | 67 |
| | B3.3 The baptism of those able to answer for themselves | 68 |
| B4 | Preparation for baptism | 69 |
| | B4.1 Postponement of baptism | 71 |
| B5 | Extra-parochial situations | 72 |
| | B5.1 Canonical matters | 73 |
| | B5.2 Pastoral matters | 73 |
| | B5.3 Schools and colleges | 75 |
| B6 | Contextual matters | 75 |
| | B6.1 Place | 76 |
| | B6.2 Occasion | 77 |
| | B6.3 Minister | 77 |
| B7 | Liturgical principles and practice | 78 |
| | B7.1 The liturgy | 78 |
| | B7.2 Liturgical furniture and movement | 79 |
| B8 | Symbols and Mode | 82 |
| | B8.1 The water of baptism | 83 |
| | B8.2 Modes for the administration of the water of baptism | 83 |
| | B8.3 Baptismal symbols | 85 |
| | B8.4 Multiple baptisms | 86 |
| B9 | Sponsors | 86 |
| | B9.1 Parental circumstances | 88 |
| B10 | Spiritual renewal | 88 |
| | B10.1 Reaffirmation of faith | 89 |
| | B10.2 'Re-baptism' | 90 |
| | B10.3 Confession and renewal | 91 |
| B11 | Baptism in emergency situations | 92 |
| B12 | 'Conditional' baptism | 93 |
| B13 | Certificates and Registers | 94 |
| B14 | Fees | 95 |
| B15 | Thanksgiving for a Child | 96 |
| C1 | Confirmation in Scripture, theology and Anglican formularies | 98 |
| C2 | Historical & contemporary developments | 100 |
| | C2.1 Historical developments | 100 |
| | C2.2 Contemporary developments | 101 |
| C3 | Who may be confirmed? | 103 |
| C4 | Preparation for confirmation | 104 |

| | | |
|---|---|---|
| C5 | Contextual matters | 105 |
| C6 | Liturgical principles and practice | 105 |
| | C6.1 The liturgy | 106 |
| | C6.2 Liturgical furniture and movement | 107 |
| C7 | Sponsors | 108 |
| C8 | Certificates and Registers | 108 |
| C9 | Fees | 109 |
| C10 | Admission to Holy Communion | 110 |
| | C10.1 The admission of adults to Holy Communion | 110 |
| | C10.2 The admission of children to Holy Communion prior to confirmation | 111 |
| R1 | Reception into communicant membership | 112 |
| R2 | Qualification for holding office | 114 |
| | Resources for Christian Initiation | 115 |
| | Readings from the Bible | 115 |
| | In print | 116 |
| | Links—preparation | 116 |
| | Links—introductions to Christianity and Anglicanism | 117 |
| | Links—liturgical | 118 |

Canon Concerning Baptism 1992 — 119
Canon concerning Confirmation 1992 — 121
Reception Canon 1981 — 122
Canon for the Admission of Children to Holy Communion — 123

**Chapter Three—Marriage** — 125

| | | |
|---|---|---|
| | Human relationships in today's Australia | 126 |
| | Marriage in the Australian context | 128 |
| | Christian responses | 129 |
| M1 | Marriage in Scripture, theology and Anglican formularies | 130 |
| | M1.1 Genesis | 131 |
| | M1.2 The New Testament teaching | 133 |
| | M1.3 The distinctive significance of marriage in Christ | 135 |
| | M1.4 The marriage covenant | 137 |
| | M1.5 Anglican formularies | 138 |
| | M1.6 Weddings in the Church | 138 |
| M3 | Marriage preparation | 140 |
| | M3.1 The rehearsal | 141 |
| M4 | Church requirements | 142 |
| M5 | Contextual matters | 143 |
| | M5.1 The minister | 144 |

- M5.2 According to the rites of the Anglican Church of Australia — 145
- M5.3 Marriages outside of a place consecrated for worship — 146
- M5.4 The time — 147
- M5.5 The marriage of divorced persons — 148
- M5.6 De facto relationships — 150
- M5.7 Particular situations — 151
- M6 Legal requirements — 154
  - M6.1 The rites and ceremonies used — 155
  - M6.2 The Notice of Intended Marriage (NOIM) — 155
  - M6.3 Happily Ever... Before and After — 157
  - M6.4 The declaration of no legal impediment — 158
  - M6.5 The Marriage certificates — 158
  - M6.6 After the wedding ceremony — 160
  - M6.7 Legally invalid marriage — 161
  - M6.8 Same sex marriage — 161
- M7 Liturgical principles and practice — 163
  - M7.1 The liturgy — 164
  - M7.2 Customs and symbols — 165
  - M7.3 Movement and posture — 167
  - M7.4 Readings — 170
  - M7.5 Other readings — 170
  - M7.6 Music and hymns — 171
  - M7.7 'Secular' music — 172
  - M7.8 Holy Communion — 173
  - M7.9 The congregation — 174
- M8 Photography, videography and webcasting — 174
- M9 The Blessing of a Civil Marriage — 176
- M10 The Renewal of Marriage Vows — 177
- M11 After the wedding — 178
  - M11.1 Ministry to those experiencing marriage breakdown — 178
- M12 Fees and charges — 180
- Liturgical resources for marriage ministry — 182
  - Readings from the Old Testament (and apocrypha) — 182
  - Psalms — 182
  - Readings from the New Testament — 182
  - Readings from the Gospels — 183
  - Hymns from 'Together in Song' — 183
  - Prayers — 184
- Resources for marriage ministry — 185

| | |
|---|---|
| Print | 185 |
| Links—Liturgical | 185 |
| Links—civil and legal | 185 |
| Links—preparation | 186 |
| Solemnisation of Matrimony Canon 1981 | 186 |
| Marriage of Divorced Persons Canon 1981 | 188 |

## Chapter Four—Funerals — 191

| | |
|---|---|
| F1 Funeral rites in the Christian tradition | 192 |
|     F1.1 Martyrs and the mass | 193 |
|     F1.2 The Church of England in Australia | 193 |
|     F1.3 Cremation | 194 |
|     F1.4 Secularisation | 195 |
| F2 Principles undergirding the funeral rites in APBA | 196 |
|     F2.1 Theological principles | 196 |
|     F2.2 Liturgical principles | 199 |
|     F2.3 Pastoral principles | 201 |
| F3 Ministry with the Dying | 202 |
| F4 Preparation | 203 |
|     F4.1 When children are involved | 207 |
|     F4.2 When the Coroner is involved | 208 |
| F5 Contextual matters | 209 |
|     F5.1 The type of service | 209 |
|     F5.2 Memorial Services | 210 |
|     F5.3 Cremation before the funeral | 212 |
|     F5.4 A vigil or viewing | 213 |
|     F5.5 The location | 213 |
|     F5.6 The time | 214 |
|     F5.7 The minister | 214 |
|     F5.8 Funeral directors | 215 |
|     F5.9 Recording and webcasting | 217 |
| F6 Liturgical principles and practice | 217 |
|     F6.1 Liturgical considerations | 218 |
|     F6.2 The liturgical 'shape' | 219 |
|     F6.3 Reception of the body | 220 |
|     F6.4 Participation of family and friends | 220 |
|     F6.5 Eulogies and tributes | 221 |
|     F6.6 Audio-visual displays | 223 |
|     F6.7 Psalms and Readings | 224 |

|   |   |   |
|---|---|---|
| | F6.8 Other readings | 225 |
| | F6.9 The sermon | 226 |
| | F6.10 The prayers | 227 |
| | F6.11 Music and hymns | 228 |
| | F6.12 'Secular' music | 229 |
| | F6.13 Holy Communion on the day of a funeral | 230 |
| | F6.14 The Farewell and Committal | 230 |
| | F6.15 Masonic and RSL rites | 231 |
| F7 | Special circumstances | 231 |
| | F7.1 The funeral of a child | 232 |
| | F7.2 The funeral of an infant who has died near the time of birth | 232 |
| | F7.3 Stillborn infants | 233 |
| | F7.4 Suicide | 235 |
| F8 | The interment of ashes | 236 |
| F9 Memorial gardens | | 237 |
| F10 Fees and charges | | 239 |
| F11 Registers | | 240 |
| F12 After the funeral | | 240 |
| F13 Times of tragedy and crisis | | 242 |
| F14 Liturgical resources for funeral ministry | | 242 |
| | Readings from the Old Testament (and apocrypha) | 242 |
| | Psalms | 243 |
| | Readings from the New Testament | 243 |
| | Readings from the Gospels | 244 |
| | Hymns from 'Together in Song' | 244 |
| | Additional prayers | 246 |
| Resources for funeral ministry | | 246 |
| | In print | 246 |
| | Links | 247 |
| A sample funeral ministry checklist | | 247 |
| | | |
| **Chapter Five—Other Pastoral Services** | | **251** |
| O1 | Ministry with the Sick | 251 |
| | O1.1 The visitation of the sick | 252 |
| | O1.2 Holy Communion with the sick | 253 |
| 02 | Ministry with the Dying | 254 |
| | O2.1 The anointing | 256 |
| | A note on assisted dying | 257 |
| O3 | Reconciliation of a Penitent | 258 |

|  |  |  |
|---|---|---|
| | O3.1 Penance and absolution | 260 |
| | O3.2 The 'seal of the confessional' | 261 |
| | Canon law | 261 |
| | Civil law | 263 |
| O4 | Abuse and misconduct | 265 |
| | O4.1 A Litany following sexual abuse | 265 |
| | O4.2 A prayer for healing after sexual misconduct | 266 |
| | O4.3 The prayer for a companion to a person who has been abused | 266 |
| O5 | The Blessing of a Home | 267 |
| O6 | Exorcism | 268 |

| | |
|---|---|
| Canon Concerning Confessions (Revision) Canon 2017 | 268 |
| General resources online | 270 |
| Appendix One—A sample parish policy for pastoral services | 273 |
| Appendix Two—Pastoral Offices and Surplice Fees policy | 281 |

# Foreword

**The Primate, the Most Revd Dr Philip L Freier**

I am personally delighted that a new edition of the widely used *Pastoral Handbook for Anglicans* has been produced under the leadership of one of my Assistant Bishops in the Diocese of Melbourne, Dr Bradly Billings. The Pastoral Handbook draws on the expertise and experience of some of our other senior clergy, together with the wisdom of the diocesan Theological Education Formation, Training and Advisory Group. Dr Billings also worked closely in putting together this new edition with the Revd Dr Charles Sherlock, who had been the editor of the two previous editions of the same *Pastoral Handbook for Anglicans*, both produced in the Diocese of Melbourne in 1988 and 2001 respectively.

We live out our faith, both individually and collectively, in challenging and difficult times. The place of the Christian Church, and the integrity of its witness, has been increasingly called into question. Despite this, many in the community continue to seek the pastoral services of the Anglican Church, both for themselves and for their children and loved ones. We continue, as a church, to exercise the deep and meaningful privilege of ministering to our fellow Australians at times of both sorrow and joy in the provision of rites of Christian initiation such as baptism and confirmation, at marriages, and funerals, and in other ways. These services of the church continue to be central to faithful Anglicans across our parishes, schools, agencies and other communities, as they have been over the course of our long history.

This new edition of *A Pastoral Handbook for Anglicans* arises directly out of the previous two, which are well used and widely trusted by

Anglicans in Melbourne, and across Australia, as a source of pastoral wisdom and authority, for ministry in these often complex situations. It has now been complemented by the extensive academic, liturgical and pastoral experience brought to it by Dr Billings, a published scholar of the New Testament and early Christianity. He served as a parish priest in the Diocese of Melbourne, prior to taking up his episcopal role, and has conducted numerous pastoral services, in particular during his time as vicar of St John's Toorak. He is now the diocesan Director of Theological Education, responsible for the training and formation of new clergy, and the professional development and wellbeing of all clergy.

I expect this new edition of *A Pastoral Handbook for Anglicans* will be a valuable and useful resource for all involved in pastoral ministry, and especially the provision of the pastoral services, across the diversity of the Anglican Church of Australia. I warmly commend it for the widest possible use, and pray it will enable all who seek its counsel to be effective in proclaiming the unchanging gospel of our Lord in the changing social environment of early 21st century Australia. It is my hope that all that is said and done in the context of the pastoral services and ministries of the Church may honour Christ, commend his gospel, and build up his Church.

# Preface to the 2018 edition

**The Rt Revd Dr Bradly Billings**

This revised edition of *A Pastoral Handbook for Anglicans* (the 'Handbook') builds on, and both updates and complements, two earlier versions: the first published in 1988 and the second in 2001, both edited by The Revd Dr Charles Sherlock. For many years *A Pastoral Handbook for Anglicans* (2001 edition) has been provided to newly ordained deacons by the Anglican Diocese of Melbourne, to assist them in the early stages of their ministry, and as a training resource for the first year program of Post Ordination Training. The Handbook is also widely used by clergy of the diocese as a point of reference and authority on the range of matters it covers, and indeed, I have extensively used it myself in the course of my own ministry. I know many others have, and still do, for when news broke that a new version was under consideration a number of colleagues were immediately in touch, eager to obtain a copy.

## Changing contexts

Since the publication of the 2001 version, much has changed in Australian society, whilst conversely, in terms of the practice and provision of pastoral ministry, it can be said that nothing much has changed at all. People are still people, with the same hopes, desires, flaws and needs, sharing equally in the human condition and in their need for God. Anglicans continue to conduct the rites of Christian initiation, weddings and funerals, as they always have, using forms of liturgy that have their source in the *Book of Common Prayer* and extend back much further in time to the rites and ceremonies of the pre-Reformation church. Even so, there have been many changes in Australian society since 2001, which have had an impact on the provision of the pastoral services in many parts of the church.

To identify just a few, there has been a marked increase in many places in adult converts seeking baptism who were not presented for Holy Baptism as infants, and there are more requests now for memorial services (funerals at which the body of the deceased is not present) reflective of recent trends in how we are dealing with grief and bereavement. Since 2001, requests for audio-visual displays at funerals have become more common, and it is now widely possible for a wedding or funeral to be webcast online in real time. Other changes have been legal—the Australian government, for instance, has in recent years amended the Marriage Act 1961 in regards to the type of identification that can be provided by those seeking marriage, and in changing the periods of time in which notice must be given to the celebrant.

Substantial changes in terms of corporate governance were introduced to the Diocese of Melbourne by the passage of the Parish Governance Act 2013, and there have been some important new Canons, and some significant amendments to existing Canons, at meetings of the General Synod since 2001, several of which have been adopted by the Diocese of Melbourne. At the 2004 meeting of General Synod, a national code of conduct for clergy and church workers, Faithfulness in Service, was adopted, this having significant implications for ministry, and ministers, across the Australian church.

## The revision team

In light of these several changes and the passage of time since 2001, together with the rapidly changing context in which we proclaim the unchanging Gospel of our Lord, a new edition of a Pastoral Handbook for Anglicans was called for, and much anticipated. This volume was commissioned by the Theological Education, Formation & Training Advisory Group (successor to the Board for Ministry) in the Anglican

Diocese of Melbourne, and is a shared work, produced by a team of experienced clergy who worked together on the material, carefully revising each of the chapters, as a ministry of service to, and as a resource for, the wider church. These included Canon Dr Colleen O'Reilly, the Vicar of St George's Malvern; Canon Dr Rhys Bezzant, Dean of missional leadership & lecturer in Christian thought at Ridley College Melbourne; and The Revd Jan Joustra, the vicar of St Andrew's Brighton and an Examining Chaplain in the Diocese of Melbourne. Colleen, Rhys and Jan have applied their significant pastoral, theological and liturgical experience and skills to the task, and each has greatly improved and enhanced the final product, including making numerous helpful and useful suggestions, and bringing clarity and accuracy to the text.

Whilst the focus in the previous two versions of the Handbook on the pastoral services (baptism and confirmation, weddings, funerals) is maintained, a new chapter has been added to include some of the 'other' pastoral services. These include Ministry with the Sick, Ministry with the Dying, and the Reconciliation of a Penitent. Another new addition to this revised edition of the Handbook is an extended reflection on 'Pastoral Ministry Today' by The Revd Dr Stephen Burns, Associate Professor and Coordinator of Research at Trinity College Theological School, Melbourne. Stephen reflects on the contextual situation of Australia, and Australians, at this time, drawing on his extensive experience and expertise in pastoral ministry, and applying this to the conduct of our mission and ministry in the form of the pastoral services.

Although revised, and in some places updated, to reflect contemporary changes, and expanded, as outlined above, this new edition has its origins firmly in the 2001 edition of A Pastoral Handbook for Anglicans edited by The Revd Dr Charles Sherlock. It retains the same framework throughout, and, in many places, much of the same text. I am especially grateful, and indebted to Dr Sherlock, not just for his past work as editor of the previous two editions of this Handbook, but for being willing also to read successive drafts of this new edition, and to apply his considerable experience and expertise to the content. As noted above, much of the 2001 text has been retained, in particular the introduction, and the pastoral, theological and liturgical principles undergirding each of the chapters on Christian initiation, marriage and funerals. These sections are as fresh and relevant today as when originally composed, and were written with a keen eye to the missional context of the Church at the commencement of the 21st century. Dr Sherlock also made many helpful suggestions, and offered wise counsel and advice on the new text, especially where it was straying from its foundations in applied pastoral ministry.

**The pastoral services and mission**

I believe this new edition of the Pastoral Handbook is timely for a number of reasons, the foremost of which is the missional context in which we find ourselves in early 21st century Australia. The insights of the mission shaped church project tell us that, whereas in the 1970s near to 70 percent of practicing Christians could trace their 'conversion' to a datable moment or event, by the final decade of the 20th century the reverse was true, with 69 percent describing their 'conversion' as a gradual process or journey that could not be dated to a definable moment or event.[1] This concords with the trend discernible in the early 21st century for converts to Christ in this post-Christian age to belong before believing, with the behaving (modification of lifestyle) often coming last of all.[2] Expecting those, who do not yet belong, to both believe and behave would seem a reactionary and unhelpful starting point in this social milieu.

---

1　Dave Tomlinson, *The post-evangelical* (London: Triangle, 1995), p. 143.
2　The Church of England, *Mission Shaped Church: Church planting and fresh expressions of church in a changing context* (London: Church House publishing, 2004).

For many who are not people of Christian faith, or whom have been in the past but have strayed from the church, a pastoral service may well be the point of re-entry, at which a seed is sown, watered, and, with prayer and the activity of the Spirit, will begin to bear fruit. Indeed, it is likely that more Australians will come into contact with an Anglican Church through attending a baptism, marriage or funeral, than the number who will come to a Christmas service. Most clergy rightly invest considerable time and energy into ensuring the Christmas services they lead are accessible to those who are not regular churchgoers and might have a focus on facilitating engagement, or re-engagement, with the Christian faith and the claims of Jesus. There is a good case, then, for thinking about the pastoral services in the same missional way.

Although this new revision, and the previous two editions of this Handbook, were commissioned by, and written for, the Diocese of Melbourne, most of the content will be applicable and relevant across the Anglican Church of Australia, being based on a shared heritage of Anglican pastoral theology, and the liturgical elements being grounded firmly in, and arising directly out of, A Prayer Book for Australia 1995. Those in dioceses other than Melbourne will only need to bear in mind whether the Canons referred to have been adopted in their own diocese, and adapt the occasional references to parish governance specific to Melbourne to their own context.

I trust this new edition of a Pastoral Handbook for Anglicans will be a useful and helpful resource for both the exercise of pastoral ministry across the Anglican Diocese of Melbourne and beyond, as well as a practical resource for mission, and a help to making known the good news about Jesus Christ among the many Australians who, every day, come to us seeking Christian ministry at times of sorrow, joy and need.

**The Rt Revd Dr Bradly S Billings**
The Feast of St Andrew, Apostle and Martyr, 2017

## Abbreviations

| | |
|---|---|
| AAPB | An Australian Prayer Book 1978 |
| APBA | A Prayer Book for Australia 1995 |
| BCP | Book of Common Prayer 1662 (and/or other versions, e.g. 1928, where specified) |

## Definitions

| | |
|---|---|
| Article | One of the 39 Articles of Religion. |
| Bishop | The bishop with whom there is an existing pastoral relationship (e.g. an area or regional bishop), and/or the diocesan bishop or Archbishop. |
| Candidate | In Christian initiation, a candidate is the person who seeks baptism and/or confirmation, admission to Holy Communion, or reception into communicant membership. |
| Canon | A law or regulation made by a church authority. In this Handbook the Canons referred to have been made and passed by the General Synod and subsequently adopted by the Diocese of Melbourne, and therefore have force in the Diocese of Melbourne. |
| Diocese | in this Handbook, the Anglican Diocese of Melbourne. |
| Minister | The person who conducts a rite or ceremony of the church—this may be a bishop, priest, deacon or authorised lay minister. |
| Parent | The term 'parent' encompasses legal guardian/s where applicable. |
| Parishioner | A person who is eligible to be on a parish electoral roll, as defined in the Parish Governance Act 2013 s 9(3), in force in the Diocese of Melbourne. |

| Rubric | An instruction or direction concerning the conduct of a service of worship. From the Latin ruber (red), because in successive books of Common Prayer such directions were printed in red so as to distinguish them from the text of the service. |

# Introduction

All people are created in the image of God and are of equal value. This is the foundation of all pastoral relationships (Faithfulness in Service 3.1).

Pastoral care is a basic facet of all Christian ministry, and is always exercised in the context of relationships to and with others. Effective pastoral ministry is, and has been throughout the long history of the Christian Church, a key factor in commending the gospel way of life, which Jesus embodied, while poor or insensitive ministry not only distorts gospel proclamation, but also brings the Church into disrepute.

This Handbook has been compiled to assist the pastoral ministry of all who work under the auspices of the Anglican Church in the Diocese of Melbourne, and will also, it is anticipated, be of usefulness and relevance (with some adaptation) to those in any of the 23 dioceses of the Anglican Church of Australia. In most cases guidelines, models and suggestions are set out rather than rules: the overall aim is to set a benchmark for pastoral ministry that commends both Christ's gospel and his Church. The Handbook thus seeks to cover the most commonly encountered situations in which pastoral care is exercised, along with policies that touch on areas of pastoral relationship.

## The Ordinal

The Ordinal describes the nature, purpose and meaning of the three 'orders' of ministry of deacon, priest, and bishop within in the life of the church (APBA p. 780). All of those who are ordained should seek to maintain an awareness of the content of the Ordinal as applicable to their ordination. Careful attention should be given, in particular, to the exhortation, and to the promises and affirmations, which are of course quite intentionally made in a public forum at the ordination service.

The full version of APBA contains the Ordinal, and sets out the text of the exhortation and examination, for each of the three orders:
- At the ordination of deacons (APBA pp. 785–787);
- At the ordination of priests (APBA pp. 793–795);
- At the ordination of bishops (APBA pp. 800–804).

It is good spiritual discipline for those ordained to actively seek out opportunities for a public 'renewal of ordination vows', to be reminded of the content of the Ordinal, and to renew one's commitment to it in a public setting, with others.

### Faithfulness in Service

The 2004 session of General Synod promulgated Faithfulness in Service to be 'a national code for personal behaviour and the practice of pastoral ministry by clergy and church workers'. The Diocese of Melbourne, along with most dioceses of the Anglican Church of Australia, has adopted Faithfulness in Service with some slight modifications to reflect legislation specific to the diocese. Faithfulness in Service, as adopted and amended by the Synod of the Diocese of Melbourne, functions as the code of conduct applicable to all clergy and church workers in the diocese. The current version is readily available via the Melbourne diocesan website (at the link below) or from The Anglican Centre and/ or via Kooyoora (the professional standards scheme company for the dioceses of Melbourne and Bendigo).

http://www.melbourneanglican.org.au/Whoweare/Governance/professionalstandards/Pages/professionalstandards.aspx

It is important that clergy and church workers are aware of their obligations under Faithfulness in Service and in particular:
- The requirement that all clergy and church workers bear a responsibility to ensure that personal behavior and practices of pastoral

ministry that are inconsistent with the code of conduct are not tolerated or covered up (3.3);
- That it is the responsibility of each cleric and church worker to be aware of, and to meet the standards of, the code (3.7);
- That those having overall authority in a church body bear the further responsibility of assuring that all clergy and church workers under their leadership and authority are made aware of the code (3.8).

It is a matter of fundamental importance that clergy and church workers are aware of the particular form of Faithfulness in Service and/or any other code of conduct in force in their diocese, and are familiar with the contents thereof.

## Pastoral ministry in today's world

In days gone by, most Australians had some idea of Christian teaching, of 'what went on in church', and could join in the Lord's Prayer and some hymns at least. Except for those who are churchgoers, this is no longer the case. Yet many have a sense of God, occasionally offer prayers, or show significant interest in spirituality. For many people in today's Australia, the initial or only contact they may have with the church is through one of the 'occasional offices'—baptism, marriage, ministry at a time of illness or crisis, or a funeral. For the sake of Christ, it is essential that those who represent the Church of God do so in such a way as to commend gospel truth.

The context of pastoral care embraces parish and sector ministries, both of which have been undergoing significant change in recent decades. At the parish level, social changes have taken place gradually, in particular affecting the ways in which local congregations relate to their surrounding community. In educational contexts, change has been faster, for example, the increasing length of schooling, the emphasis placed on vocational training in tertiary education, and the diversification of youth sub-cultures. In welfare contexts, change has sometimes been rapid, for example, developments in medical technology, or government policies such as de-institutionalisation and case-mix funding, which has shifted hospital chaplains' roles more towards emergency care than ongoing relationships. The style of pastoral ministry required in today's diverse and changing society is thus becoming more varied.

The example of Jesus, the 'chief shepherd' (I Peter 5.2) and 'great pastor of the flock' (Hebrews 13.20) is primary in all pastoral ministry. Jesus lay down his life for the sheep, loving us to the end, but is never patronising. His ministry encounters are noteworthy for their particularity and pro-active nature: it is a theological professor who is told to be 'born again', a rich young ruler asked to give away his wealth, a poor widow commended for her generosity, 'unclean' people who are touched.

In the light of this, the idea that pastoral care is basically a 'reactive' ministry must be questioned. Sometimes a reactive stance is the only option, but as a basic pattern of care it easily degenerates to merely keeping people comfortable, producing an inward looking character to ministry. Such an approach takes the 'flock' imagery of sheep blindly following a leader much too far. It creates dependent children rather than adults mature in Christ. A Christian pastoral attitude does not call for merely a reactive, 'easy options' response, but demands the cost of following the sacrificial example of Christ.

Caring for those in need is a vital dimension of pastoral ministry. The 'curative' approach is complemented by 'preventative' pastoral ministry: Christ's call to proclaim his life-transforming message and set forward what is right and just, not least by example ('by life and doctrine'). Pastoral care thus has a strongly missional dimension, seeking actively to live out the gospel in today's society, serving others so that they may know the dignity of being the child of God, and stand on their own feet in the full humanity of Jesus Christ.

## Authorised pastoral ministry

As noted above, Jesus is set before us in the scriptures as the 'good' and 'great' shepherd/pastor, who laid down his life for the sheep. Those who exercise pastoral care in the name of Christ, ordained or not, are called to a ministry involving at least these aspects:
- To seek out the 'lost' so that they may share in the fullness of life, which Christ intends for all;
- So to feed Christ's flock as to enable each member to live as an effective disciple in daily life, both in personal living and in the wider structures of society in which they take part;
- To tend and care for those who are wounded or in need, so that, knowing the love of God, they may be brought to true health;
- To be advocates on behalf of those who suffer disadvantage, injustice or neglect.

According to the Ordinal, these ministries are close to those of a bishop, the 'chief pastor' in the local church. This similarity points to the reality that no one engaged in pastoral care does so by themselves: ministering in the name of Christ, they are inseparably related to the ministry of the whole Church. Pastoral ministry thus has corporate and collegial aspects, and is undertaken in conjunction with other ministers. Therefore, those who engage in pastoral care as an authorised ministry (signified by license or authority from the bishop) are to work in such a way as to support, and be supported by, others in the ministry team of the diocese. Pastoral ministry suffers when people act as 'loners,' and also when they never show initiative.

## Pastoral relationships

People invest enormous amounts of energy in pastoral ministry, seeing it as an expression of deeply held beliefs. Human personality types vary greatly, however, and interact with different styles of upbringing, life and work experiences, and theological convictions—not least among church members and leaders. Given this, authorised ministers should be aware of, and understand, the ways in which different personality types are likely to interact: the Myers-Briggs or Enneagram analyses are useful tools in this regard.

Good pastoral relationships need to be sustained and modelled at all levels of the church. The way in which clergy have regard for one another (including bishops), for example, will commend healthy relationships to and with others, or undermine them. Courtesy (or good manners) is a significant aspect of this: those called to minister in Christ's name are called to work together, and not against one another. Sometimes relationships between clergy will be robust, but maintaining respect for one another's ministry and person, and sustaining a loyalty to the vocation to which each is called, is essential. As diversity among the church's members and leaders grows, the need for sensitivity across an increasingly wide range of issues deepens, so that communication remains open, and misunderstandings are avoided.

Courteous sensitivity includes care about forms of address. In Australian society today, many people happily operate on a first-name basis. For parishioners and priest to be on a first-name basis, for example, can be a healthy sign of mutual respect and openness in a Christian community. However, there are times when this is inappropriate, for example, when addressing the priest at a formal function, someone who in other circumstances would use the first name would not do so on this occasion. In schools, respecting policy about the use of names and titles is an important aspect of sharing in the institution's life and loyalties. Similarly, in hospitals or other community structures, it is courteous to use language that is appropriate to the institutional or corporate culture. Some Australians, and some ethnic or migrant cultures, are more formal about names and titles, and find casual attitudes towards leaders demeaning to the office they hold. It can cause needless offence to the name of Christ to be either aggressively informal or stiffly correct.

Courtesy in pastoral relationships looks beyond those immediately involved in a situation towards all who might be included. For example, when a beloved church member dies, the sensitive parish priest will not only seek to minister to present parishioners, but will instinctively notify previous clergy or lay leaders of the death, and where appropriate invite them to take part in the funeral. (A similar reciprocity of care will be shown by former clergy to those who currently bear pastoral responsibility for the parish.) Likewise, a pastorally courteous hospital chaplain will look actively for opportunities to notify parish clergy about people in their care. Such attitudes cannot be legislated for: they express an intuitive sense of the corporate, inter-dependent nature of pastoral ministry.

A further aspect of 'clergy manners' is respect for boundaries, both personal and structural. At the personal level, examples of this are keeping confidences, not spreading gossip or bad news, and recognising where intervention in a situation may be inappropriate or helpful. Geography is a sensitive structural boundary in parish ministry: one example is the way in which baptism enquiries from 'outside' the parish are handled—clergy can collude in going along with a 'rigorist' stereotype of other parish priests, so undermining both effective baptismal discipline and collegial loyalty. In sector ministries it is professional boundaries, and the relationships between church and agency (especially where the latter is the employer) that need to be given due respect.

**Dress for pastoral ministry**

How you dress says a great deal about the way you understand yourself, and your relationship to others. In community life, sensitivity is needed as to when casual or formal attire matters. The issues involved will differ between parishes, and in school and institutional chaplaincy, but the underlying principles remain.

Two particular forms of clergy dress have emerged in the Christian tradition, and been given formal expression in Anglican formularies.

The first is dress appropriate for public life—since the mid-19th century reflected in the wearing of a clergy collar, or more recently by lapel or pendant crosses. Clergy public dress has changed over the generations, and no legislative requirement governs it. Nevertheless, in many situations it is important that clergy be easily identifiable—in civic emergencies, or visiting hospitals, for example. On other occasions, however—where wearing a collar could be seen as maintaining an inappropriate 'Christendom' perspective, or as an unnecessary barrier—it may be better for clergy to be seen as 'normal' citizens.

The second area is the forms of clergy dress appropriate for the variety of public ministries. Anglican formularies and legislation require clergy normally to be robed while engaging in public ministry. This is questioned in some circles today: it is rightly argued that clergy can 'hide' behind robes, or allow distinctive dress to put up barriers to others (whether Christian or not). Some also argue that distinctive clergy dress can act as a barrier to people seeking for God. Experience indicates, however, that many people continue to welcome the public identification of Christian leaders—whether in church or in public life. The crucial issue is the quality of the ministry offered, more than the robes that are worn.

Whatever the problems, there are sound reasons for maintaining the principle that clergy exercising public ministry should continue to dress distinctively:

a) Robes indicate that clergy are representative persons. While the particular personality of a minister displays Christian truth in a personal way, there is also the danger of personality coming ahead of responsibility. Robes establish a 'distance' between the minister as a particular individual, and as someone called to exercise responsibility among God's people.

b) Robes are a tangible sign that those who are called to minister in the authority of Christ do so as part of a tradition that stretches backwards (and forwards) from our own day. Traditional designs may have derived from the court dress of earlier ages, but today's robes (notably the ecumenical 'cassalb') are cut in a 'timeless' style, which transcends particular fashions in clothing.

c) On occasions such as weddings or baptisms, where many visitors may be present, robes enable such people to identify who is presiding (the 'God-person'). When emotions may be running deep, as at a funeral, the robed officiant is more readily able to be the 'still point' in a whirling sea, and represent things that transcend the transient.

d) Robes are a great 'leveler': they remove differences between clergy of different (sub)culture or class, economic circumstance, or dress sense, and help build bridges between them. Even in Christian traditions where clergy are not required to dress distinctively, most adopt some style of 'uniform', which marks them as different. Robes avoid the unhelpful aspects of personal taste, yet can bring a splash of colour and liveliness to a drab situation, and mark the changes of 'mood' throughout the church year.

One further issue is the view that certain vestments (notably the chasuble) carry false doctrinal meanings. The 1992 General Synod 'Canon Concerning the Vesture of Ministers', adopted by the Diocese of Melbourne, declares that this Church 'does not attach any particular doctrinal significance to the diversity of vesture worn by its ministers'. In the light of this, while some will continue to prefer not to wear particular vestments, doctrinal considerations about different robes are excluded. When visiting another parish or church agency, courtesy suggests that clergy wear what is appropriate, and invitations should take this into account.

Above all, clergy public dress should be neat, clean and avoid undue show. A good dressmaker/tailor will see to it that garments fit comfortably, 'hang' and wear well, and resist soiling. Where items such as stoles are decorated with embroidery, symbols used are to point to Christian truth, and be easily recognisable to others—primarily autobiographical decoration is to be avoided.

## Care of the carers

All involved in Christian ministry will appreciate the need to develop a healthy respect for their own limitations, and to make adequate provision for their own self-care and wellbeing.

- Maintain a healthy lifestyle and do not over-commit yourself. Make sure you have adequate leisure time, through regularly taking time off, including your full holiday entitlement annually (Faithfulness in Service 4.21).

The diocesan program for clergy wellbeing includes a library of resources and referrals hosted on the website of the Bishop Perry Institute for Ministry & Mission, including details of places of spiritual retreat, spiritual direction, professional supervision, and coaching. Clergy, and the members of their immediate family (if applicable), of the Diocese of Melbourne also have access to the diocesan Employee Assistance Program (EAP), which provides up to three anonymous and fully funded sessions with a qualified counsellor, with the possibility of further sessions and/or referral as may be appropriate.

http://bishopperryinstitute.org.au/wellbeing/

In exercising Christian ministry, the effective pastor will recognise that he or she is a particular person with a distinctive personality, upbringing, skills and culture. Each has strengths and weaknesses, needs, dreams and struggles, which grow and are transformed as time passes, circumstances change and experiences deepen.

In view of this, it needs to be recognised that caring entails reciprocal ministries: those who care are ministered to in their caring, but also need to receive care apart from the ministry context. The bishop is the person who carries ultimate responsibility to see that this occurs, but it is impossible for this to be done personally. Clergy and authorised lay ministers should both expect that they will be offered structures of care, and also be open to receiving these.

Support structures need to offer confidentiality and appropriate self-disclosure at the personal level, with opportunities for revision and enhancement at the collegial level. They need to have a definite intentional character, so that growth and development can be noted and planned. A sense of playful zest will be part of healthy pastoral support, alongside creative and routine structures. Above all, support must embody a climate of trust and acceptance sufficiently robust to embrace honest critical comment, and to hear appropriate compliments.

Such support structures will usually include:

- A disciplined life of both personal and corporate prayer, including regular retreats and quiet days for spiritual refreshment;
- Opportunities for regular reading, study and ongoing professional development;
- Places to tell the good stories, as well as facing inadequacies: in short, regular accountability (for example, the pastoral report at pastoral council, the annual ministry review);
- At least one person with whom the personal life of faith can be regularly reviewed and shared (a spiritual advisor, director or mentor);
- A trained person with whom the practices of pastoral work can be reviewed regularly, and confidential professional matters can be shared, so as to help ministry be more effective (this is what is meant by 'supervision');
- A support network—in many cases informal—in which the various dimensions of pastoral ministry can be shared in a collegial environment (for example, a parish or agency staff team, the deanery, a regular lunch with other trusted clergy);
- Regular review of the 'techniques' of pastoral ministry—possibly with a ministry coach (for example, the way in which a funeral is

prepared and conducted, or how liturgical changes are assessed and integrated in a particular person's ministry);
- An openness to seek personal help when needed (for example, medical, marriage or psychological counselling) possibly at first instance through the diocesan Employee Assistance Program for clergy;
- Trusted friends and colleagues to meet with socially.

Such structures of support are particularly significant at times of transition in ministry. Some are more visible—ordination, the move from theological college to curacy, induction or retirement—and receive public recognition. Others, however, are less obvious but may be more difficult, especially where a life crisis (such as unemployment, marriage breakdown or chronic illness) is involved. Putting emergency structures in place in such situations may be a case of too little, too late. Ideally, regular structures are able to be adapted to the crisis, or augmented appropriately, so that in due course 'normal' ministry can be resumed. In all of this, it needs to be recognised that, as human beings, we never 'go back' to where we were, but journey on through good and ill, to give final account of our stewardship to Christ.

## The limits of ministry

Pastoral ministry finds its inspiration and direction in the good news of God in Christ. Yet such ministry is grounded in the realities of common life. As church and society have changed in relationship over the past fifty years, individual counselling has come to take a greater role in pastoral ministry. However, those who are authorised to minister in the name of Christ have a prime responsibility to maintain their focus on their distinctive calling to 'build up the body of Christ' through the ministry of Word and Sacraments. Further, the skills of professionals in such areas as relationship and grief counselling, industrial relations, management consultancy and the like, need to be respected and welcomed.

Pastoral ministry thus entails knowing one's own limits and priorities. It means being willing to refer people with particular needs, or in situations beyond one's competence or calling, for specific and professional help. Skills to 'read' a particular situation, and take preventative steps by appropriate referral, are a valuable asset in caring. At the heart of pastoral ministry lies the offering—in humility, joy and awe—of the resources of prayer, scripture, sacraments and godly wisdom, which the Christian tradition continues to offer.

Faithfulness in Service provides the following, helpful advice:

Recognise the limits of your skills and experience. Do not undertake any ministry (such as relationship counselling, counselling for abuse or addictions, or an exorcism) that is beyond your competence or the role for which you have been employed or trained. If in doubt seek advice. A person who requires specialised help should be referred to an appropriately qualified person or agency (4.12).

## A pastoral services policy

The chapters that follow in this Handbook seek to unfold guidelines for pastoral practice, which both maintain the integrity of this vision, and also encourage clergy and other authorised ministers—with the communities of faith of which they are a part—to shape creative initiatives of caring in the name of Christ.

It is impossible, however, for a Handbook of this nature to anticipate and address every situation that might arise in the context of pastoral ministry. Further, a wide variety of practise exists across the diocese in regards to how requests for pastoral services are handled, what fees are applied, and a range of other matters. It is highly recommended that parishes and other worship communities develop a policy for the provision of the pastoral services that has been agreed to by the parish council, or equivalent body, and which is easily accessible and available, and known to and owned by all.

A sample of such policy, which can be used as a template for adaptation at local level, is included in this Handbook in Appendix One.

**Fees for pastoral ministry**

The Anglican Church of Australia inherited from the Church of England the notion that when a priest is inducted to a 'living' he or she is entitled to the stipend and to all 'surplice fees' for weddings and funerals conducted in the parish, no matter by whom they are conducted. By 'surplice fees' is meant amounts paid to the priest, as distinct from other charges that may be made for the use of church facilities, or for the services of people other than the minister, for example, organists, cleaners, vergers, or other specialist staff.

Notwithstanding the inherited principle of parochial entitlement, significant diversity exists across the Anglican Church with regard to fees for weddings and funerals, whilst the number of weddings and funerals, and the demands for such ministry, varies considerably from parish to parish, as it does in Anglican schools and colleges. Clergy are, furthermore, bound to ensure that all their financial arrangements meet the requirements of taxation law.

The Anglican Diocese of Melbourne has produced, in 2014, a 'Pastoral Offices and Surplice Fees policy' to guide clergy and parishes in the light of these complexities—see Appendix Two.

Note: the gospel sacraments of Holy Baptism and Holy Communion should never be subject to fees, and any freewill offerings in connection with them should go into parish funds.

# Chapter One

## Pastoral Ministry Today
**Stephen Burns**

This chapter engages with trends and trajectories in Australian society, and these as they impact the church.[3] Reflection centres on:
1. Ministry around pastoral services;
2. Cross-cultural community-building;
3. Fresh expressions of church.

But by no means do all persons who seek the church for pastoral services think alike or have the same expectations; not all migrant experience is akin; and fresh expressions of church can be diverse. More than that: nor do the gifts, convictions and preferences of all congregations, public ministers or other Christians fit with only one of the modes of ministry explored in what follows. For these reasons, the words 'some' and 'may' are important in my reflections, and their configuration in phrases like 'some people may…' Regular use of provisional words reminds us that what we are exploring is not solid moulds into which all people fit, or blueprints to which all people conform, but something more complex. We need to make connections across trajectories as part of deft thinking about pastoral ministry today.

Furthermore, although these reflections do not shy away from facing the cultural flux in which the church offers ministry, here and now, in

---

3   In addition to references in the footnotes, this essay draws on various research papers published on the website of the Bishop Perry Institute (http://www.bishopperryinstitute.org.au) as well as unpublished research commissioned by the Diocese of Melbourne, which was produced by Gary Bouma ('The Church and Socio-cultural Change,' 2013) and Philip Hughes ('The Anglican Church in a Changing Melbourne: Implications for Ministry,' nd).

Victoria, it also needs to be grasped that some things stay the same: God loves the world, and God is 'infinite in mercy, welcoming sinners'[4] in Christ Jesus. Jesus is good news; he is risen, redeeming, and reliable. In Christ we might yet, as one poet puts it, 'taste bread, freshness, the honey of being'.[5] The Spirit bestowed by God is still moving over the face of the earth, making home in open hearts, breathing life through the scriptures, and giving signs of the divine reign.[6] In the strong name of the Spirit-filled Jesus, liberty from hurt and harm, justice for the last and least, new life and unusual kindness all occur. God is faithful.[7]

These starting convictions matter because confidence and joy in the gospel contains, copes with and enables the squaring up to difficulties which is necessary to flourishing in pastoral ministry amidst the 'changes and chances'[8] of contemporary cultures. And those changes are rapid. Since the last edition of this Handbook—in 2001[9]—much has shifted in Australia, and the Anglican Church is caught up in it. A lot of the church growth that has occurred in the last decade and a half is related to the incoming of ethnic minorities and other immigrants. Other growth has happened in communities with reconfigured relationships to historic Anglican forms of liturgy and polity, but that nevertheless embody deep-down Anglican verve about proclaiming the ancient and durable gospel

---

4   APBA p. 126.
5   James McAuley, 'In the Twentieth Century,' *Collected Poems, 1936–1970* (Sydney: Angus and Robertson, 1971).
6   For evocative reflection on the Spirit-giving signs—including speaking in tongues, worship after genocide, the intimate care of persons with disabilities, and joyful noise by jazz bands, see David F. Ford, 'In the Spirit: Seeking Wisdom, Giving Signs,' Jane Williams, ed., *The Holy Spirit in the World Today* (London: Alpha International, 2011), pp. 42–63.
7   The scriptural texture of this paragraph can be mapped out from Gen. 1.2, Ps. 86.15, Ps. 104.30, Isa. 61.1, John 3.16, Acts 28.2, 1 Cor. 1.9, 1 Cor. 3.16, 2 Tim. 3.16, et cetera.
8   BCP, the first collect for use after the administration of Holy Communion.
9   Charles Sherlock (ed), *A Pastoral Handbook for Anglicans: Guidelines for Pastoral Ministry in the Anglican Diocese of Melbourne* (Brunswick East, Vic: Acorn, 2001).

afresh in each generation.[10] Yet these key growth points notwithstanding, national census material for 2011[11] reveals that numbers of those identifying as Anglican, and those attending Anglican worship, are on the slide. Anglicanism is among other old-line traditions that are marked in many places by what Gary Bouma calls 'increasingly geriatric assemblies',[12] in which two or even three generations of younger persons are absent.

In the same period (since 2001) global Anglicanism has shown new fractures. In some ways, the Anglican Communion at large has been marked by features that have a long history in its Australian form: diocesanism, unilateralism, and clenched withdrawal from wider forums.[13] These have each played their part in the drama of the Communion in recent years. And the global strains in our tradition around some churches' welcome, and others' rejection, of lesbian, gay and transgendered persons, are connected to quite local issues, at least if Australian commentators are correct to point to the church's official (which is not necessarily to say, popular) views of sexuality as a stumbling-block for onlookers. For example, recent research on youth ministry in Australia contends that 'the majority of young people look at the churches with some suspicion and even disdain. Many see them as irrelevant and out of date. They see them as exclusive and intolerant, even repressive,

---

10  City on a Hill is an example in the Diocese of Melbourne, with centres in Melbourne, Geelong and elsewhere, including interstate: see https://cityonahill.com.au
11  The chapter was written just after the 2016 census, but without the benefit of access to its findings.
12  Cf. Gary D. Bouma, *Being Faithful in Diversity* (Hindmarsh, SA: ATF Press, 2011), p. 13.
13  On global Anglicanism by an Australian author, see Bruce Kaye, *An Introduction to World Anglicanism* (Cambridge: Cambridge University Press, 2009) and Bruce Kaye, *Conflict and the Practice of Christian Faith: The Anglican Experiment* (Eugene, OR: Cascade, 2009). More broadly, see Mark Chapman, Sathianathan Clarke & Martyn Percy (ed)., *The Oxford Handbook of Anglican Studies* (Oxford: Oxford University Press, 2015) for a range of relevant articles. On the situation in Australia, see, amongst other things, Tom Frame, *A House Divided? The Quest for Unity Within Anglicanism* (Brunswick East, Vic: Acorn Press, 2010).

particularly in relation to different expressions of sexuality.'[14] A particularly stark and distressing—and utterly unavoidable—truth is that, as Royal Commissions have shown us, the church's cultures have sheltered those who would abuse the vulnerable young, and so young and other people's suspicions have sometimes been sadly well-founded.

Though aspects of this situation are clearly bleak, there is nothing to be gained from evading the facts. We need to remember that if we are to engage here in pastoral theology, it involves 'resolutely refusing to engage in theological discourse that fails to engage unpleasant or inconvenient aspects of human life.'[15] Yet it also remains that despite shame and trouble, care in various modes of pastoral ministry continues to offer very precious opportunities to invite persons to Christ and the gospel, and to serve as a portal to the best that Christian communities can offer. The realities of decline and abuse do, however, invite a sturdy reframing of pastoral ministry in intentionally missional mode, and with very careful lines of accountability. In the current context of mission, neither knowledge of nor goodwill towards the churches can be presumed amongst the so-called general population. In terms of accountability, abuse and settings that enable it must be stopped. Taken together, these factors mean that what pastoral ministries involve in the current climate is not simply continuous with what they may have involved in times past when it was possible to hold quite different assumptions about the general population's religious sensibilities, their knowledge of at least key pieces of Christian tradition, and their openness to and respect for the church's representatives. This is no longer the case. So ministries of pastoral care are not for the faint-hearted, though they must be filled with gentleness; and they are not for the change-averse, as they require robustness and

---

14    Philip Hughes, Stephen Reid & Margaret Fraser, *A Vision for Effective Youth Ministry: Insights from Australian Research* (Nunawading, Vic: Christian Research Association, 2015), p. v.

15    Cf. Emmanuel Y. Lartey, *Pastoral Theology in an Intercultural World* (Peterborough: Epworth, 2006), p. 101. [My italicisation, for clarity]

grit to engage sensitively and creatively with cultural conditions that are not as before.

## Reaching Out Through Pastoral Services

In the 2011 national census something like 463,000 people in the Melbourne area identified as Anglicans, but perhaps only around 25,000 of them regularly attended a congregation of the church for public worship. The space between those who are regular worshippers and those who identify as Anglican is sometimes called cultural Anglicanism. This is a form of cultural Christianity that has, in Australia and elsewhere, at least in the past, been passed across generations with very little, or just nominal participation in congregational life supporting an Anglican identity. A mark of cultural Anglicans is that whilst they are not regularly involved in church on Sundays, they might use the ministries of the church community and of a pastor at times of significance, need, celebration and commitment. So pastoral services are important to consider with respect to persons who approach the church at the time of a death in the family, or who may exert influence upon a decision in the family to approach the church to solemnise a marriage or to seek the baptism of a child.[16]

Sympathetic studies of this kind of connection to church life suggest that at least some such persons are likely to understand themselves in relation to the Christian tradition, most especially in their embrace of the 'golden rule': 'do to others as you would have them do to you'.[17] For some, this may be a conscious way of identifying themselves with God, or with Jesus—albeit not necessarily exclusively so, as they might, and rightly, associate such a rule also with several great faiths. Such a connection is,

---

16  Pastoral services may mean something else to initiated, committed, devoted and serving members of the church, of course. The focus of this current section is on what the literature calls 'cultural Christians/Anglicans.'

17  Luke 6.31.

though, a point of contact with biblical memory and with Christian values; it is a place at which a pastoral minister can meet cultural Christians.

It ought also to be acknowledged, with gratitude, that such persons may well also pursue an active prayer life of some kind. This is another significant point of connection with what the Church represents and offers. What seems to be less common amongst cultural Christians—whichever tradition they may approach in times of need—is a feeling for very much Christian doctrine, or a prayer life informed by contemporary liturgy. That is, identification with the golden rule might be made quite apart from systematic clarity about aspects of the 'content' of the faith. The prayer of cultural Anglicans, if it is shaped at all by liturgical forms, is more likely to draw on the Book of Common Prayer (1662) than A Prayer Book for Australia (1995). The non-doctrinaire approach held by many cultural Christians may also lead to their self-identification as 'spiritual, but not religious'—though this is a descriptor that shelters a very wide variety of perspectives, of which cultural Christianity, and cultural Anglicanism in particular, is just one small strand.

When welcoming and engaging with cultural Christians, it is therefore important that pastoral ministers do not assume too much—such as doctrinal commitments—but rather focus on the point of contact that is owned and acted upon in the other's decision to seek the church's ministry for some reason. It is good that people pray; it is good that they refer to things that Jesus said; and it is good that they seek the rites of the church as their elders perhaps taught them. Nevertheless, to Christians with a lively personal sense of the abundance of divine grace, cultural Anglicanism might seem to have a somewhat minimalist faith. So it may seem strange for such Christians to listen to those pastoral ministers who see this form of engagement with the Church as well and good. (Most might agree at least that it is better than nothing.) The English Anglican theologian Alan Billings, for example, argues in his book *Lost Church*[18] that in his context (Kendal, Cumbria, in the north of England) it is a mistake to regard people as simply believing, or not, and/or attending, or not. Rather, he suggests, many people continue to think of themselves as belonging—and doing so without necessarily either believing much or attending often, at least beyond occasional pastoral services and perhaps a few festival days.

In another book, *Secular Lives, Sacred Hearts*,[19] Alan Billings writes movingly of the integrity of the 'thinking-with-small-fragments' of Christian faith that can and often does go on amongst cultural Anglicans, and it is likely that this goes on here as in Britain. For instance, in seeking baptism for their children, cultural Christians may not think of themselves as affirming the Trinitarian faith that the Church's liturgy presumes. Even so, what they are thinking may be very significant for them. For example, cultural Christians may recognise the baptism service as an important time to gather friends and family around a child, for something like a 'showing'—a thought Billings connects to the Epiphany theme of 'appearance' and the nativity story of the magi bringing gifts to the infant Jesus.[20] Families coming to baptism may connect with that story, Billings claims, as their little one is being showered with gifts by family and friends.

Of course, connecting cultural Christians' experience of baptism to Epiphany-tide stories of the magi is unusual; it is not where the baptismal liturgy places weight. But, Billings argues, it provides access to the good news of Jesus that builds upon the basics of the golden rule. And just as a sense of the golden rule may not depend much on acceptance—or awareness—of other parts of scripture or Christian teachings, so making meaning of the baptism service itself does not necessarily

---

18  Alan Billings, *Lost Church: Why We Must Find it Again* (London: SPCK, 2013).
19  Alan Billings, *Secular Lives, Sacred Hearts: The Role of the Church in a Time of No Religion* (London: SPCK, 2004).
20  Matt. 2.1–12.

much depend on the text (and explicit theology) of the service. Billings submits that a particularly profound moment can be the handing over of a newborn child into the arms of the presiding minister standing at the water. This can show an entrusting of the child, not only to a representative of Christian faith (something that may or may not figure much in the thinking of those present), but simply entrusting in a public way to another human person as a representative of the human race. What this can show is some recognition that the child is dependent on more than the immediate family, more even than the wider family and friends gathered around, but also those who may be strangers.

Just as he does for baptism, Billings makes correlations between other pastoral services—marriage and funerals—and the meaning-making that he thinks he has heard and seen going on as he has engaged in pastoral ministry. Meanings are real and operative for people, even when they may be eschewing doctrinally and liturgically 'correct' interpretations, and pastoral services are a key opportunity for churches to reach out to people engaged in rites at this level. So, then, it is important for pastoral ministers and church communities to be tender, to allow for the articulation of whatever meaning is being found, and to welcome those who voice it, not least because a request for a pastoral service can allow for the possibility of ongoing contact with a culturally Anglican family, which in turn allows for the possibility of their encountering more—and more conventional interpretations—of the Church's grateful reception of the gospel. Each pastoral service itself therefore should always be seen as part of a wider process of contact, challenge and care. This is to say that the approach of cultural Christians for ministry is not a time for ministers to assert what they may feel is lacking in what may admittedly be a partial approach to Christianity, maybe or maybe not depending much on orthodox trajectories of theological understanding.

In some cases, too, cultural Christians may also retain some loyalty to special services: things like Christmas pageants, midnight mass, possibly

Good Friday and/or Easter Day services, or occasions like 'the blessing of the pets'. If what they, in these engagements, are seeking is blessing of their lives, then that is good, and that too is to be welcomed. Such things are more points of contact allowing them, just like the rest of us, to grow into faith. What cultural Christians often seem to be rejecting, or have simply drifted from, however, is regular worship, the church's Sunday fare and, maybe most of all, the eucharist, which may be a very strange world to them. Holy Communion may be perceived as a rite of commitment that cultural Christians have never made central. It is important to realise that its resurgence as 'normal' Sunday worship for Anglicans is only a couple of generations old. At least some cultural Anglicans would have once attended services such as Mattins and Evensong, which have now fallen away in all but a few places. Therefore, a persistence of perception of Holy Communion as an exclusive rite throws down the challenge to parishes to re-invigorate some kind of non-sacramental services.[21]

Pastoral ministry at the time of a funeral, for instance, can be very effective if the funeral is followed up with invitations to a locally-crafted liturgy in which the recently departed are remembered in a service of prayers by candlelight or some such, with some gentle proclamation, in which there is space to make meaning from non-doctrinaire beginnings.[22] This can be allied in turn to careful, informal, follow-up, both visiting the family in their homes as well as inviting them to church, including to its social events. Social events can perhaps most easily be

---

21 APBA makes provision for such services in the form of Morning and Evening Prayer, and Prayer, Praise and Proclamation. It is essential to take Services of the Word seriously, including, perhaps, in some contexts at least, Evensong. At least some cathedrals point to their sung services, done well, growing—though it can then be another challenge to invite people to a sacramental spirituality and participation in Christian community. It may also mean getting involved in fresh expressions of church—on which, see below.

22 All Saints' and All Souls' Day (1 and 2 November) can be an occasion for a service to which people are invited to remember those who have died during the course of the year. Some funeral directors, and aged care residences and hospitals, have initiated rites of this kind, showing their significance for the general population.

opened up to welcome people at a time in their lives in which social relationships are difficult for the newly bereaved, who may find themselves in the midst of the new experience of loneliness.

The Anglican tradition in its English context has a long and esteemed tradition of pastoral ministry through and from the 'occasional offices', as well as accessible services of the Word. Both are rooted in the Church of England's ongoing strong commitment to local parish life. Alan Billings represents well its contemporary expression. The Church of England, he contends, has always had a ministry to cultural Christians. He is likely right, but he is also correct to note the Church of England's less certain hold on its role in English society since the 1960s, leading to its current strong concern with mission. And an Australian reading of Billings' ideas can hardly be sanguine. The future of cultural Anglicanism in Australia may be fragile for a variety of reasons: it is not just the vastness of scale that makes parish pastoral ministry harder to configure here, but the lack of formal Establishment with which notions of parish are enmeshed in England.[23]

Predicted further declines in numbers of Australians identifying themselves as Anglicans, and a fast-growing proportion of the population declaring itself in Census as holding 'no religion', conspire to mean that the proportion of people identifying as Christian at all is reducing. As already noted, it is commonly cited that the Church's embroilment in abuse of the vulnerable, and a sense of growing distance between the church and wider society about human sexuality, are reasons for un-alignment, at least among younger persons. Cultural Anglicans are

---

23   Note Billings' own discussion of how he sees the current English situation: 'establishment-lite,' in Alan Billings, *Making God Possible: The Task of Ordained Ministry Present and Future* (London: SPCK, 2010). Transporting Billings' conviction to Australia might also be troubled by longstanding memory of another Brit, the Scottish Presbyterian cleric James Denney, and his famed view of Australia, formed in 1824, as 'the most godless place under heaven.' See Ian Breward, *Australia: 'The Most Godless Place Under Heaven'?* (Melbourne: Beacon Hill Books, 1988).

more and more likely to be older persons—as Gary Bouma puts it, 'literally dying out'.[24] So what may have been a default mode of offering pastoral ministry to many Anglican elders is fast becoming dated. For some Anglicans in Australia, however, ministry around key life experiences will be a viable means of offering ministry to the wider community, for the time being at least, and especially among those who are already elders.

## Reaching Out Through Cross-cultural Community-building

Migration is a very significant part of Australian society, with roughly 430,000 people moving to Melbourne from overseas in the ten years leading up to the 2011 census. Of this number, around 21,000 migrants identified as Anglicans in the same census. Just over half of them came from the British Isles, and around 12 percent from Aotearoa New Zealand. However, significant numbers also arrived from southern, eastern, and northern parts of Africa, southern and South-East Asia, and China. At least some migrants arriving in Australia were leaving their homelands in traumatic experiences of forced migration and very stressful and dangerous circumstances. In Melbourne and other Victorian dioceses, there is testimony to this, for example, congregations have been formed that are comprised mainly of Karen people who have fled from Myanmar, or South Sudanese escaping the chaos and violence of their country of birth.

These and other migrant communities are a pivotal source of renewal. Sometimes they bring witness to the deep sustaining power of Christian faith in extremis and struggle. Sometimes they bring energy from their experience of Christian communities flourishing despite apparent odds in places of recent or still-current oppression and discrimination. The burgeoning of underground churches in China, or the hybrid forms

---

24   Bouma, Being Faithful in Diversity, p. 13.

of Anglican and Pentecostal traditions in creative collision in the 'Anglocostalism' of Nigeria[25] and other places, are just some examples.

Roman Catholic Filipino theologians Agnes Brazal and Emmanuel de Guzman very helpfully describe four kinds of churches that are, at least in part, comprised of migrants. These models from their book *Intercultural Church*[26] can be used as maps to make assessments of growth in cross-cultural sensitivity, power-sharing, and work still to do in approximating the radical welcome that is the free gift of the gospel. The first model they call 'monocultural host church'. This is a church into which migrants are incorporated, with migrants invited to become 'one' with the local community and perhaps in turn therefore become socialised into wider society. The model may draw from scripture images and ideas of unity—'all one in Christ Jesus'[27] and such like—and the hosts at least might well understand unity as being enacted in things like common worship in one language (likely, the dominant one, the language of the hosts). As de Guzman and Brazal note, 'the model assumes that if a society makes a full effort to incorporate migrants into the mainstream society, they [the migrants] will naturally work to reciprocate the gesture and adopt new customs'[28] that they have not carried with them from their previous cultures. Indeed, many migrants long for acceptance and yearn for inclusion, and are willing to strain to take up new ways.

At the same time, though, where this model is operative because long-term members retain most power, very much depends on the generosity or fickleness of the host church. Moreover, the power they hold may go unexamined or be held tight as they determine the conditions for

---

25   Jesse Zink, "'Anglocostalism' in Nigeria: Neo-Pentecostalism and Obstacles to Anglican Unity,' *Journal of Anglican Studies* 10.2 (2012), pp. 231–250.
26   Agnes M. Brazal & Emmanuel de Guzman, *Intercultural Church: Bridge of Solidarity in the Migration Context* (Alameda, CA: Borderless Press, 2015). Amidst the following references to their work, I mix in my own reflection.
27   Galatians 3.28.
28   Brazal and de Guzman, *Intercultural Church*, p. 118.

'unity', even if glossed with biblical sheen. This approach, then, needs to be seen through some critical lenses, as pastoral ministry with and for migrants must not be prone to manipulation with scriptural texts at play to mask unwillingness to scrutinise local practices, recognise vulnerability, measure how resources are shared—including gospel imperatives to 'freely give'—and track if sacrifice and compromise are being mutually engaged. It is important that long-term residents of a place, and erstwhile guardians of a church, see themselves—for a time at least—as hosts, but it is profoundly unhelpful for such a dynamic to become embedded and static.

A second model, also monocultural, is the 'ethnic-based church', which, as it were, transplants the worshipping traditions and operating styles of church from a homeland to a new place. Ethnic-based churches can allow for greater visibility for migrants than the first model, but they can also inhibit aspects of integration in a new culture, and have other weaknesses too. On the up side, they may be a crucial means of navigating massive, and perhaps traumatic, change upon confrontation with a new situation, and the shelter they offer can be a very significant act of pastoral care. But on the down side, there is a danger that over time ethnic churches embed a ritualised kind of nostalgia, a reminiscence of an another time or place ill-fit to the current context.[29]

The Windrush Generation—mid-twentieth century Caribbean migrants to the UK—were, to the disgrace of the Church of England, often made unwelcome in Anglican parishes. So these migrant Christians set up new churches—while the Church of England lost not just face, but huge cultural and spiritual enrichment. The growth of various forms of Pentecostalism in Britain is at least in part a result of this.[30] What Australian variants on this dynamic might emerge

---

29  This is, of course, what too many churches of English, Scottish or Irish heritage have become.
30  See Anthony G. Reddie, ed., *Black Theology, Slavery and Contemporary Christianity* (London: Routledge, 2010).

remains to be seen, but it can at least be said that long-term Australians (most of whom are themselves Second Peoples[31]) may or may not ensure that migrants do not feel the need to gather in a ghetto—the definition of which involves being a minority. At least part of being a 'good' host involves the host's own orientation to change, and preparedness to be changed, by the presence of new others. The arrival of migrants needs not simply to lead to an adjustment of old ways, but the emergence of a new thing. And not least, the new thing will be more deeply catholic— 'through the whole', 'according to all'—and bring great richness.

These points lead us towards the third model, which Brazal and de Guzman call 'multiculturalist'. It recognises that host and migrant cultures are different, and it encourages distinctions between them to be made, cultural particularity to be expressed, and coexistence without conformity to be the dominant ethos. In this model, much responsibility remains with the host culture, to develop policies and actions that respect difference. Appeal to the like of 'all one in Christ Jesus' needs to resist all in Christ being required, either overtly or more subtly, to become like 'us'. For migrants, dangers of ghettoising again need to be avoided. For all in a multicultural community, there is need to keep navigating the extent of blending, and the consent and desire for the changes involved. Helping communities to make such navigations consciously and equitably is a key part of contemporary pastoral ministry, just as is working towards the establishment of space for difference.

Brazal and de Guzman call their fourth model 'intercultural', which they mean to suggest a 'going beyond' multiculturalism by stressing

---

31 For some recent theological reflection on Aboriginal Australia by First and Second People, see Mark Brett & Jione Havea (eds), *Colonial Contexts and Postcolonial Theologies: Storyweaving in the Asia-Pacific* (New York: Palgrave, 2014); Chris Budden, *Following Jesus in Invaded Space: Doing Theology on Aboriginal Land* (Eugene, OR: Wipf and Stock, 2009); Jione Havea, ed., *Indigenous Australia and the Unfinished Business of Theology: Cross-cultural Engagement* (New York: Palgrave, 2014).

the positive 'mutual enrichment' that can happen in the 'in between' and hybrid space of interaction between cultures. Migrants—and the intercultural church they are helping to form—may see themselves as 'both this and that, neither this nor that'. This interculturality is able to happen, though, only when attention is paid to 'necessary changes in objective conditions' in the host culture, because advocacy towards equalising power relations is 'integral'. Brazal and de Guzman affirm this fourth model as the one in which migrants are best able to gift the whole church as 'living signs' and 'effective reminders' of the church's identity as communion.[32] These last two models outlined by de Guzman and Brazal—the multiculturalist and interculturalist—are both what they speak of as 'multiple-culture' models, and the Filipino theologians draw their own core convictions from the language of the global church as 'a community of communities' in which, at least ideally, difference is gathered without being subsumed to the mores of one particular culture.

In practice, none of these models of church is easy to enact, and even the first, least ambitious one—the monocultural host church—assumes that a 'full effort' is being made to welcome people from cultures other than our own one way or another. That may or may not be the case. At the same time, churches that begin as monocultural host communities may move, over time, to a more fulsome appreciation and inclusion of others. By the grace of God they may find themselves capable of hospitality, dialogue, exchange, and yielding more than they may at first have imagined, as Christian people from different cultures, meet, befriend, challenge, partner, and bless each other in shared endeavours, negotiating tension, and growing into understanding along the way. Whilst glorious when it happens, it is honest to say that such blessing oftentimes emerges by facing the kind of pain that marks sacrifice. It is also honest to acknowledge such a vision can be lost and churches may regress to less

---

32  Brazal and de Guzman, *Intercultural Church*, p. 129.

than the best of which they are called. And so intentional consideration is always needed about what practices are being enacted to enable welcome of those different to 'us' and to enable them to contribute to a deepening of faith and discipleship for all—indeed, give a lead in it.[33]

Ghanan (now United States-based) Methodist theologian Emmanuel Yartekwei Lartey outlines various practices which he contends contribute to intercultural pastoral leadership. These involve pastors purposefully making 'counter-hegemonic' activity key to what they do and how they act. He gives examples such as problematising and disrupting dominant structures, questioning how power is wielded, refusing to participate in the silencing of weaker voices, and deliberately promoting and intensifying diversification. All of these practices, which might have various manifestations, are crucial to sensitive pastoral ministry across cultures. Undoubtedly, they can trouble what often passes as the status quo. But they help to assert, as Lartey says, that 'diversity is God's norm'.[34]

How parishes and other communities across Melbourne Diocese might map onto models like those of Brazal and de Guzman, let alone approximate to Lartey's ideas, is a key question for pastoral ministry, given ever-increasing numbers of migrants to both city and country. But there are likely to be more monocultural host churches than intercultural ones; and too few on any kind of conscious journey to embrace migrants

---

[33] For a powerful essay on the need for 'perpetual disposition toward marginality,' see Sundar John Boopalan, 'Hybridity's Ambiguity (Gift or Threat?): Marginality as Rudder,' in Peniel Jesudason Rufus Rajkumar & Joseph Prabhakar Dayam, (eds)., *Many Yet One? Multiple Religious Belonging* (Geneva: World Council of Churches Publications, 2015), pp. 135-148.

[34] Emmanuel Lartey, "Borrowed Clothes Will Never Keep You Warm': Postcolonializing Pastoral Leadership,' in Kwok Pui-lan & Stephen Burns (eds)., *Postcolonial Practice of Ministry: Leadership, Liturgy, and Interfaith Engagement* (Lanham, MD: Lexington, 2016), pp. 21–32, drawing on his book *Postcolonializing God: Toward an African Practical Theology* (London: SCM Press, 2013).

and the wider sense of communion or catholicity they can represent.[35] Yet the realities and impact of migration and cultural diversity are not matters for just some churches to attend to, but ones for us all to take seriously and take part in. The evident under-representation of visible ethnic minorities, migrants among them, in the likes of diocesan synod, elections, and diocesan leadership, is a sign that cross-cultural dynamics need more care. As migrants tend to attend church at about double the rate of other Australians, and tend to be significantly younger than other church-going Anglicans in this country, it should be self-evident that welcoming migrants, and creating cultures in which they can and want to join, is a vital source of life and health. This will involve costly effort and change that can be uncomfortable, but it is change that is needed. It requires not least that new ways of being church, and new questions about diverse pastoral needs, must be learned.

**Reaching Out Through Fresh Expressions**

The past decade or so has seen two major reports on mission come before the General Synod of the Anglican Church of Australia—a flurry given that it was 1980 before one was produced prior to that. These reports are replete with images of urgency about the context in which the church now finds itself, depicting time bombs, burning platforms, frogs being boiled alive and (sedately by comparison) coming to a crossroad of decision that demands choices be made about which way to take. These reports, with their strong images, trouble inherited approaches to pastoral ministry.

The 2006 report *Building the Mission-shaped Church in Australia*[36] highlights a large number of changes to Australian society through

---

[35] For many helpful essays, see Susanna Snyder, Joshua Ralston & Agnes M. Brazal (eds), *Church in an Age of Global Migration: A Moving Body* (New York: Palgrave, 2015).

[36] *Building the Mission-shaped Church in Australia* (Sydney: General Synod Office, 2006). Page numbers are given in the main text.

recent decades. Not the least of what these demographic changes mean is that 'we may have too many existing churches where there are too few people and not enough new churches where population centres are growing' (p. 6). Even where parishes are active in inherited church-style, it is 'unfortunately the last place people look when searching for spirituality because it is too readily stereotyped by hierarchy, power and conformity' (p. 6). Across all demographics churchgoing may increasingly be seen as a 'leisure activity' competing for attention, time and money with a plethora of other things (p. 6), and in which 'Christian language of duty, service and responsibility may lack the currency afforded to a vision of discipleship as the finding of true abundance, satisfaction and a transformed life' (p. 6). Such comments from the report suggest not just growing challenges of providing church in growing demographic gaps, but the spiritual challenges of engaging people with new ways of being church that mediate the transforming riches of the gospel to them.

Wider studies have suggested a peculiar interior orientation to the church's life in Australia,[37] and among Anglicans a manifestation of that tendency might be in the fact that they—like those in England, until recently—have directed much of their mission work towards the baptised, 'mainly by encouraging greater participation from fringe members by putting on more attractive worship services' (p. 2). *Building the Mission-shaped Church in Australia*, by contrast, stresses that the church can no longer rely on people being attracted to church, and the need is for now '"going out" to meet otherwise distant groups' of people (p. 6), and 'reach[ing] beyond the baptised and our own cultural horizon'

---

37   See discussion in Stephen Burns, 'Formation for Ordained Ministry: Out of Touch?' in Jione Havea (ed), *Indigenous Australia and the Unfinished Business of Theology: Crosscultural Engagement* (New York: Palgrave, 2014), pp. 151–166. Note especially Philip Hughes' work *The Australian Clergy* (Hawthorn, Vic: Christian Research Association, 1989), replete with statements such as at p. 89: 'the clergy have settled into ministry within their congregations. They see their prime task as building personal devotion and caring for one another in the congregation. The locus of ministry is in the church rather than in the world.'

(p. 7). Importantly, this mission-shaped literature reminds us that in contemporary Australia, all mission and ministry are cross-cultural. This is a very serious challenge to a pastoral ministry based only or mainly on engagement with cultural Anglicans through pastoral services. So the General Synod mission report stresses the need for 'a change in parish ministry to an outward focus; from a "come to us" approach to a "we will come to you" attitude, embodying the gospel where people are, rather than embodying it where we are, and in ways we prefer' (p. 11). And it commends the ways in which 'Anglicans abroad' have 'discovered that the Anglican tradition is more nourishing and flexible than they initially imagined', reinterpreting and re-expressing it in 'surprising and creative' ways (p. 7). This is a point that can be related, more locally, to all that there is to be learned from migrant Christians.

Jeffrey Driver contributes his own significant piece of cultural exegesis and social analysis to the second of the two General Synod reports on mission in a decade, *Viability and Structures*.[38] In keeping with *Viability and Structures* as a whole, much of his attention is on dioceses, but he also draws out some implications for parishes such as 'many once viable parishes will no longer sustain the traditional parish model' (p. 63) and, given 'the dominance of the over 50s in most congregations,' the necessity of developing 'parallel expressions/ministries' in order to 'reach out to the under 40s' (p. 64). He concludes that 'broad patterns of attendance within the Anglican Church of Australia, its age profile, as well as population and immigration projections for the wider community combine to suggest that new expressions of mission are critical to Anglicanism having a vital future in Australia' (p. 67). He notes next, though, how demanding that will be, 'Effective and creative mission is much more resource intensive than maintenance of a diminishing status quo' (p. 67).

---

38  Published online at: http://www.anglican.org.au/general-synods/2014/documents/books/book%208_for%20website.pdf Page numbers are given in the main text.

*Building the Mission-shaped Church in Australia* was especially concerned to appropriate for this country what was for Anglicans abroad becoming an international and ecumenical vision of new missional initiatives fully supported as part of what Archbishop Rowan Williams called a 'mixed economy' of church, that is, related churches doing different things. So in contexts where inherited styles of church are flourishing, they are to be encouraged, but they are not to be seen as the only style of church, and new forms of church need to be established alongside inherited ones, and are to be blessed. The Australian report, in its turn, is very clear that inherited and fresh expressions of church are not in competition but needed in 'fruitful partnership and collaboration' (p. 3). Indeed, speaking of a mixed economy is, it says, '"big-tent" language which aims to help every Anglican find their place in our diverse Church' (p. 3).

It has not always been appreciated that appeals for new kinds of church made by the earlier Church of England report *Mission-shaped Church* (2006), on which the Australian report draws heavily, were not a naïve call for novelty. What the British report proposed was 'fresh expressions of church', a term that is a deliberate echo of a historic formula of the Church of England, the Declaration of Assent made by all its clergy, included in the Ordinal, and part of the liturgy for the consecration of bishops. This Declaration speaks of the Anglican vocation to 'proclaim afresh' (hence 'fresh expressions'), in each generation, orthodox, credal faith; a faith 'uniquely revealed in the holy scriptures and set forth in the catholic creeds'. It is crucial to appreciate this connection with the Declaration of Assent.[39] Fresh expressions are meant—for all their freshness, newness, and setting in a particular culture or context—to be the beginnings of a community of robust and durable Christianity, a sign of the gospel which is for everyone. While they are new beginnings of missional activity, they are by no means

---

39  See *Mission-shaped Church* (London: Church House Publishing, 2006), p. 34.

finished ecclesial states or shapes. To help them grow, careful work has been done in the UK to encourage the development of any new initiative towards what the mission-shaped literature identifies as 'mature expressions' of church. So they are seeking contemporary integration of old and new, tradition and innovation, contextual and transcultural.

The double dynamic of old- and newness can be seen well in the official definition of a fresh expression, which is (1) 'a form of church for our changing culture, established primarily for the benefit of people who are not yet members of any church' that has (2) 'come into being through principles of listening, service, incarnational mission and making disciples' and that (3) 'will have the potential to become a mature expression of church shaped by the gospel and the enduring marks of the church and for its cultural context'.[40] Much of importance is said in these three statements; about whom fresh expressions are primarily for, how they happen, and what they must manifest in order to mature. *Building the Mission-shaped Church in Australia* captured some of this as it defined terms in these ways: inherited church is 'familiar, customary and even traditional ways in which Christians have met together for worship, fellowship and mission', whereas fresh expressions 'reach out to people who are otherwise beyond the reach of our existing church community because of our cultural distance' (p. 2).

By using these descriptions of fresh expressions and inherited church alongside each other, it becomes possible to determine what is, and is not, a fresh expression. Fresh expressions are not in the first place about providing a pathway to the culture of inherited church. And so Graham Cray insists, 'We do not apply the term [fresh expressions] to bridge projects whose long term aim is to transfer people to an existing congregation'[41] and as *Building the Mission-shaped Church in Australia* makes clear, 'Fresh Expressions of Church are not intended to be stepping-stones

---

40   https://www.freshexpressions.org.uk/guide/about/whatis
41   https://www.freshexpressions.org.uk/news/grahamcray-lent12

to an existing congregation or a halfway house for someone joining a Sunday morning congregation' (p. 11). This is an important point, as it is no longer responsible to think that inherited versions of church are, on their own, going to convey the beauty of Christian faith to younger generations. It should no longer be contentious to suggest that the kinds of pastoral ministry that are offered either to Anglican elders who are part of worshipping communities, or to cultural Anglicans who belong without believing or attending much, are not going to reach out to very many young people. Indeed, according to the General Synod report, 'it appears unreasonable to expect members of Gen X and Gen Y to return to the Church or even to approach it for their pastoral needs, as so few have had any involvement with it' (p. 17).

Just what impact fresh expressions can make in Australia is an open question. Research from the UK that shows that, there at least, they are reaching out to unchurched people. It suggests that in just the first few years of the Church of England's recent missional initiative, 'those in fresh expressions of church emerge as a significant and very visible proportion of the Church of England family'. Something like the equivalent of two new dioceses have been formed by these new initiatives, and among the young, they have welcomed the equivalent of numbers in seven dioceses.[42]

Because fresh expressions are neither stepping-stones nor halfway houses, they may entail forms of church that have not often, or yet at all, been seen. This calls for re-imagining of pastoral ministry too. In fresh expressions, participation as well as leadership will oftentimes likely be more dialogical (or negotiated) than in forms of inherited church. Some of the 'trappings' of inherited church—what Martyn Percy calls clerical

---

[42] Steven Croft, 'Persuading Gamaliel: Helping the Anglo-Catholic Tradition Engage with Fresh Expressions,' in Steven Croft & Ian Mobsby (eds), *Ancient Faith, Future Mission: Fresh Expressions in the Sacramental Tradition* (Norwich: The Canterbury Press, 2009), pp. 46–47.

'plumage'[43] (clerical collars, vesture, and such like), honourifics (titles,[44] deference), sacred buildings—may well be near irrelevant, if not active impediments, to new forms of church coming to life. And existing liturgical forms may prove close to useless—though there is much to be learned from the kind of 'remixing' of liturgical traditions going on in emergent worship.[45] Apart from anything else, such remixing can resource the quest to renew services of the Word—as well as sacramental celebrations.

Whatever else fresh expressions involve, they will engage somehow in the stories of scripture, helping people to handle scripture, in order to invite faith: they will conceive of themselves as embryonic, growing, entry-points into the mysteries of faith distilled in creeds used through history by Christians the world over; one of their joys will be that in making new Christians they will come to celebrate baptism, lavishly; and in time, at the right time, they will be inviting communion with God in eucharistic meals. These central things will, if not always from the start, in time be there. Fresh expressions—whether at the pub, footy club, café, gym, gallery, mall, men's shed, caravan park, beach, toddler group, or anywhere else—will, in the end, be gatherings towards or around scripture and sacrament because these always remain the reliable gracious self-revelation of the Holy One. But ways of bible reading might not involve the full use of the Anglican Australian Lectionary schema, and the mood of sacramental celebration will not be the rigid pathway through A Prayer Book for Australia found in many parishes. Fresh expressions will be feeling a way into apt practices of engaging scripture, and shaping new ceremonial scenes for a group or culture left behind by inherited ways of church. This might well look very different

---

43  Martyn Percy, *Clergy: Origin of the Species* (London: Continuum, 2006), p. 68.
44  For devastating critique of such, see Gordon W. Lathrop, *The Pastor: A Spirituality* (Minneapolis: Fortress, 2006), pp. 1–20.
45  See Mark Earey, *Beyond Common Worship: Anglican Identity and Liturgical Diversity* (London: SCM, 2013) and Doug Gay, *Remixing the Church: Toward an Emerging Ecclesiology* (London: SCM, 2011) for two important explorations.

from Sunday morning in any number of Anglican churches to which those groups or cultures are no longer connected.

Pastoral ministry today involves not only recognising shifting opportunities for reaching out in contemporary cultures, but attempting to shape things not just for, but with, people for whom fresh expressions are intended. So it should be appreciated that the official definition of fresh expressions depends very heavily on pastoral skills: listening, service, incarnational mission, and disciple-making. Further, as incarnational mission is often described elsewhere as 'contextual—listening to people and entering their culture'—it can be imagined that they are the kind of encounter to which pastors readily give themselves. Indeed, listening turns out to be a major theme in fresh expressions, as the practices at their heart are connected together by a process the literature calls 'double listening.' This involves listening to the gospel and Christian tradition on the one hand and engaging cultural exegesis and persons immersed in particular cultures on the other.

There are clues in this thinking for evaluating inherited approaches to church. In some but by no means all, contexts, pastoral services may be exactly what the mission-shaped literature means by contextual mission. That is if in the wider environment in which they are set, there are still cultural Anglicans who relate well to such ministry and this provides some foundations for the future flourishing of the church in that place. In other contexts, though, other ways of reaching out are needed. Inherited forms of church and default modes of ministry are now best thought of as just one form of mission, and notions of their normativity need to be questioned in light of the contextual and demographic realities the church is facing.

### Conclusion: making connections

The opening of these reflections stressed the eschewal of moulds and blueprints, and highlighted attention to variables such as 'some' and 'may'. It heralded discussion of trends and trajectories, and the essay has recognised some rapid social shifts. Throughout, there has been a stress on context, culminating in openness to the mission-shaped literature's emphasis on connecting context to incarnational mission. This is the heart of effective, contextually aware, pastoral ministry today, and it will lead to different forms of presence in, connection with, and invitation to, local communities.

In some contexts, it will be apparent that one of the ways of reaching out discussed in these reflections is most apt to the setting. In many, it will be evident that what may have been default modes of pastoral ministry are becoming redundant. The scope of pastoral ministry now is more demanding and varied than it was even fifteen years ago when the previous edition of this Handbook appeared. The skills-base needed to embrace a vocation in pastoral ministry is wide and the resilience it needs, deep. The training and formation of pastoral ministers requires new foci of attention, particularly ongoing professional development for clergy, while the task for theological colleges is large, as each of the three modes of pastoral ministry discussed in the preceding pages needs to be on colleges' agenda.[46] Locally in parishes or in collaborations across deaneries and diocese, some sort of mix of approaches to pastoral ministry, some sort of mixed economy of church, will be essential. Into the future, the movement of clergy between different modes of pastoral ministry will be needed. Connections between clergy and the communities they lead will need to be galvanised as congregations age, migrants arrive, links with longstanding local communities need to be made or remade, and the world God loves continues to change.

---

46  See Steven Croft, 'Formation for Ministry in a Mixed Economy Church: The Impact of Fresh Expressions of Church in Patterns of Training,' in Louise Nelstropp & Martin Percy (eds), *Evaluating Fresh Expressions: Explorations in Emerging Church* (Norwich: The Canterbury Press, 2008), pp. 40-54, but also Jenny Daggers, 'Postcolonializing Mission-shaped Church: The Church of England and Postcolonial Diversity,' in Kwok Pui-lan & Stephen Burns (eds), *Postcolonial Practice of Ministry: Leadership, Liturgy, and Interfaith Engagement* (Lanham, MD: Lexington, 2016), pp. 183–198.

**Selected further reading**

Alan Billings, *Secular Lives, Sacred Hearts: The Role of the Church in a Time of No Religion*. London: SPCK, 2004.

Gary Bouma, *Australian Soul: Religion and Spirituality in the Twenty-first Century*. Melbourne: Oxford University Press, 2006.

Stephen Burns, *Pastoral Theology for Public Ministry*. New York: Seabury, 2015.

Steven Croft (ed), *Mission-shaped Questions*. London: Church House Publishing, 2008.

General Synod, *Building the Mission-shaped Church in Australia*. Sydney: General Synod Office, 2006.

Julie Gittoes, Brutus Green & James Heard (eds), *Generous Ecclesiology: Church, World and the Kingdom of God*. London: SCM, 2015.

Sheryl Kujaawa-Holbrook & Karen Montagno (eds), *Injustice and the Care of Souls: Taking Oppression Seriously in Pastoral Care*. Minneapolis: Fortress, 2010.

Kwok Pui-lan & Stephen Burns (eds), *Postcolonial Practice of Ministry: Leadership, Liturgy and Interfaith Engagement*. Lanham, MD: Lexington, 2016.

Emmanuel Y. Lartey, *Pastoral Theology for an Intercultural World*. Peterborough: Epworth, 2006.

Gordon Lathrop, *The Pastor: A Spirituality*. Minneapolis: Fortress, 2006.

# Chapter Two

## Christian Initiation: Baptism (B), Confirmation (C), and Reception (R)

Baptism marks the beginning of a journey with God, which continues for the rest of our lives, the first step in response to God's love. For all involved, particularly the candidates but also parents, godparents and sponsors, it is a joyful moment when we rejoice in what God has done for us in Christ, making serious promises and declaring the faith. The wider community of the local church and friends welcome the new Christian, promising support and prayer for the future. Hearing and doing these things provides an opportunity to remember our own baptism and reflect on the progress made on that journey, which is now to be shared with this new member of the Church. The service paints many vivid pictures of what happens on the Christian way. There is the sign of the cross, the badge of faith in the Christian journey, which reminds us of Christ's death for us. Our 'drowning' in the water of baptism, where we believe we die to sin and are raised to new life, unites us to Christ's dying and rising, a picture that can be brought home vividly by the way the baptism is administered. Water is also a sign of new life, as we are born again by water and the Spirit, as Jesus was at his baptism. And as a sign of that new life, there may be a lighted candle, a picture of the light of Christ conquering the darkness of evil. Everyone who is baptised walks in that light for the rest of their lives. (The Church of England, 'Pastoral Introduction to Holy Baptism', Common Worship)

These Guidelines seek to set out a coherent theology of Christian initiation, to undergird policy for pastoral and liturgical practice, set in the context of early 21st century Australia. They aim to achieve a common basic standard of pastoral practice concerning Christian initiation in the Anglican Diocese of Melbourne. They are not a set of legislative regulations, nor can they envisage or address every situation that may arise; the aim is to ensure that the Gospel is proclaimed with integrity and consistency across the range of congregations and communities that make up this diverse diocese.

**Christian initiation in today's world**

Baptism, confirmation, and reception into communicant membership, together with admission to Holy Communion, are significant moments, both in the life of the candidate, and in the life of his or her congregation, family, friends and community. The celebration of these rites of Christian initiation can and should be an opportunity for growth in understanding of both the wonder of God's gifts and the nature of our human response.

Baptism is far more than a rite of social significance, however. It is the sacrament of entry to the Church, an outward and visible sign of God's redemptive grace in the death and resurrection of Jesus Christ, working in us through the Holy Spirit. Baptism therefore speaks of our understanding of salvation and the Church: a solely 'seeker-affirming' focus risks distorting these and other key Christian truths.

The churches no longer stand in the centre of our society. They have become marginalised for many, if not most, Australians. Today we live in a missionary context, in which Christian faith is heard as one of a number of competing voices in the spiritual marketplace. This is a major factor affecting the practice of baptism. A growing proportion of candidates are adults, for many of whom the path to baptism (with confirmation and admission to Holy Communion) represents a life-changing reality of conversion to Christ. Even so, the question of who may be baptised as an infant remains. With a smaller pool of 'nominal' Christians, requests for the baptism of children are, however, growing fewer, and in many places are more likely to come from worshipping families than from the wider community.

In a missional context, baptism is more clearly seen as a gospel sacrament rather than a rite of passage—a 'new birth rite' rather than a 'birth right.' This leads to greater emphasis being placed on preparation, and concern that sponsors and godparents do not make hypocrites of themselves (and the church) by being asked to make promises that they cannot keep.

Why then do people continue to seek baptism for a baby? In the past, some parents viewed baptism as a social custom, important for their child's full acceptance in society. Some perhaps reflected folk-religious ideas and acted out of a subconscious desire to 'keep our baby safe' or to ensure a 'place in heaven' in the event of an early death. Motives such as these may still be around, but they are encountered much less often than in the past.

Despite the decline in infant baptism in recent years, it is the case that many people today will want to say 'thank you' to someone for the new child they have been given. Australian society may be increasingly secular, but interest in 'spirituality' is growing, notably among 25–40 year olds, the age group to which most parents belong. Many mothers and fathers see birth as a deeply 'spiritual' experience—'there was so much energy in the room at the birth itself' as one enquirer about baptism put it. Parents may be looking for a 'naming' or 'birth' ritual in a 'spiritual' place such as that which the church offers. The commitment to Christ which is part of baptism may be unknown or unwanted, but such parents look for a 'spiritual' ceremony for their baby from the only 'spiritual' institution they will often know—the Church.

## Christian initiation in today's Church

Due to varying social contexts, considerable variety also exists in patterns of Christian initiation in different parishes and church institutions. A small congregation in the inner city may welcome rare opportunities to celebrate baptism or confirmation, whereas a busy parish in the suburbs may find that some requests for baptism make them feel 'used'. Different Anglican schools have different traditions and policies about baptism, confirmation and admission to Holy Communion, depending on their history, parish links and other such factors.

How are such varied issues best approached in the name of Christ? One gift of the Spirit is discernment, the spiritual art of being able to analyse a situation—in humility, and out of love for all involved. Discernment involves sensitivity to what is going on spiritually when an inquiry about baptism is made. Many requests from 'outside' the church community represent a tentative step by spiritually sensitive people towards the Church, and need to be respected as such. A variety of feelings and ideas can often be found within the same family: an older generation reflecting 'folk-religious' ideas, the middle-aged being apathetic, while younger people may want something 'spiritual' for the new baby.

At one extreme is the temptation to offer 'cheap grace', at the other is the inflexible rigorism of rules. Both are failures of discernment. Some believe that baptism should be offered to all who desire it for their children, seeing any such request as a work of the Spirit. Others would wish to exclude from baptism all but the children of committed, regular worshippers. It is easy to identify the weakness of 'rigorist' or 'indiscriminate' extremes in baptismal practice. It is harder to specify theologically robust, liturgically sound and pastorally effective policies. How is proper preparation called for, without giving families the impression that they thereby 'earn the right' to baptism? What approaches will witness to the grandeur and breadth of the Gospel of Christ, yet not become unhelpfully judgemental, nor quench a smouldering wick, but rather be a means whereby the flame of faith is fanned into life?

Some more recent issues arising within the Church also need consideration. The practice of 'renewing baptismal vows' has grown in recent times. Is this a helpful way of speaking? When (if at all) may it be appropriate? What response is to be given when a baptised Anglican seeks 're-baptism'? The person may have been baptised before entering into active faith, or may have come into such a new experience of the presence of God's Spirit that their former walk with God seems to them pale or even empty. What sort of pastoral response will help this new life to be directed best into God's service, yet not compromise the 'once-for-all' character of baptism?

A number of related issues surround confirmation. Peer-group and family pressures on young people to be confirmed have now largely passed away. In some congregations, few younger people are 'coming through' to confirmation, which now takes place only occasionally, to the point where the importance of confirmation is being undermined, and its necessity for full Christian formation comes under question in some places. With growing numbers of unbaptised adults coming to commit themselves to Christ, the relationship between baptism and confirmation in their case needs to be clarified. Again, how is confirmation related to admission to the Holy Communion, especially where children who have been admitted are now grown to adult years? What understandings of confirmation are acceptable to Anglicans, and what ecumenical issues arise through our practice of confirmation?

## Renewed practice in initiation

Significant steps have been taken to restore baptism to its key place in the life of the Church. Scholarly work on baptism from biblical, liturgical, pastoral and ecumenical perspectives has deepened the appreciation of this sacrament of the Gospel, and its foundational role for Christian ministry. Likewise, much work has gone into re-integrating the key rites and symbols of Christian initiation—baptism, confirmation and admission to Holy Communion. The 1982 'Lima Statement' (Baptism, Eucharist & Ministry) of the World Council of Churches has received wide acceptance, and shaped ecumenical responses in the decades since.

A general consensus about Christian initiation thus now exists both ecumenically and across the Anglican communion. Given our missionary context, this consensus assumes the baptism of those able to answer for themselves as the primary model within which our understanding of the baptism of others (usually infants) is shaped. It also seeks to hold together the various aspects of Christian initiation—baptism (at any age), confirmation and reception into communicant membership—in an integrated rite.

Among Australian Anglicans these influences can readily be seen by comparing the services in the Book of Common Prayer (1662), An Australian Prayer Book (1978) and, especially, A Prayer Book for Australia (1995). The 1662 and 1978 services distinguish between 'infant' and 'riper years' candidates, and present baptism, confirmation and Holy Communion as separate services. The 1978 book further diversified matters by providing 'First Order' and 'Second Order' services for both baptism and confirmation, which differ in the way congregations participate, and in their liturgical shape. AAPB also included a brief service of 'Thanksgiving for the Birth of a Child, before the Baptism,' modelled on the 'Churching of Women' (BCP).

The 1995 APBA service, on the other hand, reflects the consensus noted above: the service therein embraces candidates of every age, and offers an integrated rite of baptism and confirmation in the context of Holy Communion. In addition, in APBA 'Thanksgiving for a Child' speaks to a number of situations (whether apart from or associated with baptism), and new provisions are made for the Reconciliation of a

Penitent, for the Reaffirmation of faith, and Reception into the communicant membership of the Anglican Church.

This wide range of issues, arising from the pastoral and liturgical ministry of the Church, forms the context for the policy outlined in this chapter. It is of vital importance to the ministry of the Gospel in this diocese that each congregation, within the theological and policy framework set out here, gives careful consideration to its practice of Christian initiation, as appropriate to local context and pastoral circumstances, and review it at regular intervals.

## B1   Baptism in Scripture, theology and Anglican formularies

Christian baptism has its basis in the life, teaching and work of Jesus. He underwent the baptism of John, identifying himself with sinful humans, and being identified as God's Servant and Messiah, the one who would send the Holy Spirit (Matthew 3.13–17). He taught that no one can enter the kingdom of God unless 'born anew' of water and the Spirit (John 3.3–5). He saw his own death on the cross as fulfilling his 'baptism' for us (Mark 10.32–45). After his resurrection he commanded his disciples to make disciples from 'all nations', baptising them 'in the Name of the Father, the Son and the Holy Spirit' (Matthew 28.19). The apostles obeyed this command. Peter, on the day of Pentecost, called his hearers to 'repent, and be baptised ... in the name of Jesus Christ for the forgiveness of sins'. In doing so, they would receive the gift of the Holy Spirit, and thus be made members of the new community (Acts 2.38–41).

The New Testament uses many pictures to describe baptism. The 1982 'Lima Statement,' Baptism, Eucharist and Ministry, summarises these as follows.

Baptism is:
- A participation in Christ's death and resurrection (Romans 6.3–5; Colossians 2.12);

- A washing away of sin (1 Corinthians 6.11);
- A new birth (John 3.5);
- An enlightenment by Christ (Ephesians 5.14);
- A re-clothing in Christ (Galatians 3.27);
- A renewal by the Spirit (Titus 3.5);
- The experience of salvation from the flood (1 Peter 3.20–21);
- An exodus from bondage (1 Corinthians 10.1–2);
- A liberation into a new humanity in which barriers of division, whether of sex or race or social status, are transcended (Galatians 3.27–28; 1 Corinthians 12.13).

The images are many but the reality is one.

According to the Acts, baptism was the invariable way by which people who responded to the preaching and proclamation of the apostles were admitted to the church (Acts 2.41, 8.12,38, 9.18, and so on). Baptism is, thus, an instrument of God's salvation, but its principal effect is neither external (1 Peter 3.21) nor automatic (I Corinthians 10.1-6). It is a means of grace, to be received by faith; such grace is given that we may do the works of God (Ephesians 2.10) 'until we come at last to his everlasting Kingdom' (BCP). Baptism is, therefore, also a rite of commissioning, setting a person within the whole people of God, for the purpose of identifying and exercising their ministry.

Christian baptism may be described, then, as the sacramental means of God's grace through which sinners, by faith—

enter into Christ's death and resurrection,
receive the forgiveness of sins,
are born anew into the Kingdom of God, and
receive the gift of the Holy Spirit;
thus turning to Christ from sin and evil,
they are grafted into the people of God,
made members of the Body of Christ, and
become ministers of God,

as citizens of heaven, looking for the coming of Christ in glory.

Such images are reflected in the teaching of the Catechism and the Articles, that in baptism a person is made 'a member of Christ, the child of God, and an inheritor of the kingdom of Heaven', so that he or she may 'walk in newness of life'.

This teaching is helpfully summarised at the beginning of the Holy Baptism service in APBA (p. 51, # 4).

> Baptism is the gift of our Lord Jesus Christ. When he had risen from the dead, he commanded his followers to go and make disciples of all nations, baptising them in the name of the Father, and of the Son and of the Holy Spirit. We have come together today to obey that command. Baptism with water signifies the cleansing from sin that Jesus' death makes possible, and the new life that God gives us through the Holy Spirit. In baptism, the promises of God are visibly signed and sealed for us. We are joined to Christ, and made members of his body, the Church universal.

The effect and intention of Christian baptism is further, helpfully articulated in the exhortation to the newly baptised provided for in the Church of England service of Holy Baptism (Common Worship).

> Today God has touched you with his love and given you a place among his people. God promises to be with you in joy and in sorrow, to be your guide in life, and to bring you safely to heaven. In baptism God invites you on a life-long journey. Together with all God's people you must explore the way of Jesus and grow in friendship with God, in love for his people, and in serving others. With us you will listen to the word of God and receive the gifts of God.

## B2 The sacrament of Holy Baptism

Anglicans have continued to find helpful the language about sacraments formed during the third and fourth centuries of the Church. Following Augustine's formulation taken up in the Western Church, a sacrament is defined in the Catechism as 'an outward and visible sign of an inward and spiritual grace, given to us by Christ himself, as a means by which we receive that grace, and a pledge to assure us of this' (APBA p. 817). In traditional theological terms, this entails three aspects: outward sign (element), inward grace (matter), and the pledge of this that we receive (virtue)—Article XXV. These three aspects are held together in an adequate understanding of a gospel sacrament.

The Catechism (APBA pp. 815–818) reflects Article XXV in identifying baptism as one of the two sacraments 'ordained of Christ our Lord in the Gospel'. It further teaches that baptism in water, in the name of the Trinity, is the outward and visible sign of that spiritual grace which confers 'a death to sin and new birth to righteousness', explaining that 'because human nature is sinful, a new birth is needed to make us children of God'. As a sacrament of the Church, baptism is more than a ritual or ceremony, and more than a 'badge' or 'token' of belonging. In the language of Article XXV, baptism is an effectual means of grace by which God works within us. As a sacrament, the spiritual benefits of baptism are, then, an instrument of grace; it is not something we 'do' or earn ourselves.

The water of baptism is administered in faith that God's Spirit is at work in the one baptised: this may neither be presumed (which regards the sacrament as working 'automatically') nor despised, as if the means of grace that Christ gives are empty. From time to time it can therefore be important to distinguish element, matter and virtue, so as to avoid giving the false impression that God's grace either works 'automatically,' or must be 'earned'.

## B2.1 Word and sacrament

Augustine of Hippo emphasised the key role of the proclaimed Word of God in the sacraments. Without the Word, there is no sacrament, he taught: a sacrament is verbum visible—'the Word seen'—while the preaching of the Gospel is verbum audible—'the Word heard'. By faith, itself the gift of God, the Word of God is heard, seen and heeded. Christ, the living Word, works through the Holy Spirit's use of material realities to bring God's saving grace to us. The Church thus came to speak of not only the 'element' but also the 'form' of a sacrament: the words of Christ through which the Word was active.

One other distinction came to be made about the sacraments in the early centuries. Some so over-emphasised the personal faith of the candidate that very few were regarded as having 'good enough faith' to be baptised. As a result, many delayed their baptism until they were near death. On the other hand, when baptised Christians did not live out the new life as they ought, the question arose as to whether this failure could bring their baptism into question? The distinction therefore came to be drawn between a 'valid' (i.e. properly conducted) sacrament, and an 'efficacious' (i.e. effective) one. Baptism does not depend on the candidate's faith to be genuinely baptism, but without faith baptism cannot be effective. The candidate's inward 'intention' is known fully only to God, but his or her public promises, and the Church's 'external intention' to conduct baptism (for example, by notice being given, use of an authorised service, a certificate and register entry) make it easy to tell when a 'valid' baptism has taken place.

## B2.2 Baptism and faith

When baptism is spoken of as 'a gospel sacrament of Jesus Christ', administered with water in the threefold Name of God, we view it from the divine side, as a 'means of God's grace'. Seen in human perspective, however, the role of faith comes to the fore, sometimes associated with a profound experience of God's work in conversion. One obvious issue here is the place of faith in baptism when candidates are unable to answer for themselves (usually infants): some Christian traditions would insist that baptism can only be properly administered to a person who has exercised faith publicly for him or herself. The New Testament, however, views baptism as something done to us, rather than being an expression of our own commitment.

Christian baptism has its intended effect insofar as God's grace meets with the response of lively faith in the Lord Jesus Christ, into whom we are baptised, leading to repentance from sin and evil (APBA p. 56). This is the work of the Holy Spirit, who brings us into a relationship of trust in Christ, so to become 'the child' of his Father, inheritors of his Kingdom. Faith is thus far more than a 'thing' to be weighed up in a quantitative way, but touches the quality of our life in relationship to God. When Jesus spoke of faith 'as small as a grain of mustard seed' (Matthew 17.20, Mark 4.30–32) he did not speculate about how much or little was necessary, but rejected all quantitative ideas about it. Nor is faith a human 'work': it is given by the Spirit to bring us into relationship with Christ, as sinners set right with God, in the community of faith.

As a sacrament of Christ, baptism 'doth not only quicken, but strengthens and confirms our Faith in him' (Article XXV). Such faith is more than an individual matter: it is embraced within the faith of God's people, the Body of Christ, of which the baptised person has been made a member. He or she is thus placed in a faith-relationship with new brothers and sisters in Christ, a relationship that finds its roots in the faithfulness of God in Christ. Baptism is thus 'into' faith, as well as 'by,' 'in' or 'through' faith. And this faith has content—it is the faith summarised in the Apostles' Creed, recited at baptism as 'the faith of the Church' (APBA p. 58, # 22).

At the time of baptism, the faith of every candidate is in its infancy. Nurtured by the means of grace and the common life of God's people, such faith looks to a growing relationship of trust in Christ. This will unfold over the whole Christian life of faith, until we come at the last to his everlasting kingdom. More is therefore involved than the faith of the candidate at the time of baptism. Christian faith is always 'on the way'; we look in hope to the time when faith will pass into sight. Thus even the most committed baptismal candidate is called to live by faith, not sight. It is worthwhile bearing in mind, then, that the Christian funeral service forms the liturgical conclusion of the faith journey entered in baptism (APBA p. 709, # 4; p. 719, # 14; p. 722, # 19).

Baptism is, thus, for anyone who, being set within the community of faith, is open to the grace and forgiveness of Christ. Since baptismal faith is a corporate matter, every candidate is supported by sponsors: in the case of those unable to answer for themselves, these sponsors make the baptismal promises on the candidate's behalf. These promises also involve the congregation and family of which the candidate is a part, in seeking to support the candidate in upholding such a promise. The warrant for admitting a person to baptism is thus not so much present faith, as evidence that the candidate is being set to live out the new life of faith, 'by God's grace striving to live as a disciple of Christ' until their life's end (APBA p. 56, # 17).

### B2.3  Speaking about baptism

The terms we use are important when discussing any topic, not least in the pastoral situations surrounding baptism. There is, for instance, no such thing as 'Anglican' baptism. Baptism is into the Christian faith and the whole Church of God, not into a particular denomination. Anglicans recognise as valid any baptism administered in accordance with the conditions for validity. The member Churches of the National Council of Churches of Australia (and the Presbyterian Church of Australia, which is not a member) all recognise each other's baptism, properly conducted, as valid. This means that a person baptised in one member Church is not baptised again should they seek admission to another. It is often helpful for a statement to this effect to be printed on the back of the baptismal certificate.

The terms 'Infant Baptism' and 'Adult Baptism' are misnomers, sometimes used as if they refer to different things. But baptism is baptism whatever a candidate's age, and needs no qualification. 'The Baptism of Infants' and 'The Baptism of those of Riper Years, and able to Answer for Themselves', the terms used in BCP and AAPB, state precisely the difference between the services, without compromising the truth that they are both rites of baptism. The APBA baptismal services embrace those of all ages and provides for a single integrated rite of initiation encompassing baptism, confirmation and reception into communicant membership, in the context of Holy Communion.

Another confusing term is 'believer's baptism.' If it is taken to refer only to the baptism of adults it is misleading: the validity of a baptism does not depend upon the faith of the candidate, since to say this comes close to viewing faith as a human work. Believing is primarily a quality of trusting relationship rather than intellectual effort: all baptism is 'believer's baptism'—no one advocates 'unbeliever's baptism'. Baptism is God's gift and doing: faith (itself the gift of God) is essential for a baptism to be efficacious, but not for it to be valid. It is spiritually dangerous to presume that the rite of baptism of itself brings salvation. It is equally dangerous to emphasise the human role in baptism so much that the assurance of 'the goodwill towards us of our heavenly Father' (BCP) is undermined.

Enquirers in particular will sometimes speak of having a baby 'christened'. Although this technically refers to the 'anointing' in baptism (which has not been normative Anglican practice since 1552, though it is provided for in APBA p. 82, Note 5), little is to be gained by insisting that people only speak of 'baptism' if this is clearly what they mean by 'christening'.

It has become customary to speak of 'baptismal vows', and their 'renewal'. However, many have difficulty with such terms, seeing 'vows' as carrying a legal meaning, whereas 'promises' (the term used in Anglican rites) has a more theological and personal sense (cf. Romans 4.13–25). Further, the term 'renewal of vows' could imply that baptism is primarily about human action, rather than the grace of God. On the other hand, our Prayer Books encourage all Christians to see each baptism as an opportunity to celebrate their own, and commit themselves afresh to 'walk in God's holy will and commandments all the days of our life'. It is thus more helpful to speak of 'baptismal promises' and their 'reaffirmation'.

## B3  Who may be baptised?

Baptism is commanded by Christ to be offered to 'all nations' (Matthew 28.19), to women and men of every race, occupation, ability, class—and of every age: adults young and old, teenagers and infants: to 'all who are far off' (Acts 2.38-39). As a 'means of God's grace', baptism is to be made available without restrictions such as religious upbringing ('Jew or Gentile'), social class ('slave or free'), gender ('male or female')—or a minimum age (Galatians 3.28). The baptism of a candidate unable to answer for him or herself is thus a wonderful example of the free and unmerited grace of God in Christ.

### B3.1  Some pastoral guidelines

Three groups of people typically enquire about Holy Baptism.
1. Unbaptised children or adults able to answer for themselves;
2. Active church members desiring baptism for their infant children;
3. Nominal church members, or 'cultural Anglicans', desiring baptism for their infant children.

Most clergy and parishes deal comfortably with those in the first two categories above. However some are ambivalent toward those in the third category and may want to decline such requests. In light of the theological understanding of Holy Baptism, together with Anglican polity and formularies (B1), and mindful of the variety of belief and practise across the diocese, the following are offered as principles and guidelines.

a) Every enquiry is to be welcomed as an opportunity to present the Christian faith and to introduce Christ to the enquirer/s. Those enquiring about baptism should be assured they, and if applicable their children, are welcomed by the Church and, by extension, Christ.

b) Local practise and policy should be communicated in a clear and accessible manner, and preferably made available on the parish website and/or through other forms of communication. The process to be followed by enquirers, together with the preparation to be undertaken, should be clearly set out.

c) No candidate may be baptised without evidence of faith in Christ. For those able to answer for themselves such faith is normally evidenced by participation in a program of preparation, willingness to make the Decision and give assent to the Affirmation of Faith (the Apostles' Creed), and the intention to become a communicant member of the Church with all that this implies. For those unable to answer for themselves (most commonly, but not necessarily, infants), evidence of faith will normally be provided by the sponsors' willingness to make the Decision and to give assent to the Affirmation of Faith on behalf of the candidate. In every instance, faith should be nurtured and encouraged.

d) The effect of baptism is to place a person within the community of those who share the faith of Christ. No one ever comes to baptism complete in the faith, for baptism is a beginning, not an end. All of the baptised are subsequently called to live out their faith by continually seeking God's forgiveness and grace. Baptism is the means of entering this shared journey of faith and should, therefore, be made available to anyone who is open to being set within the context of the Christian community and to beginning the Christian faith journey. The Canon concerning Baptism 1992 (6) therefore stipulates that the baptism of an infant should not be denied or delayed (except for the purposes of preparation) in situations where one parent 'professes to be a Christian'.

A refusal to baptise, where the conditions set out above have been met by those seeking the baptism, should be rare, and arise only in the context of some exceptional circumstance. In the event a cleric cannot, in good conscience, conduct a baptism, even where the canonical conditions have been met, they are to contact their bishop for advice.

## B3.2 The baptism of infants

As with all candidates, the baptism of an infant is the occasion whereby sponsors, through prayer and promises made on his or her behalf, and with the support and welcome of the church, set the face of the child towards Jesus Christ, the centre of all life. The child is thereby made a member of the people of God, the covenant community centred in Christ and the Holy Spirit. What then is the difference between candidates unable to answer for themselves (usually infants) and others (usually those 'of riper years')? Baptism remains baptism for every candidate. In the former case, rather than profess faith him or herself, faith in Christ is exercised on the candidate's behalf by the people of God, through the sponsors who make the baptismal promises on behalf of the infant baptised.

The baptism of infants has sometimes been closely linked with 'original sin'. In the popular mind, this has commonly been understood to mean that conception and childbirth are inherently sinful, so that baptism's main function is to make the child 'safe' from the consequences of sin. Such ideas go back to Augustine's misreading of Romans 5.12, a major factor in later distortions of Christian understandings of human sexuality. (The BCP phrase 'conceived and born in sin' was not intended in this way, as the change in terminology from 'Purification of Women' in the 1549 Prayer Book, to 'Thanksgiving after Childbirth' in the 1552 revision shows). The main reason given in BCP for baptism is that we may receive new birth, rather than merely dealing with 'original sin'.

'Original sin', nonetheless, points to the reality that we humans, though made in the image and likeness of God, find ourselves as a race in solidarity with sin and death. (The carefully worded Article IX recognises the reality of sin in each of us, but refuses to be drawn into the puzzle as to how 'original sin' is transmitted from generation to generation). Sins are more than habits we learn: they are the 'fruit' produced from a tree with sin-soaked roots and sin-tainted sap, encouraged by 'the world, the flesh and the devil' both around us and within. Apart from Christ, who 'knew no sin' (2 Corinthians 5.21) each of us—babies, children, young adults and old people alike—are caught up in a web of sin. Apart from Christ, each of us puts self in place of God at the centre of our lives, and needs to be 'reborn' through the Spirit. We all depend upon the grace of God to be delivered and changed.

No matter how tightly we are held by sin, nor how shocking or tawdry our sins, all are dealt with by Christ's death and resurrection, made effective in us through the Spirit who brings us to new birth. In the case of young children, Jesus' teaching that 'of such is the Kingdom of God' (Mark 10.13—BCP's gospel reading for the Baptism of Infants) means that both infants' sinful nature, as well as sins committed inadvertently by them, are covered by Christ's atoning death.

Since baptism is the sacrament in which the realities of sin and salvation are acknowledged, the renunciation of Satan and of all evil, and the public repentance of sins, form part of every baptism service.

### B3.3 The baptism of those able to answer for themselves

APBA (p. 70, Note 1) advises that 'where adults are baptised, their confirmation and first communion should take place at the same service as their baptism, making one unified rite of Christian initiation'. This is an important principle that should be considered the default or normative position in instances of baptism for those able to answer for themselves.

Some distinctive features of the baptism of those able to answer for themselves include:
a) The minister will be satisfied that the person has been prepared and instructed in the Christian faith;
b) The person to be baptised will make the responses and give the necessary promises themselves;
c) The person to be baptised will have at least one sponsor, whose primary duties will be to present the candidate and to encourage the candidate to continue in the Christian life.

In some situations, in particular involving children who are neither infants nor young adults, it may be necessary to carefully consider whether the candidate can meet the requirements set out above for the baptism of those able to answer for themselves, especially in regards to the necessary preparation and instruction, and the ability to make and give the necessary responses and promises in their own right. In some circumstances, it may be appropriate for one or more sponsors to answer in conjunction with, rather than on behalf of, the child.

## B4   Preparation for baptism

All who receive enquiries about baptism should be aware of 'Thanksgiving for a Child' (APBA pp. 43–48), as well as the service of baptism. Some inquiries may not necessarily be for Christian baptism, but for the recognition before God of the arrival of a child: in such cases 'Thanksgiving for a Child' may be more appropriate—see section B15.

The Canon Concerning Baptism 1992 (5a–b) requires that:
a) Except in emergencies and extreme circumstances, before conducting the baptism of an infant or person unable to answer for themselves, the minister shall be satisfied that at least one of the

parents have been instructed in the Christian faith and are aware of their responsibilities as sponsors.

b) Before baptising a person able to answer for themselves, the minister shall be satisfied that the person concerned has been instructed and prepared in the Christian faith.

The form, content and length of the preparation are determined at local level. It is preferable that all who are involved in the baptism of an infant, including the parents and sponsors, are given appropriate opportunity to be prepared, so that they may recognise and understand the privileges and responsibilities of baptism. It should not be assumed that parents who bring second or later children for baptism have 'heard it all before': each child is born into a distinct family context.

Those who prepare candidates' families and sponsors have a responsibility to open up to them the great issues of Christian faith and life, and to encourage them towards effective Christian discipleship. The way in which this is done will vary, but preparation may typically involve all or some of the following:

- A study of the basic truths of Christian faith, as expressed in the baptism service;
- An explanation of the shape and content of the baptism service, and any symbols used;
- Regular attendance at church over a period of time;
- An exploration of the issues of faith and life;
- Assistance with spiritual formation through personal and family prayer and scripture reading, and participation in public worship.

In all cases, preparation is to include careful working through of the relevant order of service with the candidate's family and sponsors. As well as helping parents and sponsors coming to appreciate further the meaning and responsibilities of Christian baptism, this process avoids anyone being unprepared to respond in public to the significant questions they are asked in the service.

Follow-up with candidates' families is essential and ought not be neglected. A system of visitation by 'baptism friends' can be helpful (if appropriate to the circumstances), as is a 'cradle roll' (sending birthday and baptism anniversary greetings). Most of those presenting a child for baptism will agree to be entered onto the parish mailing and email list (it is important consent is gained for this in the light of privacy laws) and can, therefore, be easily sent invitations to attend services with a particular focus on children, playgroups and outreach activities such as mainly music and messy church, and Christmas nativity services. Even so, there is no substitute for the development of quality relationships. Finding a friend in the community can make church attendance all the more likely and sustainable.

Within the above framework, each congregation needs to give careful and ongoing consideration to its policy and practice as regards the baptism of infants, as appropriate to local context and pastoral circumstances, and, ideally, to incorporate these into a pastoral services policy (Appendix One). This will include a basic pattern of preparation and follow-up for families, from the initial enquiry, through preparation in its various stages, to the service itself. One significant element to be included is a clearly written and set out welcoming letter and brochure about baptism, which introduces the church and its initiation practice to those not previously associated with the life of the church. This can be provided to those seeking baptism at the point of enquiry, and also uploaded in a generic form to the congregation's website. Being able to point to a clear policy that is shared and owned at local level, and reflective of Canon law and the guidelines and principles set out here, can be pastorally helpful in a range of ways, for enquirer/s as well as the clergy and congregation.

### B4.1  Postponement of baptism

Baptism should be administered within a reasonably short time following a request, unless there is good reason for acting otherwise. During the time intervening from request to the baptism itself, it is expected that appropriate preparation will be undertaken. Where baptism is postponed through a casual approach to Christian responsibilities, opportunity should be taken to remind those concerned of the significance and importance of baptism.

Some Anglican parents do not wish their children to be baptised until they are of sufficient age to participate actively in the baptism, and be admitted to Holy Communion. Such desires are to be respected, but the anomalous standing of an unbaptised person in the congregation and the Christian home should be discussed in a pastorally sensitive way.

Candidates' sponsors and families may benefit from an extended period of preparation using the catechumenate pattern. Requests for such a preparation should be honoured unless there are sound reasons for not doing so. In these cases, it may be helpful for candidates to be 'enrolled' when they commence pre-baptismal instruction.

## B5  Extra-parochial situations

The system of dividing a diocese into parishes for the delivery of pastoral care and the provision of the pastoral services such as baptism has a very long history for Anglicans. The parish continues to be 'the geographical unit for organising the mission of God throughout the Anglican Church within the Diocese of Melbourne' (Parish Governance Act 2013 s 5). Whilst the parish system continues to have a high degree of importance to Anglican polity, its importance to those attending services of worship, whether on Sundays or at other times, is much diminished. Even among observant Anglicans, many people, in some places the majority of the congregation, do not live in the geographical area of the parish in which they are regular worshippers.

In these circumstances it is not surprising, then, that an enquiry for baptism may come from persons who are geographically removed from the place in which baptism is sought, and who may not be worshipping members of that congregation. They may have some connection to that place of worship, perhaps through their own baptism, through being married there, or through attending occasional services in the past. No matter how tenuous the link, it is better to nurture it rather than dismiss and sever.

### B5.1  Canonical matters

The Canon Concerning Baptism 1992 (7) stipulates that a minister will not normally baptise a child whose parents are not resident in the geographical area of the parish in which it is proposed the baptism take place.

Two exceptions are made:
a) If at least one of the parents 'attends divine service in the parish'.
b) If the advice of the minister in the parish where the parents reside, or, if applicable, the parish in which they usually attend divine service, has been sought.

In circumstances where one or both of the parents presenting a child for baptism normally attend divine service in the place where the baptism is sought, as stipulated by the canon (above), the baptism can proceed with no further action being necessary, regardless of where the parent or parents are physically resident.

### B5.2 Pastoral matters

A variety of pastoral sensitivities, and potential difficulties, can arise in situations where baptism is sought by persons who are geographically removed from the place in which baptism is sought, and where one or both parents are not worshipping members of that congregation. The principle of welcoming all enquiries as an opportunity to nurture faith should be adhered to in every situation, and an open and respectful conversation entered into with those seeking the baptism with a view to exploring the reasons for the request. Questions such as 'how will you stay connected to this or another faith community in the future?'

or 'have you considered a parish church in your area?' can be helpful discussion starters. A range of options is possible, but will not cover every situation.

a) The minister may form the view, having consulted with the churchwardens or other lay leaders as may be appropriate, that those seeking the baptism are not part of any other church or Christian faith community, and that they understand the parish in which the baptism is sought to be their spiritual home, and so proceed with the baptism.

b) The minister may make contact with the minister of the parish in which the enquirer/s presently reside, with a view to conducting the baptism and referring the enquirer/s to that parish for a liturgical welcome and pastoral follow up after the baptism.

c) The minister may refer the enquirer/s to the parish in which they worship or reside for baptism.

d) In some situations, the reasons for seeking baptism may lie in a refusal, or what was experienced as a refusal, or perceived to be the imposition of an unreasonable burden, in the parish in which the enquirer resides or possibly attends divine worship. Such incidents should be treated sensitively and professionally, with care taken to avoid criticism of colleagues in ministry, whilst recognising that refusal always causes hurt and reverberates through family and friends long after the word 'no' is spoken.

e) Where a candidate lives interstate or overseas, but there are good pastoral reasons for conducting the baptism in another place, the parish in which the candidate worships or resides should be consulted, with a view to arranging for preparation prior to baptism, and for a liturgical welcome and pastoral follow up after baptism.

## B5.3 Schools and colleges

Requests for Holy Baptism from students at an Anglican school or college are to be welcomed. Thorough preparation should be given, along with information about parish membership. If this preparation can be undertaken by the school/college and parish together, so much the better.

Where baptism is to take place at an Anglican school or college, the chaplain should advise the candidate's home parish of the proposed baptism, and invite it to be represented and/or involved in the service in some way, acknowledging at that time the presence of the parish representatives. Conversely, the baptism may be administered in the parish church during a regular Sunday service, with school or college representatives present and/or taking part. Such practices take up the opportunity to link the baptised person with a local faith community, and to deepen the links between school and parish.

When confirmation is administered to students or staff in Anglican schools, it is both a professional courtesy and pastorally helpful for the chaplain to contact the priests of candidates' parishes. Parish and school may be able to share together in preparing candidates, with the parish priest and parishioners being present at the school for the confirmation, taking appropriate parts in the service.

When students come to leave school or college, they should be encouraged to link up with a local parish congregation, with assistance from the school's staff as appropriate.

## B6    Contextual matters

Baptism is a sacrament of the Gospel and the rite of initiation into the Christian community. The congregation in the place where the baptism is administered have an important role in the service, especially to welcome the new Christian into the community of faith on behalf of the wider Church. In most cases the rite of baptism will be administered in a place of worship by a cleric licensed to that congregation.

### B6.1 Place

Unless an emergency, baptism is normatively conducted in a place dedicated or consecrated for Christian worship. Usually, this will be the place where the candidate's congregation or home parish meets for worship.

The rise in incidence of adults coming to faith who were not baptised as infants has meant that it is increasingly common for there to be requests for baptism to be conducted in a place not dedicated or consecrated for Anglican worship such as a river, pool, or the sea. The issue that arises in such circumstances is the balance between baptism as an act of the church, and its personal significance. Baptism is a community event, in which new members of Christ's flock are welcomed; it also provides an opportunity for all the baptised who are present to renew their promises. Where the request comes from an adult candidate, confirmation and first communion will normally be associated with the baptism, which may raise considerable difficulties in an outside setting. Nonetheless, baptism in such places is still very much capable of being a community event, with members and representatives of the congregation present, often in significant number, to welcome the newly baptised into the family of God. Such circumstances are increasingly common as fresh expressions of church, new church plants, and the variety of pioneer ministries are established under Anglican auspices.

Where the primary reason for seeking to conduct a baptism in a place other than an Anglican Church is to facilitate baptism by submersion (see B8.2), arrangements enabling this to occur in the candidate's place of worship should be considered. The bishop may be consulted for advice about other parishes with experience in practising baptism by submersion. One congregation, for instance, has hired a portable hot tub for this purpose; a child size inflatable pool will also suffice.

### B6.2 Occasion

APBA (p. 70, Note 1) describes 'baptism as a community event, welcoming new members of Christ's flock, and providing an opportunity for all the baptised to renew their vows', and states that baptism 'should therefore take place within the regular pattern of congregational worship'. Notwithstanding the possible exceptions discussed above, clearly APBA anticipates that baptisms will normatively be conducted as part of a regular Sunday service of worship as stipulated by the Canon Concerning Baptism 1992 (6)—'the sacrament of Holy Baptism shall normally be administered at public worship'.

Where a baptism does take place outside the context of a public service of worship, the person baptised should be welcomed by the congregation in the context of a public service of worship at the next opportunity. Sections 18–19 and 26 of the baptism service (APBA pp. 56, 60) may be used for this purpose. When there has been an emergency baptism, for example of a baby in hospital, the liturgical welcome can include a prayer of thanksgiving for the child's recovery from danger and be a joyous time to welcome the family and friends who may well have been distressed and fearful at the time of the baptism.

### B6.3 Minister

The administration of Holy Baptism is an act of the Church rather than a private occasion. Requests for a particular person to conduct a baptism, arising out of prior or current relationships are understandable. However baptism is a public rather than a private or domestic rite, in which the minister represents the wider Church. The minister at baptism will normally be the priest who has pastoral charge of the congregation in which the baptism takes place, or another cleric licensed to that congregation. A deacon may also minister baptism in appropriate pastoral circumstances. Except in the case of emergency baptism (B11), a layperson is not authorised to baptise without permission of the bishop.

## B7 Liturgical principles and practice

All services of Christian initiation in the diocese will follow the rites of baptism, confirmation and reception into communicant membership provided in APBA, AAPB, or BCP, in accordance with the oath and declarations made by all licensed and authorised clergy.

### B7.1 The liturgy

A variety of liturgical resources for Christian initiation are provided for by APBA.

a) The main service for baptism in APBA (commencing on p. 51) is a single integrated rite of Christian initiation encompassing baptism, confirmation and reception into communicant membership, in the context of Holy Communion. The service is highly adaptable and suitable for the main service on a Sunday. Where the service includes baptism only, the shaded portions relating to confirmation are omitted. Where baptism and confirmation are both part of this service, the shaded areas relating to confirmation are used. Where reception into communicant membership is also part of the service, the liturgy on pp. 96–97 of APBA is incorporated at the appropriate point.

b) A service of Holy Baptism (only) in the context of Morning and Evening Prayer is also provided for in APBA (p. 73). This service is used in instances where the baptism takes place in the context of a public service that does not include Holy Communion, and in situations where the baptism is being administered outside of a regular Sunday service.

c) Revised forms for the Baptism of Infants were produced by the Liturgy Commission in 2009 at the request of some of the bishops, and to correct misunderstandings about the place of the Creed: they are available on the General Synod website (see 'Resources for Christian initiation'). These services are also commended for use in this diocese.

The readings for a Sunday service including Holy Baptism will normally be those of the day. Some further options for readings specific to baptism are given by APBA (p. 71, Note 8).

### B7.2 Liturgical furniture and movement

The placement of church furniture and the arrangement of the worship space, together with the 'choreography' concerning the movement of those involved in a service of baptism, requires careful thought and planning.

a) The font is the place of baptism and should be highly visible during the service, both when in use and not in use. The location of the font should declare baptism to be one of the sacraments of the Gospel. Each location provides both opportunities and challenges, however, wherever the font is placed, space should be left around it.

   The 'traditional' position for the font is at the back near the 'west' door, this speaking of entry into God's household, reminding worshippers of their own baptism as they enter and leave the church building. This position also provides a balancing focus to the holy table, so that worshippers are physically 'included' between the major symbols of each gospel sacrament. On the other hand, the font in this position is usually out of worshippers' view, and provision will need to be made to enable the whole congregation to see the baptism itself, and participate actively. This may mean asking the congregation to move to surround the font, which movement can itself be a powerful symbol of our shared 'journey' in God.

   Some contemporary/multipurpose buildings employ movable furniture. The font should always be present during each main

Sunday service, whether a baptism is taking place or not, though its location can vary depending on the season and occasion. During Easter, for example, it is helpful for a paschal candle to be placed next to the font, as a reminder of the opportunity for baptismal renewal that this season provides.

The design of the font should reflect both the meaning of baptism, and practical usage. The traditional eight-sided design points to the resurrection of Christ, which baptism symbolises, as the new 'first day' of the new creation—the 'eighth day'. Some contemporary designs employ modern plumbing so that water runs continually through the font, adding to the aural as well as visual environment of the church building (a good example of this is to be found inside Holy Apostles, Sunshine). The font should be large enough to hold a reasonable amount of water.

b) Thought and attention needs to be given by those planning the service to where the candidates and their sponsors will stand, how the baptism and the after-baptism ceremonies will be administered, and who will assist the clergy with this part of the service. Included in this are considerations as to how, and when, the baptism party will reach the font, whether this means those involved being 'called forward', or entails a procession to the font.

c) Normally the paschal or Easter candle will be lit and prominent at a baptism, and often placed near or behind the font. If candles are given to those baptised, thought should be given as to where this will be done and who will light and present them (the logical place is during the after baptism ceremonies—APBA p. 60, # 25). After the presentation of candles, the candidate and/or parents and sponsors may need some instruction as to when they should be extinguished during the service, and may be provided with advice as to when the baptismal candle may be used again (e.g. on the anniversary of baptism, at confirmation).

d) The rubrics (APBA p. 55, # 11) require the candidates and their sponsors to stand in view of the congregation. They should be both seen and heard. This will usually entail a rehearsal or instructions of some nature, even if it is brief and on the day of the service, to ensure those making promises, especially those unfamiliar with the customs of the church, are fully aware of their part in the service, and of how and when it will happen. Care should be taken to ensure that those who may not be used to being in a church, let alone actively involved in a church service, are treated with courtesy and respect, and with appropriate hospitality, and not embarrassed or put into awkward situations.
e) A ewer (jug), filled with water, together with a towel, should be prepared and ready before the service.
f) At a Sunday service including a baptism there will often be significant numbers of people present in the congregation for whom the church and its customs are unfamiliar and alien. Those leading the service should carefully plan all aspects of the liturgy, and conduct the service in such a way that all present are able to clearly follow the service without embarrassment. This may mean giving page numbers if using the physical books, or preparing a printed service booklet or a digital order of service to be displayed on a screen. It can be helpful to clearly advise the congregation when to stand, sit or kneel, and (if applicable), to give clear instructions about who is welcome to receive Holy Communion and how the sacrament will be administered.
g) If used, the oil of chrism should also be prepared and ready for use.
h) Certificates with all relevant details filled in are to be provided for each candidate, and thought given as to when and how these will be presented to both the candidate/s and their sponsor/s. It is important to make sure the Baptismal Register is kept up to date

as well as making an entry into the Services Register. The parish will inevitably receive requests, usually years later, to confirm that a person was baptised. Keeping records is a serious responsibility, which the Parish Governance Act 2013 s 53 vests in the minister having pastoral charge for that congregation.

i) In the baptism of an infant, it is helpful for the minister to have clarified who will hold the child to be baptised—for some families the expectation is that the minister will do so, others may desire to follow the tradition that a male godparent holds the child. In some cases it may best for one of the parents to hold the child. It is more important that the child be calm and comfortable with whoever is holding them than that a particular custom is kept.

j) Where the baptism is by submersion or immersion particular issues arise around the need for the candidate/s to dry off and/or change clothes after the baptism. Careful thought will need to be given as to how and where, and at what point in the service, provision will be made for this to occur.

## B8 Symbols and Mode

Baptism shall take place by immersing a person in water or by pouring water upon the candidate and by pronouncing the words, 'I baptise you in the name of the Father, and of the Son, and of the Holy Spirit' (Canon Concerning Baptism 1993, 3).

Baptism is, therefore, valid when a person has been baptised with water (the proper element), in the name of the Father, the Son, and the Holy Spirit (the proper form), with public (external) intention to baptise (met by the candidate and/or sponsors stating their desire for baptism and making the required responses).

### B8.1 The water of baptism

The 'element' of baptism is water. Scripture begins and ends with images of water (Genesis 1.2, Revelation 22.1–3, 17). Water is the great universal symbol of both life and danger, of refreshing rain and destroying flood. We speak of the 'waters of birth' and the 'river of death'. For the Hebrews, in particular, 'sea' and 'the deep' were fearsome images of the powers of chaos. The flood (Genesis 6–8) and the exodus (Exodus 14–15) became paradigmatic examples of salvation from water, and through water images used in Christian baptismal liturgy as 'types' of the salvation of God's people through Christ's death and resurrection. They are prominent in the prayer over the water in APBA (pp. 57–58, 76–77).

Jesus taught the theologian Nicodemus that 'no one can enter the Kingdom of God without being born of water and the Spirit' (John 3.5), a teaching long associated with baptism. We who have passed through the waters of 'fleshly' birth must be 'born from above' through the Spirit, of which baptism into Christ is the sign and seal. Jesus thus spoke of 'living water' as a picture of the gift of the Holy Spirit (John 7.37–39), and of Jonah's 'burial' in water, to interpret his death and resurrection (Matthew 12.40–41). Jesus calmed storms and walked on the sea, so demonstrating his power over 'the deep' and its terrors. Great richness is found in the biblical and liturgical use of water symbols: consider stories such as the healing of Naaman, Jesus' healings at the Pool of Bethesda, his meeting with the woman at the Samaritan well, and Paul's experiences at sea (also note Revelation 21.1).

### B8.2 Modes for the administration of the water of baptism

As to the way in which the water of baptism is administered, nothing is prescribed in the New Testament. A number of modes have scriptural precedent behind them, however.

In the Hebrew Bible (the Christian Old Testament), 'sprinkling' of water, oil or blood was the sign of 'sanctification': it was the way by which the people of God were made 'clean' once more (Leviticus 16.14; Numbers 8.7; 19.18; and Ezekiel 36.25). The water of baptism is sometimes described as being 'sprinkled,' but this is problematic: it minimises the dramatic symbolism associated with water in the scriptures, and applies a metaphor to do with ongoing spiritual life (sanctification) to the sacrament of its beginning. The ritual sprinkling of a person, congregation or object with water (aspersion) may occur as part of a rite reaffirming baptismal promises, or as part of the consecration or blessing of a new building, an item of liturgical furniture or a sacred vessel and the like. These are cognate with scriptural usage, and may remind us of our own baptism. Sprinkling as a mode of baptism is, however, not authorised by Anglican formularies or canons.

'Immersion' refers to a candidate standing in water while more water is poured over them; 'submersion' means the person goes under the water. These modes bring out the symbolic characteristics of water to the fullest extent, especially our being buried with Christ in baptism (cf. Romans 6). In the rubrics of BCP, being 'dipped in water' refers to either of these modes.

'Affusion' (pouring) symbolises the love of God, 'poured into our hearts by the Holy Spirit which has been given to us' for whom Christ died (Romans 5.5). It is allowed by the rubrics of BCP and, over time, became common practice, usually by pouring water over the candidate's head from a 'shell' (the symbol of pilgrimage).

For baptism to be valid, either immersion and submersion in water, or the pouring of water in affusion, must take place in accompaniment with the Trinitarian formula ('in the name of the Father, and of the Son, and of the Holy Spirit') in the context of a publicly made intention. Affusion—the pouring of an amount of water over the candidate's forehead—will normally and easily take place at the font. If immersion or submersion is desired, other suitable arrangements will need to be made—there are, for instance, immersion fonts available in the Diocese of Melbourne, notably at St Paul's Cathedral.

### B8.3 Baptismal symbols

Christian baptism is a sacrament of the Church, and so should be celebrated in ways that bring out the richness of the symbolism present.

a) Water is the primary and essential symbol in baptism. APBA (p. 70, Note 3) requires that, 'in the celebration of baptism the symbolism of water should be emphasised. Immersion or the pouring of a significant quantity of water shows this clearly. The pouring of the water both into the font and over each candidate should be done deliberately and with care.'

b) BCP and APBA provide that the sign of the cross is used at baptism. Although the Anglican Church retains the practise, it 'holds and teaches that the sign of the cross used in baptism is no part of the substance of the sacrament' (Canon Concerning Baptism 1992, 10). For a fuller explanation of the sign of the cross at baptism see APBA p. 822, Note 3.

c) Oil of chrism (olive oil with balsam added), normally that dedicated by the bishop in Holy Week prior to Easter, may be used at the signing of the cross (APBA p. 70, # 6).

d) A candle, often lit from the paschal or Easter candle, and symbolising the light of Christ, may be presented to the candidate as part of the after baptism ceremonies (APBA p. 60, # 25; see p. 70, Note 7).

e) In some circumstances particular clothing such as a 'chrisome' (white robe or gown) may be worn by the candidate. There is no requirement regarding the clothing worn by infants or adults in baptism, other than that clothing worn at a baptism by immersion or submersion preserve the dignity and sacred nature of the occasion and not be overly revealing or immodest.

f) The full Christian name/s of the person being baptised, without the surname, should be used. APBA does not provide for the 'naming' of the candidate since that now happens when a birth is registered with the state.

In some instances parents or sponsors may request that objects such as a necklace or other item, be dedicated (or blessed) and/or placed on the candidate at a certain point. Such a request should be dealt with outside of the baptism, so as not to give the impression this is occurring as part of the rite of Holy Baptism.

### B8.4 Multiple baptisms

Where there is more than one baptism, the 'after baptism' ceremonies (APBA p. 60) are conducted after all the baptisms have been completed. It is, further, helpful to the flow of the service that the congregational words of welcome (APBA p. 60, # 26) are said once, for all the newly baptised as a group (after the words and symbolic actions at # 24 and # 25 have been conducted for each). As APBA (p. 70, Note 4) advises, 'when all have been baptised, the ministers, the newly baptised and their sponsors may move to a position in the centre of the congregation', at which time the congregational welcome may be said by all.

## B9 Sponsors

'Sponsor' is the term generally used in the Anglican Communion to describe those who support candidates for baptism (and confirmation). It has the same meaning as 'godparent' and both terms are used interchangeably by the Canon Concerning Baptism 1992.
   a) Each child or person to be baptised who is unable to answer for themselves is to have at least one, and normally three, sponsors, of whom two will be of the same gender as the child, and one of the opposite gender (Canon Concerning Baptism 1992, 8).
   b) Either one or both of the parents of a child may act as sponsors.

c) The parent/s directly 'sponsor' their child or children by bringing them for baptism and should, therefore, be invited to make the responses along with the sponsors, in circumstances where one or both parents are not formally acting as a sponsor (APBA p. 71, Note 11).

d) For every candidate for baptism who is able to answer for himself or herself one sponsor shall suffice, whose responsibility shall be to encourage the candidate to continue in the Christian life (Canon Concerning Baptism 1992, 9).

e) Sponsors must be baptised (in any Church that professes the apostolic faith and uses the Trinitarian formula—this will embrace almost all Christian traditions). The sponsors should be persons who will faithfully fulfil their responsibilities both by their spiritual nurture and instruction of the children committed to their charge and by the example of their own godly living (Canon Concerning Baptism 1992, 8). Ideally, sponsors will, then, be regular communicants, whether of the Anglican communion, or of another Christian tradition.

f) If a sponsor is unable to be physically present, their role may be performed by proxy by another person, providing the candidate and/or the candidate's other sponsors, and the minister, agree to this.

Note: It is sometimes thought that, should a child be orphaned, or be in a situation where the parents cannot offer appropriate care, then the sponsors/godparents carry a legal responsibility to look after him or her until the child or children concerned become adults. While this is an admirable ideal, no basis exists for this custom in Anglican formularies, nor in Canon law or civil law.

### B9.1 Parental circumstances

The personal circumstances of the parent/s (whether a single parent; a married, divorced, or unmarried couple; or a couple of the same gender) presenting a child for baptism do not impede the provision of the sacrament to that child where all of the canonical requirements have been met. The pastoral issues that might arise are to be considered separately to the provision of the sacrament to an infant or child.

Occasionally parents may ask the cleric who is to baptise their child, to marry them at the same time. Theologically and pastorally, it is a good practice to conduct the baptism first in such circumstances, and then the wedding, as this demonstrates that God's grace is offered without preconditions and that baptism is on the profession of faith, not the marital status of the parents.

## B10 Spiritual renewal

A person may go through a life-changing spiritual experience, leading to a re-awakening or a re-birth of faith after spending a period of time, sometimes many years, away from the worshipping life of the church. Others may have continued their involvement in the church, but undergone an especially meaningful experience of God's gracious presence in some way. In such circumstances, a person may quite naturally desire to make a public act of commitment to faith, and may seek a public opportunity to express their gratitude to God for this new and deepened understanding in the context of the community of faith. This should be recognised and affirmed, and opportunity offered for the faith community to celebrate the person's new experience of God. If the person concerned is made to feel spiritually 'strange' or even rejected, their Christian life may become distorted, and the Church may be denied the God-given gift of its renewed member.

## B10.1 Reaffirmation of faith

APBA (p. 62, # 30) provides for prayer and the laying on of hands by the bishop, in the context of baptism and/or confirmation, for those who have been baptised and confirmed who may wish to make a public reaffirmation of faith (APBA p. 71, Note 12). This act is designed to link the new spiritual experience with the wider Church, and with God's primary 'means of grace.' In Reaffirmation, a person's experience and desire for new commitment can be recognised appropriately: as well as the bishop's prayer, this could include an act of repentance and recommitment, appropriate testimony, special music and songs, or particular prayer following the reception of communion. Pastoral sensitivity may need to be exercised so as to avoid placing too great a focus on the person concerned. The service will need to be carefully prepared, in consultation with the person or people who seek to reaffirm their faith in Christ through it.

At the corporate level, the custom of congregations reaffirming their baptismal promises at Easter offers an opportunity for spiritual growth to be celebrated, and fresh commitments to be made.

Any act of Reaffirmation (whether personal or corporate) will be strengthened by the use of appropriate actions. These could include the laying on of hands, anointing, lighting and giving a candle, or the presentation of symbols.

Sometimes there is a request for water to be used in an act of reaffirmation: provided that it is clear to all present that the service is not 're-baptism', this may be appropriate. As noted above (B8), the modes of baptism provided for in Anglican formularies are affusion or immersion/submersion. To avoid all confusion, where water is utilised in an act of reaffirmation, these modes are not to be used. On the other hand, since sprinkling carries the idea of sanctification (being 'made holy'), it is a most appropriate way to use water for reaffirmation.

### B10.2 'Re-baptism'

From time to time people may ask to be 're-baptised'. Someone baptised in infancy may regard their baptism as invalid because they were too young to exercise faith for themselves. Others may feel that the faith exercised at their baptism was not Spirit-based, because it was not associated with an experience such as 'speaking in tongues'. They therefore may ask to be re-baptised with an emphasis on the Spirit. At other times, a request for re-baptism comes because a person has had a life-changing spiritual experience, which they wish to acknowledge. As noted in the previous section (B10.1), every such enquiry is to be welcomed as a sign of spiritual need and growth, and positive approaches to such opportunities can be taken up as described there.

Baptism, however, is an unrepeatable act. Just as Christ died and rose once for all, so we are baptised into that death and resurrection once for all. To suggest otherwise runs counter to the teaching of the New Testament (Ephesians 4.5)—may imply that Christ's completed earthly work was insufficient—and so undermines our assurance as Christians of having a stable foundation for life in Christ. Baptism is the effectual sign of the full adequacy of God's provision for us in Christ: as the imagery of 'drowning' and 'burial' suggests, it is the sacrament of new life in Christ, a unique beginning. Further, to seek 're-baptism' as a way of expressing renewed commitment misunderstands the nature of baptism: it does not in the first place concern our commitment to God, but God's gracious call to discipleship.

It may help the person who has made the request for re-baptism to realise that no baptism is ever perfectly efficacious: the baptism of a mature adult convert is as much a matter of faith as that of the youngest baby. Likewise, no spiritual experience (including baptism) brings to us all the blessings that God may give: in this life we see 'as in a glass darkly', and look to the future to see Christ 'face to face' (1 Corinthians 13.12). The warrant for baptism is not perfect faith or experience, but the intention—no matter how feeble—to lead the life of faith, hope and love. Baptism sets us at the beginning of Christian life, and calls us to 'live as a disciple of Christ' and to 'fight the good fight, finish the race, keep the faith' (APBA p. 60, # 24).

### B10.3 Confession and renewal

In some circumstances it may be appropriate pastorally for a person seeking to reaffirm their faith to receive absolution in the context of a 'private confession'. This is provided for in ' Reconciliation of a Penitent' (APBA pp. 774–778; see O3). Sometimes a person (including regular worshippers) may be deeply concerned that they have 'grieved the Holy Spirit' through a particular sin, and so feel that they have lost touch with God. Responding to such a situation calls for considerable discernment, but the person may be assured that God will never let them go, and that their baptism cannot and will not be invalidated from God's side. It may be helpful to explain that the willingness to explore the sense of God's 'absence' is itself a sign of the active presence of the Holy Spirit within them. Such enquirers need to be helped to know that, through the ministry of God's Word, anyone may receive grace to repent of their sins, and rededicate themselves to the service of God in the power of the Holy Spirit. This ministry is made available in Anglican formularies in the public reading and preaching of the scriptures, and through both 'general' and 'private' confession and absolution.

The most suitable way for someone to confess both renewed faith and forgiveness from sin is by participation in the eucharist. The ministries of the Word, prayer and Holy Communion speak both to the forgiven sinner and to the renewed saint: all alike humbly feed on Christ, and joyfully feast with him. Christ crucified and risen offers repentant sinners the forgiveness of sins through his body and blood, and calls all disciples to be 'celebrants' of God's saving work in the power of the Spirit.

On private confession and reconciliation, see Chapter 5, O3—Reconciliation of a Penitent.

## B11  Baptism in emergency situations

Emergency events lead to situations for which pastoral guidelines cannot be formed ahead of time. As it is not, therefore, possible to provide comprehensive guidelines in advance that will meet all of the circumstances in which emergency baptism may be administered, the following are to be considered as general principles.

a) A request to conduct the baptism of a person for whom it is reasonable to suppose that life is under threat should be agreed to and expedited without delay, unless there are exceptional and compelling reasons not to proceed.

b) The minister of a baptism in emergency circumstances will normally be a priest or deacon who has a pastoral relationship with the person concerned, or with their family or sponsors, or who has pastoral responsibility in the place in which the rite is to be administered. If it is not possible for a priest or deacon to attend in a timely manner, a layperson may administer baptism.

c) If it is possible, and if the candidate is of an age and in a condition in which they are able to understand, brief instruction about the meaning of baptism and the significance of the symbols, may be undertaken.

d) The guidelines in APBA (p. 71, Note 9) must be adhered to in order for the baptism to be valid. These stipulate that, where possible, sections 16, 17 and 18 of the baptism service commencing on p. 51 of APBA should be used, with one or more of the parents or sponsors responding if the candidate is a child; where possible sections 21 and 22 should also be used, or at least the last paragraph of section 21; whilst section 23 must be used.

e) Details of the time and place of the baptism, together with the minister who conducted the rite, should be written down so that they can be entered into the appropriate register later, and the required certificates issued (see B13).

f) Where circumstances make it possible (i.e. in the event of recovery from the emergency), the person baptised in emergency circumstances should come to, or be brought to, a service of public worship, to be formally welcomed by the congregation (APBA p. 71, Note 9).

g) In situations where there is less urgency, but the person concerned is unable to come to, or be brought to, a place of worship, the whole of the baptism service, or as much as practical, should be conducted in the home, hospital, or other place, with the sponsors taking up their roles as appropriate.

Particular pastoral difficulties exist where baptism is sought in situations where a person has already died. All Christian traditions affirm that baptism concerns the exercise of faith in living persons. Where death has occurred it should be carefully and sensitively explained that baptism is not necessary, as it remains only to commend the person concerned to God's loving care. Where the person concerned is an infant there are strong scriptural grounds on which to offer a 'warm' assurance of this nature. The material in the Funeral Service for an Infant (APBA pp. 752–764) may provide some helpful prayers and other resources in such situations.

For circumstances where baptism is sought for a stillborn child, see Chapter 4, F7.3.

## B12 'Conditional' baptism

Circumstances occasionally arise in which some doubt exists as to whether a person has been validly baptised. This may be due to the lack of reliable evidence that a baptism ever took place, or where questions have arisen as to whether the rite undergone by the person constituted Christian baptism.

Where genuine doubt exists that a valid Christian baptism has been administered, the rubric and formula set out in BCP is followed—the minister baptises the candidate with water using the words 'If you are not already baptised, Name, I baptise you in the name of the Father, and of the Son, and of the Holy Spirit. Amen.'

The following considerations apply:

a) In many situations it may be necessary to conduct a sensitive investigation to ascertain whether a ceremony performed constituted valid baptism. There may have been, for instance, a 'naming ceremony' conducted by a civil celebrant that might have been thought of as being equivalent to Christian baptism in some way.

b) If there are grounds on which to believe the baptism performed was in fact valid, it may be pastorally appropriate to treat the candidate as having received 'private baptism' and arrange for them to be brought to a place of Christian worship in order to be formally welcomed into the community of faith.

c) 'Baptism' conducted according to the rites of, and under the auspices of, groups such as the Unitarians, Mormons, Jehovah's Witnesses, Christadelphians, and others who deny the Trinity, does not constitute valid Christian baptism. Christian baptism is into the catholic faith as summarised in the ecumenical creeds, and is always in the name of the Trinity.

Further advice concerning valid baptism and the administration of conditional baptism may be sought from the bishop.

## B13  Certificates and Registers

Canon Law (the Canon Concerning Baptism 1992, 11) requires that:

a) The details of each baptism are to be entered into the Baptism Register of the congregation concerned.

b) The service in which the baptism took place is to be entered into the Service Register of the congregation concerned.
c) Each candidate for baptism is to be given a certificate signed by the minister who conducted the rite. The certificate is to show the full name of the candidate, the name of the minister, the names of the sponsors, the date on which the rite was conducted, and the place.
d) The sponsors are also to be provided with a certificate.

The Parish Governance Regulations 2014 (7.1) require the following details to be entered into the Baptism Register:

a) The next consecutive number of the entry in the registry;
b) The date on which the person was baptised;
c) The candidate's date of birth;
d) The candidate's full name;
e) The first name and surname of each of the candidate's parents (if known);
f) The occupation of each of the candidate's parents if the candidate is aged under 18, or of the candidate if the candidate is aged 18 or older;
g) The first name and surname of each godparent;
h) The candidate's residential address;
i) By whom the baptism was performed.

## B14    Fees

The sacraments of the church should never be subject to 'fees' or 'charges'. Those coming for Holy Baptism, or presenting a child for baptism, may make a donation to the parish or Christian community in which the baptism takes place if they wish to.

## B15 Thanksgiving for a Child

The birth of a child is the occasion for great thanksgiving on the part of all people, Christian or not. All societies have celebrated rituals around the birth of a child, and the need for such in our society has not diminished. In previous times, a rite of birth was provided in BCP, originally called 'The Purification of Women' in the first 1549 Prayer Book, then 'The Thanksgiving of Women after Childbirth, commonly called the Churching of Women' in the 1552 revision. The same rite is present, with the same title, in BCP (1662). These relate more, however, to the safe delivery of the mother from the dangers of childbirth, rather than to the arrival of the child. In AAPB and APBA the emphasis has shifted towards 'Thanksgiving for a Child' (whether born or adopted), with prayers and thanksgivings for the mother in particular continuing to be included.

Where parents enquiring about baptism seem uncertain about what they want for their child, or unclear about their reasons for seeking baptism, they should be encouraged to consider whether 'Thanksgiving for a Child' might better meet their needs. The relationships between church and home that are built up initially through such a service may well culminate in Christian baptism at a later date.

In contemporary Australia, research has revealed that while some couples seek out a 'civil celebrant' for a birth ceremony, or hold a party to welcome a new child, a growing number do not mark the birth of a child in any way at all. Anthropologists would regard this as most unusual in terms of the wider human community, and the reasons for its coming about are not yet clear, but the loss of a sense of 'tradition' and 'ritual' in daily life would seem to be one factor. In this situation, the offer of a 'rite of passage' for birth by Christian churches can be a significant service to the common good, pointing people to the wonder of life as God's gift. 'Thanksgiving for a Child', held at times and places suitable for parents, can form the basis for a public service to this end, quite distinct from Christian baptism.

Parishes that intend to make significant use of 'Thanksgiving for a Child' are encouraged to promote it widely, and consider using it as a first-stage or 'enrolment' rite where baptism is envisaged. It may also be used after a baptism, particularly where the baptism took place in an emergency situation, or if there has been any danger to the life of the parents or child.

'Thanksgiving for a Child' provides an opportunity:
- To express to our Creator the joy and wonder of human birth;
- To acknowledge our dependence upon God for safety and health, and to thank God for safety in child-bearing;
- To formally announce and publicly affirm the name of the child;
- To affirm people in their calling to be parents (whether by birth or adoption);
- To give a positive moral and spiritual start in life to the child.

'Naming' is included as part of the service in APBA (p. 44, # 8). From ancient times the giving of a name has been associated with baptismal practice, derived from the biblical picture of the 'new name' given to the one who overcomes (Revelation 2.17, cf. Isaiah 62.2), and the notion of being baptised 'into the Name' of God. Where a candidate's birth-name reflects a non-Christian world-view, or is associated by the candidate with a past life that they wish to leave behind, taking a new name makes sound pastoral sense.

Yet naming is a significant symbolic act for all human beings, apart from baptism: 'naming ceremonies'—regular practice among African Christians especially—can be both impressive and pastorally helpful. The two notions behind 'naming' should not be confused, but the rich dimensions of biblical understandings of its significance may be of some assistance in offering the possibility of 'naming' a child within 'Thanksgiving for a Child'. (Note that in Anglican formularies, 'naming' is restricted to what is necessary for the minister to address the person being baptised directly and personally).

It is important to note and understand that the liturgy provided in APBA (pp. 43—47) titled 'Thanksgiving for a Child' is distinguished from Holy Baptism, and is not to be considered a rite of Christian initiation. It is available to anyone who desires it, including children who are to be, or who have been, baptised. As APBA (p. 48, Note 1) indicates, the purpose of 'Thanksgiving for a Child' is not to 'replace baptism,' but to provide the congregation with an opportunity to welcome the birth or adoption of a child, and for the parent/s to give thanks for that child and its safe arrival into the world. The service reflects the natural human desire to give thanks for these important life events.

## C1 Confirmation in Scripture, theology and Anglican formularies

As APBA (p. 94, Note 1) advises, 'Christians should be willing to confess their faith publicly (Romans 10.9–13). Those baptised as infants need to profess for themselves the faith into which they have been baptised.' The Anglican tradition provides for this in confirmation, the rite in which a person who was unable to answer for themselves at their baptism affirms and renews those promises made on their behalf by others, and receives the strengthening of the Holy Spirit through prayer and the laying on of the bishop's hand.

> In confirmation those who have been previously baptised come to confirm their baptismal promises and join with the other candidates to receive the laying on of the bishop's hand with prayer (APBA p. 52, # 4).

Holy Baptism is normally performed in a local congregation, most commonly by the parish priest, but its significance transcends the boundaries of both the parish and the Christian tradition. Confirmation offers the necessary opportunity for a baptised Christian to profess publicly the faith of the whole Church, represented in the person of the bishop. Recent theological thinking about the meaning of confirmation has suggested we should be asking 'what' rather than 'who' is confirmed. The rite can thus be understood as the confirmation of a person's baptism through the laying on of the bishop's hand, together with a commissioning and setting apart for ministry through the prayer invoking the strengthening of the Holy Spirit for continuous Christian life and ministry. For many this will occur some years after the baptism, but for an increasing number it may immediately follow baptism, depending on the person's circumstances, age and understanding.

Confirmation is not, then, to be seen as an 'optional extra', but a necessary stage in a baptised person's journey to full discipleship. For this reason the APBA baptism service (p. 52) includes an exhortation for the parent/s and sponsor/s of those presenting an infant for baptism to complete the process of Christian initiation in the rite of confirmation.

Children are baptised in response to God's all-embracing love. Parents and godparents who have responded to that love come now to bring their children for baptism. Before this congregation they must express their own trust and commitment to the promises of God, and their intention to bring up their children in the faith and practice of the Church. In due time these children should make their own response to God, and be prepared for confirmation (APBA p. 52, # 4).

Each minister who has pastoral charge of a community of faith therefore bears a responsibility to ensure that all baptised members of the community are given an opportunity to consider being prepared for confirmation on a regular basis as may be appropriate to the circumstances of that congregation: so the Canon Concerning Confirmation 1992 (3)—'every minister who has a cure of souls shall encourage those baptised as infants to affirm the Christian faith for themselves and to present for confirmation.'

## C2 Historical & contemporary developments

Whilst the historical picture is incomplete and at times contradictory, it is likely that the rites of Christian initiation were originally celebrated together, in the context of a single service including both baptism and confirmation. As time passed, and as the number of candidates increased, baptism and confirmation were separated into distinct services. Initially, at least, this seems to have been for practical reasons, to enable the priest to conduct the baptisms within the parish area, and the bishop to visit to confirm in groups those previously baptised, a custom that continues to the present day.

### C2.1 Historical developments

In its early centuries, and in England until the end of the first millennium, the Church's initiation rites (baptism in water, the laying on of hand/s, anointing with oil, and initial participation in Holy Communion) seem to have been mostly celebrated in the one service, in the manner noted above. In the East, baptism (always by submersion) and 'confirmation/consignation' (i.e. anointing) have remained immediately related down to the present time, both for adults and children. The priest became the usual minister of both parts of the rite: the link between 'confirmation/consignation' and the ministry of the bishop is preserved by the use of oils consecrated for this purpose.

In the West, however, the ministry of baptism (by submersion, immersion or affusion) was increasingly delegated to the priest, while the bishop administered 'confirmation' (i.e. anointing and/or the laying on of the bishop's hand/s) at some later convenient time. Thus the Western separation of 'confirmation' from baptism was at first not linked to the age of candidates, but arose from the practical reality of the bishop's unavailability (the bishop could only visit so often!) A custom gradually developed in the western Church whereby confirmation was typically celebrated around the age one moved from childhood to early adulthood, and linked to admission to Holy Communion (or 'first Communion'). The meaning of confirmation as a distinct rite, and its relationship to admission to Holy Communion, thus came to be understood in the Western churches in a variety of ways. Where confirmation was described as a 'sacrament', the emphasis was on prayer for strengthening by the Holy Spirit. The English Reformers, on the other hand, largely saw confirmation as the ratifying and confirming of one's baptismal promises, and as the normal rite of admission to Holy Communion, emphases prominent in Anglican formularies.

## C2.2 Contemporary developments

In the middle decades of the 19th century, in the wake of the Evangelical and Tractarian/Anglo Catholic revivals, the rite of confirmation came to greater prominence in the Church of England, with more regular visitation by the bishops, and preparation being taken with some seriousness. An understanding of confirmation as the bestowal of the Holy Spirit became widespread, interpreted by some as a 'conversion' experience following a public decision for Christ, and by others as a sacramental act at the bishop's hand, with Acts 8 seen as the scriptural warrant for such views. If baptism had come to be closely associated with the birth of a child, confirmation came to be seen as an 'initiation rite' from childhood, and, as the 'teenage' years emerged as distinctive sub-cultures after World War II, as a marking of the life-cycle changes associated with puberty.

Such ideas gradually came to be questioned, however, not only by scholars, but also from the pastoral experience of young people seeing confirmation as 'graduation' from church rather than into it. Further, the requirement that communicant members of non-Anglican churches be confirmed in order to become Anglicans was felt to call into question their standing as Christians. A series of English and American reports saw these views gradually come under question, particularly as the significance of baptism was more deeply appreciated. The Diocese of Melbourne formed its own perspective through the 1970 Report on Christian Initiation. In the 1970s and 1980s this crystallised into Canon law, with the passage of the General Synod Canon intended to regularise Admission to Holy Communion, and then with a further Canon enabling the Reception of baptised Christians of other traditions into the Anglican Church.

As noted above, church and society have been gradually growing apart in the Western world for some time. In this context, it is now widely accepted that, while confirmation remains a necessary aspect in Christian formation, baptism is the sacramental sign of full incorporation into the Church, and thus forms the only universal prerequisite for admission to the fullness of Church life, inclusive of the sacrament of Holy Communion. Alongside this, increasing emphasis has been placed on the need for more formation-oriented preparation for adult Christian life, notably through the catechumenal process. In the Anglican Communion alternative patterns of Christian formation have emerged, and the close nexus between confirmation and admission to Holy Communion has been eased, but not completely severed.

In recent years, the awareness that every Christian is called by God to ministry has grown apace. While baptism is the sacrament by which such ministry is entered, confirmation is a key way by which each Christian, in the power of the Spirit, can affirm and embrace a mature, considered commitment to Christian service. Further, confirmation is an occasion in which each local church recommits itself to God's call to be a ministering community. Confirmation is thus a rite in which personal and corporate growth in Christian faith, development in godliness, and empowerment for Christian service, are to the fore.

However understood, confirmation continues as a vitally significant aspect of initiation into Christ through the Spirit, a necessary part of full Christian formation. In post-Christendom missionary contexts there has been a growing sense that the various dimensions of Christian initiation belong together in an 'integrated rite' of baptism, confirmation and Holy Communion, an ideal which finds expression in the APBA service for 'Holy Baptism and Confirmation in Holy Communion together with provision for Reaffirmation of Baptismal Vows and Reception' (from p. 51).

## C3   Who may be confirmed?

The realisation that baptism is the sacramental sign of full incorporation into the Church has gained wide support in the Anglican Communion, this being reflected in the Diocese of Melbourne. Yet confirmation is not an optional extra, but forms a normal and necessary part of Christian formation towards full discipleship.

As noted above, each priest who has pastoral care of a congregation bears the responsibility to ensure that baptised church attenders, especially communicants, are regularly encouraged to consider confirmation, and be suitably and adequately prepared for it. Ideally, this process of notification and preparation will take place annually. Where candidates have not been baptised, and are able to answer for themselves, they are to be prepared to enter Christian life through an integrated rite of baptism and confirmation in the context of Holy Communion, as provided for in APBA. In the case of those baptised as infants, confirmation should take place at an age when the person concerned is willing and able to make a mature commitment to Christ. Pressure from parents, peers or parish towards young people being confirmed too early may need to be resisted.

It is not the case that there is an 'age limit' or 'appropriate age' for confirmation, and nowhere in the canons and formularies of the Church has one been set. The Canon Concerning Confirmation 1992 offers the following guidance, advising that the priest should only present to the bishop those candidates who:

- Have reached 'years of discretion';

- Are ready to make public affirmation of their commitment to the Lord Jesus Christ;
- Are able to render an appropriate account of the faith and life expected of a Christian.

This will ultimately be a matter of discretion for the parish priest at local level, and will rely to a large extent on appropriate and suitable preparation.

## C4  Preparation for confirmation

The Canon Concerning Confirmation 1992 (4) requires that 'every minister who has a cure of souls must instruct or cause to be instructed all who wish to be confirmed in the Christian faith as set forth in the Scriptures and in the Catechism.' Preparation is, however, to be seen as a shared task of each congregation. Care and attention given to the occasion, and the preparation and follow-up of all involved—candidates and sponsors especially—shows out the significance of baptism and confirmation for Christian life. It also mirrors a congregation's understanding of its own identity, ministry and mission in Christ. Preparation is an essential part of the process of growing in faith and confidence therein, and should give time and space for the developing of personal relationships with the minister/s and congregation, whilst also seeking to mutually discern the particular ministries that the new candidate brings to it.

While systematic structures of education are necessary and helpful, they may often need to be adapted to suit each candidate's situation: factors such as background, personality, lifestyle and Christian knowledge need to be taken into account. Such a process cannot be undertaken quickly, and typically takes some months, but a course of preparation for confirmation should not normally extend beyond a year. Whatever resource or program is used, whether one developed elsewhere or adapted for use at the local level, preparation for confirmation should maintain a clear focus on the life, work and significance of Jesus Christ, the Holy Spirit, and the Christian understanding of God.

Preparation should, therefore:
- Enable candidates to affirm the faith of the Church as set out in the Apostles' Creed;
- Introduce the scriptures and their use, with practical teaching on discipleship and prayer;
- Explain the significance of baptism, confirmation and Holy Communion;
- Give guidance on Christian life and ministry in the world;
- Celebrate and explore the particular life and calling of each candidate;
- Outline the basic responsibilities of church membership.

## C5   Contextual matters

Confirmation, like Holy Baptism, is a public act of the Church, and should normally take place in the context of a public service of worship, whether a regular Sunday service, or a service dedicated to confirmation occurring at another time. The parish priest has responsibility for preparing those who have been baptised, and who are now able to answer for themselves, for confirmation.

The minister at confirmation will be the bishop, and the service must therefore be planned in close conjunction with the relevant bishop. This will normally entail contact with the bishop's office well before the desired date of the confirmation, often at least twelve months before, to ensure the date can be added to the bishop's diary of engagements. The bishop's office will provide an engagement summary that is to be completed and returned at least one week prior to the service.

## C6   Liturgical principles and practice

As with baptism, services that include confirmation (and/or reception) require careful thought and deliberate planning, which is to be undertaken in consultation and dialogue with the bishop who will lead and preside at the service. The minister responsible will normally advise the bishop at least one week prior to the service, and preferably earlier, of the readings (as the bishop will deliver the sermon), as well as further details of the order of service, ideally providing a digital version of a printed order of service or PowerPoint slideshow or other form of projection, if one is to be used. The order of service to be used must be approved by the bishop prior to it being distributed or finalised for printing or projection. It is normally very helpful also for the bishop to be provided with the full names of those to be confirmed and/or received, their gender and age, sponsor or sponsors, together with a brief summary of the candidate's involvement in the life of the church and Christian formation.

### C6.1   The liturgy

Where those able to answer for themselves are baptised, their confirmation and first communion should take place at the same service as their baptism.

a) APBA (commencing p. 51) provides for a single integrated rite of Christian initiation encompassing baptism, confirmation and reception into communicant membership, in the context of Holy Communion. The service is highly adaptable and suitable for the main service on a Sunday. Where baptism and confirmation are both part of this service the shaded areas relating to confirmation are used.

b) Where reception into communicant membership is to be included, the form in APBA (pp. 96–97) is inserted into the service at the place indicated by the rubrics.

c) APBA (commencing p. 84) provides for a service of confirmation only, which may or may not include Holy Communion.

Where the same service is to include the baptism and confirmation of some candidates, and the confirmation only of other candidates, careful thought will need to be given to balancing the two rites, and to ordering the liturgy in such a way that all the candidates make the Decision and Affirmation of Faith together, and are welcomed together.

## C6.2 Liturgical furniture and movement

The placement of church furniture, and the arrangement of the worship space, together with the 'choreography' concerning the movement of those involved in a service of confirmation, as with baptism, requires careful thought and planning. A rehearsal will be necessary in most cases, involving both candidate/s and sponsor/s.

a) As with baptism, the rubrics require that candidates for confirmation stand in view of the congregation at the time of the presentation and decision (APBA p. 87, # 10). Thought should be given to how and where this will occur.

b) The rubric (APBA p. 87, # 11) asks the bishop to invite the sponsor/s to present the candidate/s using the form of words indicated. Thought should be given to how the sponsor/s will physically do this, and in what sequence the candidate/s will be presented. All concerned should be informed of the arrangements (usually at the rehearsal).

c) If the bishop is to use a chair it needs to be ready for use, together with a place for the candidate/s to kneel, and kneeling cushion if necessary.

d) If oil is to be used it needs to be prepared and accessible, together with a towel.

e) Certificates with all relevant details filled in are to be provided by the parish or congregation in which the confirmation takes place for each candidate, and thought given as to when and how these will be presented to both the candidate/s and their sponsor/s.

f) Where the service is to include baptism as well as confirmation, much of the detail at B7 will be relevant also.
g) At a service of confirmation there will often be significant numbers of people present in the congregation for whom the church and its customs are unfamiliar and alien. Those leading the service should carefully plan all aspects of the liturgy, and conduct the service in such a way that all present are able to clearly follow the service without embarrassment. This may mean giving page numbers if using the physical books, or preparing a printed or digital order of service, and giving advice to the congregation about when to stand, sit or kneel, and (if relevant) giving clear instructions about who is welcome to receive Holy Communion and how the sacrament will be administered.

## C7 Sponsors

APBA (p. 94, Note 2) advises that candidates for confirmation ought to have at least one sponsor to 'help them prepare', and further suggests that at least of one the candidate's sponsors 'be a member of the congregation'. It can be especially significant and meaningful that, where possible, one or more of those who acted as sponsor (or godparent) for a person baptised as an infant, act as a sponsor for that person at their confirmation.

## C8 Certificates and Registers

a) The details of each confirmation are to be entered into the register of the congregation concerned kept for this purpose.
b) The service in which the confirmation took place is to be entered into the Service Register of the parish or ministry context concerned.
c) Each candidate for confirmation is to be given a certificate signed by the bishop who conducted the rite. The certificate is to show

the full name of the candidate, the name of the bishop, the name/s of the sponsor/s, the date on which the rite was conducted, and the place.
d) The sponsor/s are also to be provided with a certificate.
e) A form for the purposes of registering the confirmation in the diocesan register is to be prepared also. This is usually available from the bishop's office. This form is completed in advance of the service, for the bishop to sign and take on the day of the service.

The Parish Governance Regulations 2014 (7.3) require the following details to be entered into the register for each confirmation and reception:

a) The next consecutive number of entry in the register;
b) The date and place of the candidate's birth;
c) The date and place of the candidate's baptism;
d) The date of the confirmation or reception;
e) Whether the service was confirmation or reception;
f) The names of the sponsors or presenters;
g) The signature of the confirming or receiving bishop.

## C9   Fees

There is no 'fee' or 'charge' for confirmation (or reception into communicant membership), as the rite is intrinsically related to the sacrament of baptism. Those coming for confirmation, or sponsoring a candidate for confirmation, may make a donation to the parish or Christian community in which the confirmation takes place if they wish to, and will normally have an opportunity to give to the ministry of the place in which the confirmation/reception takes place through the offertory at the service.

## C10 Admission to Holy Communion

Many provinces and dioceses across the global Anglican Communion have, in the past few decades, come to the view that baptism is the sacramental sign of full incorporation into the Christian community and, therefore, constitutes the only prerequisite for admission to Holy Communion. The common practise in the Anglican Communion in the past had been for baptism to be administered primarily to infants, and for confirmation with admission to Holy Communion to be administered upon reaching 'an age of discretion'. This has changed rapidly in the past few decades in light of the missional environment in which the church finds itself, the breakdown of denominational identity, the imperatives for ecumenical hospitality, and, in the Australian Church, the widespread adoption of canons enabling the admission of baptised children to Holy Communion prior to confirmation.

### C10.1 The admission of adults to Holy Communion

Those who come to faith as adults will generally be admitted to Holy Communion at the same time as their baptism and confirmation, ideally in a single integrated service of initiation, as envisaged by APBA (p. 70, Note 1).

The widespread practise, since the adoption of the Admission to Holy Communion Canon 1973, is that adults who have been baptised in other Christian traditions that hold 'the Apostolic faith', who are or have been communicant members of that church, are welcome to receive Holy Communion in Anglican churches in accordance with the discipline and practise of their own tradition.

Where a communicant Anglican has been baptised but not confirmed, and where a non-Anglican becomes a worshipping member of an Anglican church, the minister with pastoral charge of the congregation should invite such persons to consider confirmation or reception into communicant membership as appropriate to their circumstances.

**C10.2 The admission of children to Holy Communion prior to confirmation**

The Canon for the Admission of Children to Holy Communion 1981, adopted by this diocese, allows for the admission of baptised children to Holy Communion 'while awaiting confirmation', with the following conditions:

a) The child, with the sponsorship of his or her parents or other confirmed members of the congregation, seeks admission;

b) The minister 'is satisfied that the child has been adequately instructed' and 'gives evidence of appropriate understanding of the nature and meaning of the Holy Communion' (no specific age is set down);

c) The Bill accompanying adoption of the canon in this diocese requires that a change in policy regarding the admission of children to Holy Communion in a parish be a decision of the Parish Council, supported by a Parish Meeting convened for this purpose.

The Canon presupposes that some preparation will be provided to children desiring to be admitted to Holy Communion prior to confirmation. The form this takes is at the discretion of the minister and the parish concerned and is normally undertaken primarily by the family, with the help of priest and congregation, who should assume special responsibility for nurturing new communicants within its usual framework of Christian education.

There is no provision for a formal rite or ceremony of admission in the Canon, and the custom at local level will normally prevail. Whatever form this takes, it should not be confused with confirmation, nor take place during a service of confirmation. The admission of a child to Holy Communion is not to be seen or understood as an end point in the wider process of Christian initiation. It is not independent of either baptism or confirmation, but forms one part of the whole process of Christian formation. This process is designed to lead towards mature commitment to Christ and commissioning for service as a member of the whole Church, the aspects of initiation which confirmation represents.

Note: A baptised child who has been admitted to Holy Communion shall not be excluded from Holy Communion anywhere in the Anglican Diocese of Melbourne. The determination of the Australian bishops on this matter is that any discrepancy in practise that might arise in the event of movement to a different diocese, or parish, is more tolerable than the exclusion of a person from Holy Communion after admission.

The Parish Governance Regulations 2014 (7.3) require the following details to be entered into the register for each child admitted to Holy Communion under the provisions of the Canon:

a) The date of admission;
b) The name of each child admitted;
c) The name of the vicar;
d) The signature of the vicar.

## R1  Reception into communicant membership

From time to time non-Anglican Christians who have been validly baptised ask to become Anglicans. Many choose to take this step by being confirmed in the Anglican Church. Others may have already been confirmed by a bishop in another Church that has retained the threefold order of ordained ministry. A good number of others, however, will not have been confirmed by a bishop, but are, or have been, communicant members of another church. They may see an insistence on confirmation as raising questions about their status as Christians in full standing: this would be ecumenically insensitive and may be pastorally unhelpful. Where a person is, or has been, a communicant member of another church which holds the apostolic faith, such Christians may be 'received and welcomed' into the Anglican Church by the bishop, who then prays that they may be strengthened by the Holy Spirit through the laying on of hands.

Christians from other traditions who have been fully initiated in that tradition may be admitted to communicant membership of the Anglican Church through the rite of reception into communicant membership (APBA p. 98, Note 1). By 'fully initiated' is meant that the person concerned has been baptised and has made a public profession of faith through means of confirmation or another such public rite or ceremony.

Where the person concerned has been baptised, but has not made a public profession of faith, confirmation may be more appropriate.

Those who have been received as Anglicans have equal standing alongside those who have been confirmed. They are thus eligible to be authorised as a lay minister, ordained, to be appointed as churchwardens, and as members of Anglican governing bodies such as the parish council.

The Reception Canon 1981, as amended in 1995, requires the following:

a) The vicar or minister who has pastoral charge of the congregation concerned should be 'assured' of the candidate's desire to be received into communicant membership of the Anglican Church;
b) Appropriate 'due preparation' should be provided;
c) The reception is to be recorded in the registers of the church;
d) The Canon further requires that the minister in reception is the bishop, and conveys the expectation that candidates will normally be presented to the bishop in the context of a service of confirmation. The liturgy provided for in APBA (pp. 96–97) is inserted into the confirmation service at the appropriate place, as indicated by the rubrics (see p. 91, # 22);
e) The Canon stipulates that a person who has been received into communicant membership of the church has the same status as a person who has been confirmed.

The Parish Governance Regulations 2014 (7.3) require the following details to be entered into the register for each confirmation and reception:

a) The next consecutive number of entry in the register;
b) The date and place of the candidate's birth;
c) The date and place of the candidate's baptism;
d) The date of the confirmation or reception;
e) Whether the service was confirmation or reception;
f) The names of the sponsors or presenters;
g) The signature of the confirming or receiving bishop.

## R2 Qualification for holding office

Both the scriptures and Anglican formularies teach that the ministries of leading and administration in the church should be undertaken by mature Christians who are committed to Christ's service, called by God, and open to the enabling of the Holy Spirit (Romans 12.1–12, 1 Corinthians 12.27–28; 1 Timothy 6.6–19). The Articles Religion (XXIII), therefore, require that those exercising public leadership in the Church be 'lawfully called and sent' and do so in accordance with a 'public authority' conferred upon them. The notion of authorised ministry finds expression in several ways in the diocese, all having their source in the rites of initiation.

a) A person cannot be ordained deacon unless they have been baptised and either confirmed or received into communicant membership (Canon Concerning Holy Orders 2004, 5).

b) In the Diocese of Melbourne, a person cannot be provided with an authority as a lay minister unless they have been baptised and either confirmed or received into communicant membership of the Anglican Church of Australia.

c) A person is not eligible to be on the electoral roll of a parish (Parish Governance Act 2013 s 9) unless they are baptised, regularly attend services of divine worship, and affirm in writing, by completing the required application form, that they consider themselves to be a 'member' of an Anglican parish or authorised congregation.

d) Members of parish council and churchwardens must further be 'communicant members' of the Anglican Church (Parish Governance Act 2013, Rule 13.1), this being defined as persons who are baptised and eligible to receive Holy Communion in accordance with the canons of the church. This will normally be through the rite of confirmation or reception into communicant membership, unless the person concerned is a member of a church in full communion with the Anglican Church (for instance, the Church of South India).

## Resources for Christian Initiation

### Readings from the Bible

Whilst APBA (p. 71, Note 8) advises that the readings will normally be those 'of the day,' the following readings are especially suitable for a service including Holy Baptism.

Genesis 9.8–17, The covenant after the flood
Exodus 14.19–31, Crossing the Red Sea
Ezekiel 36.25–28, A new heart I will give you
Acts 2.37–42, Repent and be baptised
Romans 6.1–11, Dying and rising with Christ
Galatians 3.23–29, All are one in Christ
Matthew 28.18–20, The great commission
Mark 1.1–11, The baptism of Jesus
John 3.1–8, Born from above

In print

Booker, Mike & Mark Ireland. *Evangelism—which way now? An evaluation of Alpha, Emmaus, Cell church and other contemporary strategies for evangelism.* London: Church House Publishing, 2010.

Best, Thomas F. & Dagmar Heller. *Becoming a Christian.* Geneva: WCC, 1991.

Browning, Ron. *Taking the plunge: seeking accompanying baptising.* Melbourne: Spectrum, 2008.

Green, Michael. *Baptism: its purpose, power and meaning.* London: Hodder, 1987.

Holeton, David (ed). *Walk in Newness of Life. Christian Initiation in the Anglican Communion, from the Inter-Anglican Consultation on Liturgy.* Cambridge: Grove Books, 1991.

Jones, Simon. *Celebrating Christian Initiation.* London: SPCK, 2016.

Whitehead, Nick & Hazel. *Baptism matters.* London: Church House Publishing, 1998.

Links—preparation

CPAS 'First Steps' (baptism preparation guide)
https://www.cpas.org.uk/church-resources/first-steps/#.Wfu6ePmWbIV

Church House Publishing (confirmation resources)
https://chbookshop.hymnsam.co.uk/features/confirmation-preparation

Confirmation Book for Adults (Sharon Swain, SPCK)
http://spckpublishing.co.uk/confirmation-book-for-adults

Faith Confirmed (Peter Jackson & Chris Wright, SPCK)
http://spckpublishing.co.uk/product/faith-confirmed-2/

Faith Inkubators
http://www.faithink.com/

Going to the Supper of the Lord (preparation for admission to Holy Communion)
http://shop.genesisdirect.com.au/eshop/eshop-educational-and-books/
    going-to-the-supper-of-the-lord-teachers-booklet

Making the most of your child's Baptism (Ally Barrett, SPCK)
http://spckpublishing.co.uk/product/
    making-the- most-of-your-childs- baptism-3/

Sparkhouse re:form
https://www.wearesparkhouse.org/teens/reform/core/

The New City Catechism
http://newcitycatechism.com/

## Links—introductions to Christianity and Anglicanism

Alpha
http://australia.alpha.org/

Alpha—Youth
https://alpha.org/alpha-youth-series

Anglican: Introducing the faith, history and practice of the Anglican Church
http://shop.genesisdirect.com.au/

Australis Certificate of Ministry
http://www.bendigoanglican.org.au/australis-certificate-of-ministry/

Education for Ministry (EFM) Australia
http://www.efmaustralia.org/

Pilgrim
http://www.pilgrimcourse.org/

The Anglican Way
https://adom.talentlms.com/catalog/info/id:122

## Links — liturgical

General Synod Liturgical Commission (Anglican Church of Australia): Updated forms of the APBA baptism services
https://www.anglican.org.au/baptism

Broughton Publications issues packs of Certificates (approved by the House of Bishops) for Baptism, Confirmation, Reception and Re-affirmation
www.broughtonpublishing.com.au/about/

## Canon Concerning Baptism 1992

Canon 21, 1998 (passed provisionally as Canon P5, 1992)

The General Synod prescribes as follows:
1. This Canon may be cited as 'Canon Concerning Baptism 1992'.
2. The sacrament of Holy Baptism shall normally be administered at public worship.
3. Baptism shall take place by immersing a person in water or by pouring water upon the candidate and by pronouncing the words, 'I baptise you in the name of the Father, and of the Son, and of the Holy Spirit'.
4. Due notice must be given to the minister of a church before a child is brought or a person comes to the church to be baptised.
5. Except in extreme circumstances—
   a) The minister, before baptising any person able to answer for himself or herself, shall be satisfied that such person has been instructed and prepared in the Christian faith; and
   b) The minister, before baptising an infant or person who cannot answer for himself or herself shall be satisfied that at least one of the parents or guardians of the infant or person have been instructed in the Christian faith, and that they are aware that the same responsibilities rest on them as are required of the godparents.
6. Subject to sections 4, 5, 7 and 8, no minister may refuse or, except for the purpose of preparing or instructing the parents or guardians or godparents, delay baptising a child who has a parent or guardian who professes to be a Christian.
7. A minister shall not normally baptise a child whose parents or guardians are not parishioners of or resident in the parish where it is proposed the baptism be administered unless at least one of the parents or guardians attends divine service in the parish or the

minister has sought the advice of the minister of the parish where the parents or guardians reside or usually attend divine service.
8. Every child to be baptised shall have at least one, but usually three godparents or sponsors of whom at least two shall be of the same sex as the child and of whom at least one shall be of the opposite sex. Either or both of the parents of a child may act as godparents or sponsors. Godparents or sponsors shall be baptised persons and should be persons who will faithfully fulfil their responsibilities both by their spiritual nurture and instruction of the children committed to their charge and by the example of their own godly living.
9. For every candidate for baptism who is able to answer for himself or herself one such sponsor shall suffice, whose responsibility shall be to encourage the candidate to continue in the Christian life.
10. This Church holds and teaches that the sign of the cross* used in baptism is no part of the substance of the sacrament but retains that sign in baptism.
11. The minister shall, in a Register kept for the purpose, record or cause to be recorded the name of each person baptised, and the date and place of baptism, and provide the person and his or her godparents or sponsors with a certificate of baptism.
12. A diocesan synod may promulgate rules and guidelines not inconsistent with this canon for the administration of baptism within that diocese.
13. The Godparents Canon 1977 is repealed as regards a diocese that adopts this canon.
14. The canons numbered 29, 30, 68, 69 and 70 of the Canons of 1603, in so far as the same may have any force, have no operation or effect in a diocese which adopts this canon.
15. The provisions of this Canon affect the order and good government of this Church within a diocese and shall not come into

force in a diocese unless and until the diocese adopts this Canon by ordinance of the synod of the diocese.

*A fuller explanation of the sign of the cross at baptism is set out in A Prayer Book for Australia (p. 822).

## Canon concerning Confirmation 1992

Canon 14, 1998 (passed provisionally as Canon P7, 1992)
A canon concerning confirmation.
The General Synod prescribes as follows:
1. This canon may be cited as 'Canon concerning Confirmation 1992'.
2. The bishop of a diocese must personally or by a bishop authorised by him confirm throughout his diocese as often and in as many places as convenient, laying his hands upon those who have been baptised and instructed in the Christian faith and life as set forth in the Scriptures and in the Catechism and praying over them.
3. Every minister who has a cure of souls shall encourage those baptised as infants to affirm the Christian faith for themselves and to present for confirmation.
4. Every minister who has a cure of souls must instruct or cause to be instructed all who wish to be confirmed in the Christian faith as set forth in the Scriptures and in the Catechism.
5. A minister normally must present to the bishop only those who have come to years of discretion and who are ready to make public affirmation of their commitment to our Lord Jesus Christ and who can render an appropriate account of the faith and life expected of a Christian.
6. The canons numbered 60 and 61 of the Canons of 1603, in so far as the same may have any force, have no operation or effect in a diocese that adopts this canon.

7. The provisions of this canon affect the order and good government of this Church within a diocese and shall not come into force in a diocese unless and until the diocese adopts this canon by ordinance of the synod of the diocese.

**Reception Canon 1981**

Canon 1, 1985 as amended by Canon 14, 1995 (passed provisionally as Canon 4(P), 1981 and amended by Canon 14, 1995)

A canon to authorise the use of a service for the reception into communicant membership of this Church of baptised persons who were formerly communicant members of other churches.

The General Synod prescribes as follows:

1. This canon may be cited as the 'Reception Canon 1981'.
2. When a person who has been baptised and who is or was a communicant member of another church that holds the apostolic faith but which is not in full communion with this Church desires to become a communicant member of this Church, the priest, being assured that such is his desire, shall after due preparation present that person to the bishop at the time of confirmation or some other time. The bishop may receive and welcome him into communicant membership of this Church, laying hands on him with prayer for the strengthening of the Holy Spirit, using the form of service set out in the schedule to this canon, or in some other form of service authorised for use in this church by canon, in accordance with the rubrics incorporated therein.
3. A person received into communicant membership in accordance with this canon shall have the same status in this Church as a person who has been confirmed in accordance with the rites of this Church.
4. The reception of a person into communicant membership in accordance with this canon shall be recorded in the registers of this Church.

5. This canon affects the order and good government of the Church within a diocese and shall not come into force in any diocese unless and until the diocese by ordinance adopts the canon.

## Canon for the Admission of Children to Holy Communion

Canon 6, 1985 (passed provisionally as Canon 14(P), 1981)

A canon for the admission of children to Holy Communion.

The General Synod prescribes as follows:
1. This canon may be cited as the 'Canon for the admission of children to Holy Communion'.
2. A child who has been baptised but who has not been confirmed, is eligible to be admitted to the Holy Communion if the minister is satisfied that the child has been adequately instructed, gives evidence of appropriate understanding of the nature and meaning of the Holy Communion and has fulfilled the conditions of repentance and faith; and if the child, with the sponsorship of his or her parents or of other confirmed members of the congregation, seeks such admission while awaiting confirmation.
3. (1) The bishop of the diocese may make regulations, not inconsistent with ordinances (if any) made under subsection (2), concerning the practice and procedure in relation to the admission of children to the Holy Communion under this canon.

    (2) The synod of the diocese may, by ordinance, regulate the practice and procedure in   relation to the admission of children to the Holy Communion under this canon.
4. This canon affects the order and good government of the Church within a diocese and shall not come into force in any diocese unless and until the diocese by ordinance adopts the canon.

# Chapter Three

## Marriage and Weddings (M)

It is important to note that marriage is to be distinguished from the wedding ceremony by which a particular marriage may begin. The term 'wedding' is used in this Handbook of the ceremony or ritual that marks the commencement of the marriage relationship and brings it into being, whilst the term 'marriage' is used to describe the 'estate' into which the couple enter at the wedding, ideally for the rest of their lives.

Social patterns and mores around human relationships have changed dramatically in Australia, as in the Western world in general, over the course of the past few decades. This has inevitably had a dramatic effect on marriage customs, with many people now living together, often for extended periods of time, before entering into a marriage, and sets of relationships that do not constitute the traditional understanding of marriage being commonly accepted. Whilst there are a wide variety of views, both traditional and alternative, and many cultures and sub-cultures, it is still, however, the case that the concept of marriage as an exclusive relationship entered into for life remains important for a great many Australians, and significant numbers continue to enter into marriage in Australia each year.

A further change in relation to marriage has been the rapid decline in the number of couples seeking the rites of the Christian church, something that is not overly surprising in the context of a social environment less shaped and influenced by Christian principles and perspectives than in the past. It is now the case that a little less than one third of all wedding ceremonies in Australia are solemnised in a Christian church or according to Christian rites.⁴⁷ Consequently, it is now common for many parishes to have no requests for weddings outside of the members of their congregation and those connected to them. In some places, however, wedding requests continue to be an important ministry and means of outreach.

Whatever the level of demand, a wedding can be a prime missional opportunity for Christian churches. Andrew Body goes so far as to say:

> There is no greater mission opportunity for the Church of today than a wedding. Not only does the couple come wanting something from us, and open to what we can offer, but most of the people who gather for the service will never step inside a church for any other reason. In a country that is largely 'unchurched' this is a moment, however brief, when people experience what the church does rather than what it looks like, what it is rather than what it is perceived to be. It is sometimes difficult for church people, for whom services, prayers, hymns and clergy are part of their weekly experience, to remember how alien this is for the majority, who haven't sung hymns since they were at school, and who may never have spoken to a priest in their lives.⁴⁸

### Human relationships in today's Australia

Considerable change has taken place in Australia in recent decades regarding human relationships. Many Australians have come to accept as valid a wide variety of living and partnership arrangements, reflecting differing understandings of the roles of women and men, and changing

---

47  McCrindle Research  http://mccrindle.com.au/the-mccrindle-blog/marriages-in-australia
48  Andrew Body, *Making the most of weddings: a practical guide for churches* (London: Church House publishing, 2007), p. 1.

family patterns. Factors such as the questioning of traditional structures, and the ready availability of reliable contraception, have significantly shaped the contexts in which marriage is understood. The Family Law Act (1973/1975) gave institutional expression to these changes, and accelerated changed attitudes to marriage breakdown (for good as well as ill), but more far-reaching developments have taken place since.

Sexual mores have also shifted considerably, especially, but not only, among younger people. Peer pressure towards casual sexual encounters seems to be stronger than in previous generations, whilst short-term relationships among young adults are regarded as normal practice. An outcome of these developments has been a significant shift in the publicly accepted meaning of sexual relationships, reflected now in most 'young adult' mass media and social media, and in the rise of dating apps and online forums enabling 'hook ups' and casual encounters. The prevalence and permeation of Internet pornography among younger Australians, and across the world, has also served to shape the attitudes of young minds towards sex and sexuality.

A wide variety of attitudes to what constitutes appropriate sexual activity thus exists in contemporary Australia. Seen against this background, the Christian understanding of marriage as the exclusive context for sexual relationships may be seen and understood as overtly counter-cultural, as is the requirement of clergy and church workers prescribed by the 2004 national code of conduct Faithfulness in Service (7.2)—'Sexuality is a gift from God and is integral to human nature… it is appropriate for clergy and church workers to value this gift, taking responsibility for their sexual conduct by maintaining chastity in singleness and faithfulness in marriage.'

Whatever the challenges and context, the contribution which a sound marriage makes to society is priceless. Stable, loving, and loyal long-term partnerships undergird the nurture of children, and their growth to maturity as well-balanced, outward-looking men and women with a healthy sense of personal identity. Healthy marriages thus make an inestimable contribution to community, society and the human race. Conversely, marriages in which there is violence, abuse or mere tolerance between partners do considerable damage to the families and community they touch. Christian ministry that supports health in marriage thus makes a significant contribution to church and society.

### Marriage in the Australian context

Marriage has undergone significant change in Australia in recent decades. As noted above, non-religious rites conducted by civil celebrants are now far more prevalent than religious rites led by clergy. Couples are getting married older than in previous generations, with the average age for men being around 30 and for women around 28.[49] For many (if not most) couples, formalising the relationship in the context of a wedding ceremony is considered only after they have lived together for some time. Whilst living together for a period of time was, at one time in the recent past, widely seen as a precursor to making the commitment of marriage, it has become, for many, socially and legally acceptable in itself.

The steady increase in life expectancy has also brought tensions within marriage. In previous generations, 'till death us do part' was a promise made with a much lesser life expectancy than today and in a very different social environment. Increasing numbers of older adults have experienced two, three or more medium-term marriage or marriage-like relationships over the course of their lifetime. This may reflect a longing for marriage to 'work', but it also introduces long-term tensions into family relationships. The children involved grow up in 'separated' or 'blended' families, while former 'in-laws' may not know how to regard one another when their children have parted ways. While such developments have left behind some oppressive features of marriage, the longer-term effects in society are not at all clear.

---

49   McCrindle Research   http://mccrindle.com.au/the-mccrindle-blog/marriages-in-australia

## Christian responses

We live and work in a world very different from that experienced by those who drafted the rites of Holy Matrimony present in the 1662 Book of Common Prayer and its earlier antecedents. The vast majority of Anglican congregations today include worshippers who have experienced marriage break-up, or who live with marital stress. Recent enquiries, including a Royal Commission in Victoria, have revealed the shocking prevalence of family violence, on both marriage and marriage-like relationships.

Churches have often found it difficult to deal with this. When both partners in a divorce are parishioners, it can be difficult for them to remain in the same congregation. In seeking not to take sides, other church members can find themselves at a loss to know how to be supportive. In any situation involving sexual relationships, some worshippers' embarrassment or inability to cope may mean that pastoral contact is not made, and those involved come to feel 'judged'. On the other hand, refusal to face the difficult task of responding to broken loyalties can bring the gospel itself into disrepute. Learning to respond appropriately when relationships are broken remains a major challenge to all churches.

Changes have also come about in wedding services in response to changes in society. As long ago as 1928 the word 'obey' was made optional; the modern language revisions of the middle 1970s, which crystallised in the two forms for marriage in An Australian Prayer Book (1978), took place in the shadow of 'second wave' feminism and the Family Law Act. The Marriage services in A Prayer Book for Australia (1995) reflect more deliberately the influence of some of the changes noted above, and ecumenical experience. While retaining the deposit of the Anglican tradition and features consistent with that heritage, they offer great diversity for the ways in which marriage may be celebrated liturgically. Whatever the shifting contexts, week by week Anglican clergy use such forms to solemnise the marriage of numerous couples. How are these time-honoured rites to be employed so that 'marriage may be held in honour among all' in our day, without a sense of nostalgic unreality?

Further questions inevitably arise. What of the marriage of those who have a previous partner still living? What is the status of longstanding de facto relationships? What of inter-church or inter-faith marriages? Is it appropriate to bless a couple married in a civil ceremony? Questions also arise about the forms used. Should a 'giving away' of the bride be allowed? May weddings be conducted by Anglican clergy outside church buildings? All of these questions, and many others, revolve around the particular question raised when any couple approaches the church about a wedding: namely, is Holy Matrimony the appropriate state of life for this man and this woman? It is in response to questions such as these, and with the social context of today's Australia in mind, that these guidelines have been formulated.

## M1 Marriage in Scripture, theology and Anglican formularies

The social world in which the BCP rite for the Solemnisation of Matrimony took shape was, needless to say, very different to the social world of early 21st century Australia. Despite that, its majestic words and liturgical shape continue to inform the celebration of marriage in Anglican churches today, whilst the BCP rite (generally the 1928 revision) is itself still used in some places, albeit in modified form, most prominently in recent years in the marriage of Prince William to Kate Middleton in April 2011 at Westminster Abbey.

The prevalence of marriage in all societies means that we tend to assume that we know what we mean by it. Yet wedding customs and family relationships vary widely across societies and cultures. Until recently, a substantial consensus as to what marriage is prevailed across Western societies, especially in Europe and the United States. Various roles and rights (or lack thereof) were assigned in law to the partners, but out of a growing and changing tradition and historical reality, not on the basis of a settled definition.

Surprisingly little theological discussion has taken place as to what marriage actually is. The Book of Common Prayer, for example, does give reasons 'as to why matrimony was ordained': procreation, control of sexuality, and companionship. While true, they are reasons, causes or purposes for marriage: they do not constitute a definition, nor do they provide the basis for a clear liturgical shape for a wedding. Conversely, considerable effort has been put into understanding what marriage is not, and to recognising when a marriage has broken down.

The present situation in Australian society, whereby marriage is no longer, and has not been for some time, the all but universally accepted and normative form a committed relationship of a sexual nature may take, is of relatively recent origin. There is thus a pressing need in our day for substantial theological discussion concerning marriage, not least to foster appropriate discernment in the variety of pastoral situations encountered in Christian ministry, but also in the light of the extended engagement in Australia with the question of same sex marriage.

### M1.1   Genesis

Christians have looked to Genesis 2, especially verses 18–24, as the scriptural basis for marriage. The classical 'conditions' for a marriage to be valid derive from the concluding verse (24) of that pivotal text: a 'leaving' of the old household (the founding of a new family unit), a 'cleaving' of the partners (the free, exclusive choice), and 'becoming one flesh' (sexual union as the unitive seal of marriage). The biblical term for such a partnership is 'covenant', an idea that includes the notion of contract but also transcends it, as having an enduring, personal and communal character marked by love-in-action more than duty.

This basis is not as obvious as might appear at first sight, however.

No wedding ceremony is mentioned in Genesis 2, and the context is the creation of the human race as a whole, more than merely the story of the first two members of it. According to the scriptures, Jesus only offered teaching about marriage in response to a (trick) question about divorce. The teaching he does give, however, is based on Genesis 1–2 (Mark 10.6–8). It is significant that he moves from Genesis 1.27 straight on to Genesis 2.24, passing over the intervening verses, which concern the making of the woman. Jesus thus avoids the possible implication that the woman is 'under' the man in creation: instead, he appeals to the statement of the preceding chapter, 'God made them male and female, in the image of God' (Genesis 1.27), noting that this was the divine intention 'from the beginning'. Thus for Jesus, marriage was based in the partnership of male and female, expressing one aspect of what it means to be 'made in the image of God'.

The distinctive relationship of man and woman that Christians describe as 'marriage' is set against the background of God's creative work. The unity of man and woman in the completeness of their new life together reflects one aspect of humanity as being made in the image of God as male and female (Genesis 1.26–28). This notion is not merely individual: we are made in the image of God as a race of like-yet-unlike, male-and-female. Humankind is directed to be 'fruitful' (1.29-31), not only in the bearing of children, but in contributing to the creative development of human society. Marriage thus belongs to the order of creation, in which human faithfulness mirrors the faithfulness of God, in whose image we are made.

Genesis 2 then explicates this 'image' from the ground up (literally): we are 'earthlings' ('adam) from 'earth' ('adamah), then living beings (2.7), having a task over creation (2.8–9, 15). Note that verses 15–18 do not refer to 'one male human' so much as 'humanity as a whole' ('adam)—and it is 'not good that humanity should be solitary' (2.18). No companionship amongst the animals is found: so humankind is divided, and the outcome—'woman' ('ishshah) and 'man' ('ish) (2.23)—is acknowledged as being truly one, yet different. Genesis 2.24, the text on which scriptural teaching about marriage is grounded, concludes a closely-textured discussion of what it means to be made in the image of God, and needs to be read in such a context.

Whatever the scriptural ideals may be, marriage as we have received it is marred, as is clearly recognised in Genesis 3. The primordial relationship broken after disobedience is between the man and woman, who hide themselves from each other by clothing (3.7). Nothing is said about the first sin being particularly related to sex—a misunderstanding which supports the false idea that sexual sin is worse than others—though one of its consequences is shame, while blame rather than trust characterises the attitudes of the woman and man to each other (3.12). Pain, domination and toil result in their dominion and multiplying functions (3.15–19).

Thus marriage as we experience it may reflect the interests of only one partner, or be abused in the power struggles that characterise sinful humanity, or become an instrument of social control or oppression. In our own day marriage has become increasingly privatised, losing its wider communal setting and purpose, turning inward upon itself. The element of commitment therefore needs particular stress in the world in which we live. When pursued as an end in itself, marriage can become an idol, the dominant thing in a person's life, transcending even what God demands. Marriage thus calls for our 'penultimate' rather than our 'ultimate' allegiance, which belongs to God alone.

## M1.2 The New Testament teaching

Jesus gave little direct teaching about marriage, and is depicted in the scriptures as an unmarried man. When pressed with questions about divorce, he sought to return his listeners to reflect on the original goals of marriage, directing them back to the ideals of Genesis 1–2 (Matthew 19.1–12; Mark 10.1–12). These were seen to be so demanding as to invite the disciples' comment, 'then it is better not to marry'. Jesus bore great respect for marriage, but called his disciples into a wider 'family' or 'household' (oikumene), that of the 'reign of God'. So, responding to a (ridiculous) case brought by some Sadducees to trap him, Jesus taught that 'in the resurrection in heaven they neither marry nor are given in marriage, but are like the angels' (Mark 12.25). The Book of Common Prayer, in describing marriage as 'a holy estate [which] Christ adorned and beautified with his presence and first miracle that he wrought, in Cana of Galilee' (John 2.1–11), points to the truth that marriage itself is blessed by Christ, not only marriages between Christians. Thus, according to the traditions about Jesus received and passed on in the early Christian communities, marriage (and kinship) were to be honoured, but not given ultimate honour.

Pauline teaching on marriage is likewise only given in response to questions raised with the apostle. Consistent with Jesus' teaching, he holds that marriage, though important in this age, is not of eternal significance. One misunderstanding of his teaching is that people are 'called' to marry. The New Testament speaks of our Christian 'calling' only in terms of us being called to be 'in Christ', not as any particular lifestyle within that. As regards marriage, Paul—mindful of 'the impending crisis'—tells his readers in 1 Corinthians 7 to remain 'in the state in which you were called', with no encouragement to seek marriage, except to avoid immorality. This teaching about marriage assumes that it is a possible lifestyle for a Christian, about which Paul gives advice of a practical nature, distinguishing his own opinion from what is 'of the Lord'.

More positively, in Ephesians 5 the union of man and woman in Christ is described as displaying the faithful love and service of God in Christ through the Church, which is described as the 'bride of Christ' (5.21–33). Marriage, which (in traditional terminology) belongs to the 'order of creation', can thus point beyond this to the 'order of redemption', reflecting the 'great mystery' of the intimate relationship between Christ and the Church. In Christ, therefore, marriage can serve as a practical bridge between faith and life.

In summary, the scriptures present marriage as grounded in what it means to be human. According to Christian teaching, marriage is the one-flesh, life-long covenantal relationship of a man and woman in an exclusive commitment. In Christ, marriage points to a deeper significance, showing visibly something of the love and unity between God and the church.

### M1.3 The distinctive significance of marriage in Christ

The preceding section points to the profound Christian understanding of the significance and importance of marriage, whomever the partners may be. Marriage between Christians is often spoken of as 'Christian marriage'. However, this term might suggest that 'Christian marriage' is a distinctive kind of marriage, different from marriage generally, and is avoided in this Handbook. Marriage between Christians does, however, have a distinctive significance and can properly be described as 'Holy Matrimony', the term used in BCP ('to join together this Man and this Woman in Holy Matrimony'). For people of Christian faith, Holy Matrimony is, essentially, marriage 'in Christ'. It does, of course, fully meet and satisfy the whole definition of marriage as described in the preceding section, as a one-flesh, life-long covenantal relationship of a man and woman in an exclusive commitment; but other factors are also involved.

Firstly, Holy Matrimony is not the only state of life in which a Christian may live, but is to be entered into 'soberly, having in mind those purposes for which it was ordained' (BCP). A Christian disciple enters marriage as an act of costly obedience to what he or she understands to be God's will and gift for them. Marriage in Christ forms a partnership between 'joint heirs of the grace of life' (I Peter 3.7), characterised by common prayer and witness, and a willingness to bear the lifelong costs that such commitment entails. Sexual relations are not seen as 'unspiritual' or carnal, but form an important dimension of marriage, characterised by mutual concern for one another, without abuse or 'rule' of each other (cf. 1 Corinthians 7.3–7). The New Testament writers are realistic about marriage as Christians experience it, recognising that marriages in which one partner only is a believer are of special concern in the churches of the time (1 Corinthians 7.12–16; I Peter 3.1–6). Further, marriage may be ended, but only as a last resort (I Corinthians 7.10–11).

Secondly, Holy Matrimony is a sign of the unity between Christ and the Church, the 'bride without spot or wrinkle' (Ephesians 5.25–26). In Christ, marriage does not exist for its own sake, but as a sign in this age of God's new creation (cf. Revelation 19.6–9). It is not only a 'covenant' between two human beings who happen to be Christians, but is also a sign of the 'new covenant' to which they belong in Christ, an anticipation of the coming 'marriage supper of the Lamb' (Revelation 21.1–2) to which all humankind is invited. Marriage in Christ thus points outwards and forwards, as well as inwards and backwards. It makes visible the love of God in Christ in creation, its redemption and the consummation of all things.

Thirdly, Holy Matrimony is not a private but a communal matter, lived out within the people of God, and the wider human community. It is a relationship in which the couple mutually develop and enable their gifts for the service of God. Since marriage in Christ belongs to the 'orders' of creation and redemption, such ministry extends to the wider community and world. As the Church receives the gifts of the Spirit for the work of ministry, so does a marriage between Christians, seen as the church in microcosm. 'Church' weddings thus invoke God's blessing upon the couple—symbolised in some Christian traditions by the couple being 'crowned'—so that they may be fruitful in their service. One aspect of this fruitfulness is the task and responsibility of raising children (where given by God).

Seen in this way, marriage can be situated in a Trinitarian framework:

it is lived in obedience to God, signifies our relationship with Christ, and embodies the fruitful ministry of the Spirit. Yet marriage—and family—do not constitute the Christian's ultimate allegiance: this belongs to God alone, and is expressed in participation in the household of faith. Thus, while giving marriage a very high place in human priorities, in Christ it does not have ultimate standing. There are greater claims, and wider callings. Holy Matrimony involves a life-long covenantal commitment 'for better for worse, for richer for poorer, in sickness and in health', which nevertheless points beyond itself to the kingdom of God.

In the light of this, in every marriage conducted under the auspices of the Anglican Church of Australia, one or both of the couple must be baptised, and will normally be expected to demonstrate in some way an adult Christian faith.

### M1.4 The marriage covenant

Each person is fully human, and 'made in the image of God' (Genesis 1.27) whether married or not, since this pivotal teaching of Scripture applies to all humanity. Marriage is one estate into which a man and a woman may enter. The teaching of the Christian church is that, for those who are called to enter it, marriage is a covenantal relationship of exclusivity entered into for life, in which a new family unit comes into existence and wherein children (if given by God) may be brought up and nurtured. The preface to the service for the Solemnisation of Matrimony in the BCP (1662), which continues to be the basis of the Anglican understanding of marriage to the present day, makes the following statements.

Marriage is:
a) A 'holy' and an 'honourable' estate between a man and woman;
b) Instituted of God in the time of human innocence (i.e. prior to 'the fall' of Genesis 3);
c) Not to be entered into lightly or unadvisedly, but reverently and in the fear of God;

d) Ordained for the purposes of the procreation of children and the raising of children;
e) A means of avoiding the sin of fornication;
f) For the mutual help, society and comfort that 'one ought to have for the other'.

The promise (troth) 'till death us do part' makes it clear that the ideal is that the marriage covenant is intended to be a lifelong one.

### M1.5   Anglican formularies

Article XXV teaches that marriage is not a sacrament of the gospel, as it does not proclaim the gospel of Christ crucified and risen (as do the 'gospel sacraments' of Holy Baptism and Holy Communion). On the other hand, marriage was blessed by Christ's presence at Cana, and approved in his teaching. For Christians, it proclaims the love and faithfulness of God in Christ, and the intimate relationship between Christ and the Church. These are consequences of the Gospel, pointing to the profoundly spiritual dimensions of marriage in Christ. The BCP presents marriage as a 'holy estate [which] Christ adorned and beautified by his presence and first miracle that he wrought at Cana in Galilee'. The Anglican theological tradition thus came to regard the marriage covenant as 'blessed' (by Christ). Holy Matrimony may then be properly thought as being 'sacramental' in nature.

### M1.6   Weddings in the Church

A marriage will normally begin with a ceremony (the wedding). It is not the ceremony in isolation, but the life-long, one-flesh covenant relationship of a woman and man, which expresses the unity of Christ and the Church. The form of a Christian wedding needs to express a Christian understanding of marriage, but we are not given in scripture or early Christian tradition any particular form for this, and those authorised in the churches have varied considerably throughout history.

It is important to understand that it is the couple who enter the marriage covenant, and who are the proper 'ministers' of the marriage. Only when abuses arose did it become necessary (in the West) for a priest to be present, to ensure that the marriage was entered into freely, and publicly witnessed. As time went on, the priest also came to give the 'nuptial blessing', which had traditionally been offered by a leading member of one of the families concerned. Today, the ordained minister presides not only for these reasons, but because a Christian wedding takes place as an act of divine worship, in the context of Christ's people. The one who presides in the people of God is a sign of Christ's presence among his people, and so may be termed a 'co-minister' of the marriage along with the couple. The ordained minister's presence is a reminder and sign that the couple's promises are made in the presence of Christ, as an act of commitment by a man and woman affirmed to be joint heirs of God's grace.

Over the last century 'arranged' marriages have all but disappeared in western societies, with romantic love becoming the dominant factor in the choice of a life partner. From a Christian perspective, love is a most significant factor in the ongoing life of a marriage, but not the sole factor, especially where it is wholly identified with emotional feelings.

Those with experience in marriage education find that couples need to be focussed on love as an act of the will rather than an emotion— indeed, some couples are relieved and empowered by this learning. In Anglican and other mainstream Christian rites, the man and woman are not asked 'do you love?' but 'will you love?'. Unlikely marriages often succeed because of this realism. Marriage forms the context in which we will act out and learn our capacity for loving, rather than the culmination of a love that is already shared.

## M3  Marriage preparation

In a social context in which slightly less than one in three marriages are solemnised in a Christian church, and in which civil celebrants are plentiful in a highly competitive 'market', an approach to a Christian church for a wedding represents a deliberate choice on the part of the couple concerned. Often such an approach will be reflective of significant longings for stability, community, and spirituality. It will almost always be itself an expression of genuine faith, however nascent. Further, given that many couples remain living together unwed, the decision to enter into the marriage covenant is to be recognised and affirmed.

Marriage preparation is a vitally important aspect of pastoral ministry. It is an enjoyable 'growing experience' for the majority of those who participate. The health of a marriage and the quality of future family life can be deepened when a couple is helped to reflect on their relationship in some depth prior to marriage. The myth that 'problems will go away when we are married' needs to be creatively challenged. In Australia today, around one third of all marriages will break down irretrievably.[50] The churches have a responsibility towards such a situation. We need to take seriously those aspects of a couple's relationship that will enable them to see each other more realistically prior to marriage, and also enhance their marriage in future years.

The desirability of marriage preparation should, then, be communicated as an expression of concern for the couple's welfare, rather than as a rigid rule. Attention needs to be given to more than the legal and liturgical aspects. Christian ministers are obliged to be faithful pastors, keeping the welfare of the couple to the fore. Many find marriage preparation to be a rewarding ministry, offering the privilege of working at a deeply personal level with the couples concerned, presenting significant opportunities for sharing the truths of Christian faith, and often leading to ongoing pastoral relationships.

Preparation may be conducted by the minister who will conduct the marriage or his/her delegate, or by referral to a suitably qualified person

---

50   McCrindle Research   http://mccrindle.com.au/the-mccrindle-blog/marriages-in-australia.

or agency. Lifeworks Victoria provides such programs, whilst Prepare/Enrich is a widely used tool for ministers who will conduct the marriage preparation themselves—see further at 'Resources for marriage'.

Marriage preparation will have several aspects, generally encompassing:
a) An initial meeting and conversation at which the minister may form a view as to whether he or she can solemnise the marriage and may agree to do so;
b) Pastoral preparation of the couple for their life together as husband and wife, which will rightly have priority and possibly extend over several sessions;
c) Ensuring all of the legal requirements are met;
d) The liturgical preparation and arrangements for the service itself;
e) The rehearsal.

It is recommended that, as part of a wider pastoral services policy (Appendix One), a comprehensive written document setting out the basic canonical and legal requirements for marriage, together with the course of preparation to be undertaken and other relevant matters as determined by the ministry context, be made easily accessible via the website and/or through other means to those enquiring about marriage. This will be especially important for those experiencing consistent or high demand for marriage ministry.

## M3.1  The rehearsal

It is common practise for there to be a rehearsal prior to the wedding ceremony and this is to be considered an important element of the wider preparation. In some exceptional circumstances, where the wedding may be simple and straightforward, for instance, or if one or both parties are unavailable or absent until close to the day of the wedding for some reason, it might not be possible to hold a rehearsal. Apart from the missed opportunity to guide the couple through the mechanics of the service, the significant practical issue of when the 'Declaration of no legal impediment' (M6.4) will be read and signed arises. This must be done prior to the wedding commencing.

The rehearsal provides an opportunity to practise the elements of the service that will need some planning and preparation, however slight. This will normally include the commencing procession (if there is one), some instruction as to where the bride and the groom and their attendants will stand, and practical matters such as when or where the wedding party will sit or kneel and at which points in the service. Importantly, the matter of how the vows will be said (read from a script, said after the minister or memorised) can be clarified, together with the actions specified by the rubrics such as the joining of hands.

The rehearsal also provides a good opportunity for any questions or concerns the couple may have to be dealt with, and for the minister to provide advice on how to approach the day, and hopefully some encouragement to the couple to find time to relax and reflect on the nature of the occasion, and its importance, beforehand. To be useful, it will normally be necessary for the rehearsal to take place during the course of the week prior to the wedding, with many couples wishing to avoid the night immediately prior.

## M4  Church requirements

The Anglican Church has developed requirements around the eligibility of who may be married under its rites and auspices and in a place consecrated for Anglican worship. These are separate to, and distinct from, the legal and civic requirements imposed by the State and promulgated in Australia under Commonwealth law (M6). The Church requirements take priority in every instance.

The Solemnisation of Matrimony Canon 1981 sets out the following prerequisites regarding weddings conducted according to the rites and ceremonies of the Anglican Church.

a) The celebrant must be a minister registered on the nomination of the Church as an authorised celebrant according to the law of the Commonwealth of Australia;
b) At least one of the parties to the marriage must be baptised;
c) The marriage must be solemnised in the presence of at least two witnesses;
d) The parties to the marriage must not be in a 'prohibited relationship' under the provisions of the Matrimony (Prohibited Relationships) Canon 1981, which prevents the marriage of those closely related either by descent, affinity or adoption. The BCP contains, usually at the very end, a 'Table of kindred and affinity wherein whosoever are related are forbidden by the Church of England to marry together' that may be consulted for guidance.
e) If one or both of the parties are divorced and the previous spouse is still living, the marriage cannot be solemnised unless permission has been sought and received in writing from the bishop;
f) If one of the parties to the marriage is aged under eighteen, the marriage cannot be solemnised unless the appropriate legal permissions have been sought and received in writing;
g) If it is intended that the marriage be solemnised outside of a place consecrated for Anglican worship, permission must first be sought and received in writing from the bishop.

## M5    Contextual matters

The complexities around wedding ceremonies have escalated in recent decades, with many couples heavily influenced by the 'wedding industry' and media portrayals of the 'ideal' or 'dream' wedding. This will often lead to particular requests in relation to the time, place, celebrant and liturgy used. These should always be met respectfully, and with a view to nurturing faith, however fragile that faith may seem, and in the light of the following policy guidelines which are reflective of Anglican polity, and of both canonical and civil law.

## M5.1 The minister

In order to be recognised legally as an 'authorised celebrant', a minister must be nominated as such by the diocese in which he or she is licensed. Upon registration as an authorised celebrant, the minister will receive an individual registration number (in the State of Victoria, this is 'the V number').

a) In weddings conducted under Anglican auspices, the 'authorised celebrant' will be the parish priest or another cleric licensed to that parish, a chaplain, or a priest holding another licence or authority issued by the Archbishop.

b) Where the couple have a relationship with an Anglican minister who is an 'authorised celebrant' and who holds the Archbishop's licence in the diocese in which the marriage is to be solemnised, the extent of the participation of that minister is at the discretion of the minister who has pastoral charge of the congregation where the wedding is to take place.

c) If the intended minister is an 'authorised celebrant' and an ordained minister of the Anglican Church of Australia holding a licence in another diocese, permission for that minister to conduct the wedding, if desired, must be sought in writing from the diocesan bishop. An 'authorised celebrant' is legally able to solemnise marriages in any State or Territory of Australia, including a State or Territory outside the one in which they are registered.

d) It is not normally possible for an Anglican minister holding a licence in a diocese overseas (i.e. that is not part of the Anglican Church of Australia) to conduct a marriage in Australia, as the minister concerned will not be registered as an 'authorised celebrant' according to the laws of the Commonwealth of Australia.

e) The minister who conducts the wedding will normally have prepared the couple for marriage.

Requests for ministers ordained in Christian traditions other than the Anglican Church are sometimes made. As a marriage in a place consecrated for Anglican worship must be conducted according to the rites of the Anglican Church of Australia, and as this is a matter of both Anglican polity and Commonwealth law (see M6.1), it is not possible for a minister who is not ordained in the Anglican Church to conduct a wedding in a place consecrated for Anglican worship. Ministers of other Christian traditions may, however, be invited to participate in the wedding in a variety of ways—by robing (if appropriate) and standing and/or sitting alongside the Anglican minister who will conduct the service, by giving the homily, by leading the prayers and adding prayers of blessing for the couple as may be appropriate and desired, or by performing (in consultation with both the couple concerned and the Anglican minister who will conduct the service) particular rites or ceremonies associated with another Christian tradition such as the Orthodox crowning ceremony.

### M5.2 According to the rites of the Anglican Church of Australia

Marriages are solemnised according to the rites of the Anglican Church of Australia. This is both a church (ecclesiastical) and civil requirement. By this is meant that one of the services for marriage in BCP, AAPA, or APBA will be used.

On some occasions there may be requests for the liturgy to be 'softened' or altered in some way. This is often around matters of conscience raised by a party who is unable to say 'in the presence of God' or similar such words. Whilst the person's honesty and integrity should be respected, so also must that of the Church. An Anglican minister is not at liberty to agree to any changes, re-wording or alterations to the liturgy that diminish the wedding as an act of Christian worship without reference to the bishop. Altering the wording can also have serious legal consequences (see M6.1).

Couples may also request that the vows be 'personalised' in some way, often under the influence of highly individualised vows they may have witnessed at other wedding ceremonies, in movies or on television. The consent and vows are clearly an important part of what constitutes marriage according to both the rites of the Anglican Church of Australia and Australian law, and cannot be changed or amended in any substantial way for this reason. To do so would violate the liturgical integrity of the Church and potentially threaten the legal validity of the marriage, which does rest to a significant extent on authorised words being used, in particular at the point of the consent and vows. Both the celebrant and the couple can have full assurance that the form of words prescribed by BCP, AAPB and APBA meet the requirements of Australian law. Where this is a pastoral matter of some import a possibility, at the discretion of the minister, is that the couple be invited to add some words they wish to say to each other after the exchange of the vows, although such discourse is usually more appropriate at the wedding reception afterwards in the context of the speeches.

### M5.3 Marriages outside of a place consecrated for worship

The policy position of the diocese is that weddings solemnised according to Anglican rites, with an Anglican minister officiating, are normatively to be conducted in a place consecrated for Anglican worship. This will typically be an Anglican parish church, a school chapel, or another similar such place consecrated for Anglican worship. The possibility exists, however, for a wedding solemnised according to Anglican rites, with an Anglican minister officiating, to be conducted somewhere other than a place consecrated for Anglican worship if the bishop has given written permission for this occur.

Should the minister to whom the request is made be willing to conduct a wedding outside of a place consecrated for Anglican worship, the minister should request the form used for making such application from the bishop's office. The prescribed form will request details such as:

a) The full names and addresses of the couple concerned;
b) The proposed date of the marriage;
c) The proposed place;
d) The reason put forward by the couple for the marriage to be solemnised in that place;
e) The recommendation of the proposed celebrant and/or a statement as to the proposed celebrant's willingness to conduct the marriage.

Where permission to solemnise a marriage in a place not consecrated for Anglican worship is granted by the bishop:

a) The preparation should be the same as that which would have been provided for any other marriage;
b) An authorised service must be used;
c) The marriage should be entered into the marriage register of the parish in which the marriage took place, or if this is not practical or not possible, the marriage register of another parish church;
d) The minister who is to conduct the wedding should be satisfied that the venue and practical arrangements such as audibility, music, seating etc. are conducive to the solemnity of the occasion.

**M5.4 The time**

There are no legal or canonical restrictions on when marriages may be solemnised, however the nature of the marriage service as a public rite of the Church means that the wedding should be held at a time a congregation can reasonably be expected to gather.

    a) Most marriages take place on Friday afternoon or early evening, Saturdays, or Sunday afternoon, but other times are possible also (e.g. some couples may request a service on the eve of a public holiday).

    b) There is no impediment to marriages being solemnised on a Sunday, indeed BCP assumes they will be.

    c) The custom of not solemnising marriages in Lent, or requiring permission from the bishop to do so, has not been widely observed in this diocese for some time, however the matter is at the discretion of the proposed minister.

    d) A marriage will not normally be solemnised during Holy Week, but again, this is at the discretion of the proposed minister.

### M5.5   The marriage of divorced persons

The Marriage of Divorced Persons Canon 1981 3(1) requires that the marriage of any person who is divorced shall not be solemnised by a minister of the Church during the lifetime of the person's former spouse 'unless, upon application made by the proposed celebrant, the bishop of the diocese in which the marriage is to be solemnised has consented to the solemnisation of the marriage'.

De facto relationships are not within purview of the Canon even if one or both parties of the couple concerned have previously been in a long term committed relationship, but were never legally married, regardless of whether any children resulted from that union. In these situations, the minister will normally explore, in a pastorally appropriate and sensitive way, the reasons for the end of any prior long term relationships, in the same way as the reasons for a prior marriage ending in divorce might be explored.

The following policy and guidelines apply to requests for marriage

where one or both parties to the marriage are divorced with a former partner still living:
a) All requests for marriage should be honoured as expressions of faith and representing a desire to seek the blessing of the church, and of God, on the union;
b) The minister's main consideration will be to discern if the couple concerned are genuinely seeking Christian marriage;
c) The minister should ensure the request meets the condition of canonical law as set out above (M4), and of civil law (M6);
d) If the minister is satisfied this is the case, and if one or both parties to the marriage have been previously married with one or both of the previous spouses still living, the minister should seek written permission from the bishop to solemnise the marriage, as required by Canon law;
e) In the Diocese of Melbourne a form, available from the bishop's office, is used for the purpose of seeking the bishop's permission to solemnise the marriage of a divorced person. The form will request details such as the full names and addresses of the couple concerned, the date and place of the proposed marriage, the nature of the relationship the minister has established with the couple, and an indication of the minister's willingness to solemnise the marriage;
f) The minister is responsible for arranging for a suitable course of marriage preparation for the couple.

There may be circumstances in which a minister cannot, in good conscience, solemnise the marriage of a divorced person. The Marriage of Divorced Persons Canon 1981 recognises this, and provides (at section 6), that 'a minister of this Church may refuse to solemnise the marriage of any divorced person during the life of the person's former spouse'.

Note: A person who has been divorced, and whose previous partner has died, is regarded as a widow or widower. No permissions will need to be sought from the bishop to solemnise any subsequent marriage after the death of the previous spouse, however evidence of the end of the previous marriage, in the form of a death certificate, will need to be provided to the celebrant in accordance with civil law (see M6.2).

### M5.6  De facto relationships

The diversity of relationship types and arrangements is increasing across Australia and the western world in general, a trend that includes Christian couples and families of origin also.

Many factors may have led a couple to live together: a repudiation of marriage as 'institutional' or 'irrelevant', gradual growth of a 'casual' relationship into a long-term relationship, Centrelink rules, or simply the cost of a wedding. It is important to acknowledge that women and men may approach relationships with different understandings of the commitment involved.

It is hardly surprising, then, that many requests for marriage today are made by couples who are already living together. In general, such approaches should be welcomed, since they indicate that a mature decision about marriage has been made by the couple. Whatever the history of any couple, it is essential that the clergy who receive the request offer a warm and open reception to every inquiry about marriage, so they can engage with the couple's relationship, its realities and possibilities.

The pastoral response to those already living together should be shaped and informed by a range of factors. There are many situations, for instance, in which the conditions of marriage have effectively been fulfilled by the couple, and to all intents and purposes they are married. Indeed, long-term cohabitation of a couple recognised by their community as married was a legal way to be married in England until 1753. Further, most (if not all) de facto couples would regard their relationship as excluding others, and would treat unfaithfulness as if it were adultery. It needs to be assumed that if a couple approaches a Christian minister they are serious about their relationship, and committed to it.

Often a significant life event, most prominently the birth of a child, will be the catalyst for a re-appraisal of a couple's marital status, and lead to them approaching a Christian minister for marriage. Of course, the same preparation will apply as to any couple, however the minister or other person conducting the preparation may need to sensitively adapt or shape the preparation to the couple's actual situation, with an emphasis perhaps on how, and why, marriage may change the nature of their relationship.

### M5.7 Particular situations

In today's multicultural social world it is not uncommon for those of Christian faith, whether lived out in the Anglican tradition or not, to marry members of other Christian churches, people of other faith traditions, or those of no professed faith. The Anglican Church of Australia stipulates one basic requirement upon a couple seeking to be married under its auspices, namely that at least one partner is a baptised Christian. In the light of this, and subject to the policy applying generally to any wedding in an Anglican church, no particular restrictions are placed on an Anglican marrying a non-Anglican. When one partner is not an Anglican, however, particular issues arise about the wedding itself, and more especially about preparation for marriage.

### Inter-church marriages

'Inter-church' marriage means one in which husband and wife are regular worshippers, but maintain separate loyalty to different Christian traditions (one being an active member of the Anglican tradition). Such marriages represent a concrete expression of the unity we share as Christians, despite our divisions. They should be seen as foretastes of the ecumenical future of God's people, no matter what practical tensions may arise for the couple and their family. In most cases personal discussion with the couple, and contact between any clergy involved, is sufficient to clarify matters. A meeting in which the couple and both Anglican and non-Anglican ministers are involved can open up communication over the issues, both as regards the wedding and married life.

The larger questions in such situations will probably not concern the wedding, but the way in which the couple faces their married life. The easiest path is to ignore the differences, and regard them as merely 'church regulations', but such approaches fail to grasp the ecumenical opportunities opened up, and the serious theological issues involved.

Typical questions raised include the following:

a) Will wife and husband continue to worship separately? If not, what may be the standing of the member from the 'other' church? If they do worship separately, how will the couple sustain their life as 'joint heirs of the grace of God'? In either case, what ecumenical contribution can be made to their respective churches?

b) Can their children be baptised/confirmed in a joint service (and if so, in which church)? How may the Christian nurture of children be sustained in an ecumenical and practical way? What happens if one church will not accept the other partner (or children) as regular communicants?

Unless exceptional circumstances prevail, it is recommended that a wedding involving a non-Anglican partner not take place in the context of Holy Communion. This is only likely to be considered in the case of an inter-church marriage, but may obscure rather than illuminate ecumenical relationships.

### Inter-faith marriages

'Inter-faith' marriage means one in which one partner is an Anglican, and the other is not a Christian. Growing numbers of Australians are members of a faith or ideology other than Christianity, or profess no particular faith. Marriage belongs to the whole human family—it is not a distinctive of Christian belief, though it does concern matters central to it. Marriages that cross cultural and religious boundaries can be seen as bridges between different races and communities—such marriages join more than the couple concerned. Particular difficulties and tensions are likely in such marriages, however, due to contrasting perspectives coming to the surface in the close life of a married couple.

Two inter-related issues arise here: the pastoral counsel of Anglicans considering marriage to someone of a non-Christian faith, and requests for inter-faith marriage in the Anglican church.

The Anglican Church teaches that the Christian ideal is a household in which all members seek to serve Jesus Christ, but it does not forbid Anglicans marrying those of another faith or ideology. Anglican clergy are, nevertheless, responsible for ensuring that all those in their pastoral care who are considering marriage to a member of another faith understand its possible implications.

The scriptural teaching that marriage is to reflect the unity of Christ and the church presupposes that the intimacy of marriage should include the intimacy of shared faith in Christ. The raising of children will involve similar questions about the sharing and transmission of faith.

The other faith community involved, and the non-Anglican partner's family, may have difficulty in receiving the Anglican partner into their fellowship. In Australia at present, because of their minority position, the bonds defining such communities may be drawn more tightly than elsewhere. There may be unanticipated expectations about marital/parental roles and relationships.

### Requests for an inter-faith marriage under Anglican auspices

From time to time a request is made for a Christian wedding involving an Anglican partner and a member of a non-Christian faith. Canon law requires that at least one of the partners in each marriage conducted under Anglican auspices must be baptised. It does not specify any particular categories into which the unbaptised partner may fall, although it assumes that the unbaptised partner is willing to take part in the Christian ceremony.

An inter-faith couple is unlikely to approach a minister for a Christian wedding without thought, but several matters will need serious consideration.

a) The non-Anglican partner's perspective will need to be sought and clarified, since prayers and blessings in Anglican weddings are offered in the name of the Trinity. The potential inability of the non-Anglican's family to join in the service also needs to be thought through.

b) Where the non-Christian partner is by conscience unable to say the words of the Consent and Vows referring to God, these words may be amended or changed for that partner, with the permission of the bishop. It is expected, however, that both parties to the marriage are willing to have prayers offered on their behalf, and to receive the nuptial blessing.

Where the conditions set out above cannot be met, but the couple wishes the wedding to take place under Anglican auspices, a civil ceremony followed by a blessing in the church may meet the needs of the couple concerned (see M9).

## M6   Legal requirements

The 'authorised celebrant' at a marriage has a duty to ensure that everything is done according to current Australian law, and that every step is taken to ensure any marriage they solemnise is legally valid. All marriages in Australia are regulated by two pieces of Commonwealth (federal government) legislation—the Marriage Act 1961 and the Marriage Regulations 1963.

## M6.1 The rites and ceremonies used

The Marriage Act 1961 section 45(1) stipulates that the 'authorised celebrant' of a recognised denomination may only use the form and ceremony recognised by that denomination. This means that Anglican clergy are not at liberty to use other rites or those of their own devising and, further, that an Anglican minister may only solemnise marriages using the authorised liturgies of the Anglican Church of Australia (that is, those in BCP, AAPB, or APBA). These authorised liturgies of the Anglican Church have been affirmed by the federal government to satisfy the requirements of Australian marriage law. To signify that the requirement to use an authorised liturgy has been met, an Anglican minister will indicate on the marriage certificates that the marriage was solemnised 'according to the rites of the Anglican Church of Australia'. This is a legal requirement that cannot, and should not, be altered or ignored under any circumstances.

## M6.2 The Notice of Intended Marriage (NOIM)

The Notice of Intended Marriage (NOIM) is the first legal document that needs to be completed, and in Victoria is now provided online to registered celebrants.
  a) The NOIM must be received and signed by the authorised celebrant at least one month before the date of the wedding, and not more than eighteen months before the wedding.
  b) In some cases the time requirement may be shortened, but only in rare and exceptional circumstances (e.g. on medical grounds) after application to a prescribed authority, and upon receipt of permission for a shortening of the time frame from that authority.
  c) The celebrant should record the date on the NOIM on which he/she received the document from the couple; this date must fall within the time specified above in (a).
  d) It is possible to begin filling out the NOIM even if one or both

parties of the couple are unable to provide the required documents, or can only provide a scanned, faxed or photocopied version of their documents. The authorised celebrant must, however, sight the original documents before the marriage is solemnised. Partially completed NOIMs can be saved online.

e) The names entered into the NOIM by the couple will normally be their names as they appear on their respective birth certificates, unless the name has been changed by deed poll or a prior marriage.

f) Both parties must give to the authorised celebrant evidence of their date and place of birth, and these details must be entered into the NOIM. Acceptable documents are a birth certificate or extract, or a passport, or if neither can be provided for a valid reason a statutory declaration may be made.

g) The authorised celebrant must be satisfied of the identity of each party to the marriage. This is additional to the requirement that each party to the marriage provide evidence of their date and place of birth. The 'authorised celebrant' meets this requirement by asking for, and recording on the NOIM, a form of photo identity for each party to the marriage (e.g. driver's licence, passport, proof of age card).

h) The couple bear the responsibility of satisfying the authorised celebrant that they are free to marry and must provide evidence of the end of any previous marriage. This will normally be in the form of a court order if divorced, or a death certificate if a widow or widower. The authorised celebrant can accept a request for marriage and sign the NOIM if one or both of the parties are still married to another person at the date of receipt of the NOIM. In such cases it is sufficient that the married party or parties note when filling in the NOIM that he/she is still married, that a divorce order is being sought, and the date upon which the divorce is expected to be finalised. The marriage cannot, however, be solemnised unless evidence of the finalisation of the divorce is given to the authorised celebrant prior to the solemnisation of the marriage.

i) When the NOIM is complete, the document will be printed out and signed by the couple in the presence of the intended authorised celebrant, who witnesses their signatures. Where necessary, the NOIM can also be witnessed by another person authorised to witness statutory declarations and by an Australian diplomatic or consular officer overseas.

In Victoria, the NOIM may be completed and lodged online. Comprehensive detail covering a range of situations regarding completing the NOIM, and other matters, is provided in the current version of the document Guidelines on the Marriage Act 1961 for Marriage Celebrants published by the Attorney-General's Department, which is available for download.

See further at 'Resources for marriage ministry—links, civil and legal'.

### M6.3 Happily Ever... Before and After

As soon as practical after signing the NOIM, and ideally at the same time, the authorised celebrant should provide the couple with a document issued by the Australian government currently titled Happily Ever... Before and After, which sets out the obligations of marriage and provides detail regarding marriage preparation and some legal matters concerning marriage. This is referred to on the NOIM as being required under subsection 42(5A) of the Act, and is to be given to each party to the marriage. Happily Ever... Before and After is available in PDF format for download.

See further at 'Resources for marriage ministry—links, civil and legal'.

### M6.4 The declaration of no legal impediment

The 'declaration of no legal impediment' is on the reverse of the official certificate of marriage. This declaration must be read out and signed by each party to the marriage, and by the authorised celebrant, before the wedding takes place. This will typically be done at the rehearsal. If there is not a rehearsal, the minister must ensure this declaration is completed and signed at another time before the marriage. The signed declaration is sent with the official certificate of marriage to the Registry of Births, Deaths and Marriages in the State or Territory in which the marriage took place, after the service. The form is available for download.

See further at 'Resources for marriage ministry—links, civil and legal'.

Note: The Registry of Births, Deaths and Marriages advise that this document is the one most commonly omitted by authorised celebrants. If not completed and signed before the marriage, the authorised celebrant will receive written advice from the Registry together with instructions about what must now be done in order for the marriage to be registered. Repeated failure to lodge this form, or other documentation, may result in authorisation to act as a marriage celebrant under Australian law being removed.

### M6.5  The Marriage certificates

The Marriage Act 1961 section 50 requires the authorised celebrant to prepare and sign three certificates for each marriage they solemnise. The names on all three certificates should be exactly the same, and should correspond exactly with the names on the NOIM. The three certificates are:

    a) The official 'certificate of marriage,' signed by the parties to the marriage, two witnesses (over 18 years of age), and the authorised celebrant, usually during the marriage service, which is sent to the Registry of Births, Deaths and Marriages in the State or Territory in which the marriage took place, after the service. (This certificate, if a hard copy is being used, may have on the reverse the 'declaration of no legal impediment' that must be made prior to the marriage—see M6.4).

b) A second official 'certificate of marriage', which is kept by the authorised celebrant, and must be exactly the same in every detail as the official marriage certificate referred to in (a). This will normally be in the form of a Register kept in the place where the marriage was solemnised. Every wedding conducted by an Anglican minister must be entered into the Register of a parish or other agency such as a school or chapel. If this is not possible, the minister must purchase and maintain his/her own Register.

c) The 'Form 15 certificate of marriage' bears the coat of arms of the Commonwealth of Australia and is imprinted with a unique identifying number on the reverse. This certificate is signed by the parties to the marriage, two witnesses (over 18 years of age), and the authorised celebrant, usually during the marriage service or immediately afterward, and handed to the couple by the minister. The certificate constitutes proof of the marriage, but will not displace the need for the couple to purchase a certified copy of the official certificate of marriage from the Registry of Births, Deaths and Marriages for some purposes (e.g. if applying for an Australian passport or new driver's licence).

d) The authorised celebrant must record the number of the Form 15 certificate of marriage (c) given to the couple at the marriage ceremony, what happened to the certificate, and the date on which it was used. The Record of Use document used for this purpose is available for download.

The official certificate of marriage, the declaration of no legal impediment, and the form for recording the number of each Form 15 certificate of marriage used, are available for download. The Form 15 certificate of marriage and marriage registers for use by the celebrant, together with hard copies of other forms, must be purchased from the Australian Government printer, CanPrint Communications.

See further at 'Resources for marriage ministry—links, civil and legal'.

### M6.6 After the wedding ceremony

The authorised celebrant has a legal responsibility to register each marriage solemnised by sending the required documentation to the Registry of Births, Deaths and Marriages in the State or Territory in which the marriage took place no more than fourteen (14) days after the date of the marriage. The documents to be sent to the relevant registry office are:

a) The official certificate of marriage;
b) The declaration of no legal impediment (either as a separate form if downloaded or on the reverse of the official certificate of marriage if using a print version);
c) The signed Notice of Intended Marriage (NOIM);
d) Any supporting documents such as statutory declarations, or documentation concerning the shortening of time for lodgement of the NOIM, or for the marriage of a person aged between 16 and 18.

Some States, including Victoria, require that the NOIM be completed online, and then printed out and signed by the couple and the minister. It is then forwarded to the Registry of Births, Deaths and Marriages with the official certificate of marriage and the declaration of no legal impediment after the marriage has been solemnised. Information about this can be sought from Births, Deaths and Marriages Victoria.

See further at 'Resources for marriage ministry—links, civil and legal'.

## M6.7 Legally invalid marriage

There are some circumstances that all authorised celebrants, including of course Anglican clergy, should be aware of that will prevent a marriage from being solemnised on legal grounds. If aware of such circumstances the authorised celebrant must not solemnise the marriage to avoid committing an offence.

a) A prior unresolved marriage—if one or both of the parties are still legally married to someone else at the time of the proposed marriage.

b) Prohibited relationships—if the parties are closely related in some way (Canon law also prevents this—see M4, d).

c) If consent is not real consent—where the intended celebrant becomes aware one or both of the parties may be entering into a 'forced' marriage.

d) Marriageable age—the marriageable age in Australia is 18 years for males and females. It is possible that one party to the marriage may be aged between 16 and 18 years if a judge or magistrate has issued an order giving permission for the underage party to marry and the parent/s of the underage party have also given consent. A person under the age of 16 years cannot marry under any circumstances. Two persons under the age of 18 years cannot marry each other under any circumstances.

## M6.8 Same sex marriage

The marriage of two persons of the same gender became legal in Australia following the passage of legislation through the federal parliament in December 2017. The passing of the enabling legislation did not, however, change or affect the longstanding exemptions under Australian law that, in general, allow churches and their clergy to determine for themselves whether they will conduct a wedding or not, in accordance with their own teaching, beliefs and practice. In some Christian traditions, for instance, both partners to the marriage must be baptised before the wedding can proceed; in others it may not be possible for a person who has been previously married and whose former spouse is still living, to be married in the church.

The Attorney-General's department has published, on its website, a helpful guide to the implications of the amendment to the *Marriage Act 1961* enabling the marriage of two persons of the same gender.

   https://www.ag.gov.au/marriageequality

The information published by the Attorney-General's department also includes a factsheet summarising the protections that continue to be available under Australian law to ministers of religion who are authorised marriage celebrants.

   https://www.ag.gov.au/FamiliesAndMarriage/Marriage/Documents/Fact-sheet-Protections-for-ministers-of-religion-and-marriage-celebrants-with-religious-beliefs.pdf

In light of the debate in the general community on the matter of same sex marriage, the Anglican Church of Australia, at the September 2017 meeting of the General Synod, which convened as the postal survey on the matter was underway, affirmed the doctrinal position of the Anglican Church of Australia (arising out of the *Book of Common Prayer*) as being that Holy Matrimony is a lifelong union between a man and woman. Regardless of the change in Australian law referred to above, it is not possible, then, for an Anglican minister to officiate at, or participate in, the wedding of two persons of the same gender, whether the ceremony is in a place consecrated for Anglican worship or another venue. There is no authorised Anglican liturgy for the conduct of, or for the blessing of, a same sex union. This situation can only change in the future if the position taken by the General Synod in September 2017 is amended in some way at a subsequent meeting of the General Synod.

This summarises the position legally, under both civil law and canon law, but does not, of course, address the pastoral dimensions, which demand a careful response exercised in accordance with the doctrine and discipline of the Anglican Church, that is shaped and informed by the fundamental Christian conviction that all people are created in the image of God and loved by God.

**M7  Liturgical principles and practice**

The broad liturgical shape of a Christian wedding ceremony is informed by the language and nature of a covenant, in which a man and woman make a solemn agreement before God to enter into the marriage and to live together as husband and wife. All weddings will require careful planning with the couple concerned, with most couples expecting to have a degree of input, in consultation with the minister, into elements of the liturgy such as the music, hymns, and readings. Whilst a relatively high degree of flexibility can be allowed, the guiding principle is that nothing should be done or said that is contrary to Christian belief and practice, and that the ceremony as a whole constitutes an appropriate act of Christian worship.

The 'pastoral introduction' to the marriage service in the Church of England's Common Worship, intended for the congregation attending a wedding in an Anglican church, sets out a Christian understanding of what is about to take place.

> A wedding is one of life's great moments, a time of solemn commitment as well as good wishes, feasting and joy. St John tells us how Jesus shared in such an occasion at Cana, and gave there a sign of new beginnings as he turned water into wine.
>
> Marriage is intended by God to be a creative relationship, as his blessing enables husband and wife to love and support each other in good times and in bad, and to share in the care and upbringing of children. For Christians, marriage is also an invitation to share

life together in the spirit of Jesus Christ. It is based upon a solemn, public and life-long covenant between a man and a woman, declared and celebrated in the presence of God and before witnesses.

On this their wedding day the bride and bridegroom face each other, make their promises and receive God's blessing. You are witnesses of the marriage, and express your support by your presence and your prayers. Your support does not end today: the couple will value continued encouragement in the days and years ahead of them.

## M7.1  The liturgy

The BCP marriage service is rarely used today, but may be requested by some couples, in which case the 1928 revision will be what is actually being sought. It is anticipated, however, that most wedding ceremonies will follow APBA, which provides two options:

a) The First Order (APBA pp. 647–653) preserves the shape and sequence of BCP and much of the language, in contemporary prose, giving it a more traditional feel. The consent and vows occur early in the service, followed by the readings and sermon (or at least the reading of Ephesians 5.20–33), and the prayers and blessing.

b) The Second Order (APBA pp. 657–674) is more commonly used, and utilises a 'eucharistic shape' (whether Holy Communion is included or not—see M7.8). The main structural difference is that the marriage occurs after the reading/s and sermon, followed by the prayers and blessing and (optional) Holy Communion.

It is important that the couple being married are provided with the Order of Service to be used at an early opportunity, and that time and space is provided for them to discuss this in an open and honest way with the minister. This will normally be an important part of the preparation. It can be very helpful to have 'user friendly' versions of the two services in APBA prepared, showing, in a clear way, what will be said and by whom (the minster, the couple). It is important that the couple have read and been made aware, for instance, how the Preface describes marriage. It is, of course, extremely important also that they know what they will say to each other at the point of the consent, vows and the exchange of the ring or rings.

## M7.2 Customs and symbols

A large number and variety of customs and symbols are associated with marriage, some arising out of tradition, others out of contemporary practices, and some in the context of the couple's particular backgrounds and life experience. The following is not exhaustive and does not address every situation. Whilst all requests should be received seriously and respectfully listened to, the principle that nothing be done or said that is contrary to Christian values and beliefs, and that the ceremony as a whole is to constitute an appropriate act of Christian worship, should always prevail.

a) Banns. The issuing of marriage banns goes back to Roman times, and whilst required to the present day in the Church of England (in England), banns are not required canonically or legally in Australia. It can be helpful, however, that forthcoming marriages are advised through the pew slip or another means of communication so that the couple concerned can be prayed for, and the congregation made aware of the marriage.

b) The attendants. The number of attendants is normally at the discretion of the couple. The attendants do not have a large role in the wedding service, but will normally be more actively involved in the reception. The custom of the best man or another groomsman having charge of the wedding ring/s is useful, but not essential, and another may be given this task. It is increasingly common for children of the couple being married, and/or a child or children from previous relationships, to be involved in the wedding party in some way.

c) Dress. How the couple and their attendants dress is normally at their own discretion, with the expectation that it be consistent with the nature of a public service in a place consecrated for Christian worship.

d) The 'giving away' of the bride. In the BCP rite, after the consent has been given, the priest asked 'Who giveth this woman to be married to this man?' and took the woman's hand from either the hand of her father or another male and then caused the bridegroom to take her hand in his. This custom, often known as 'the giving away' of the bride is sometimes expected, and at other times specifically rejected as preserving social and legal constructs that have long since lapsed. APBA First Order (p. 648, # 4) preserves the custom, with 'brings' replacing 'giveth' but places the whole section in parenthesis indicating that it is optional, and further admits the possibility that, where the custom is observed, 'the man may be similarly presented by his family or friends' (p. 654, Note 3). APBA Second Order leaves the possibility of a presentation of the bride and/or bridegroom by their family and/or friends open at the very beginning of the service (p. 657, Note 1), and provides a form for inviting the blessing of the respective families (p. 675, Note 3). This is a matter for the minister to clarify with the couple concerned as part of the preparation for the liturgy.

e) A Bible may be presented to the couple by the minister 'at a suitable point in the service such as before or after the readings' (APBA p. 675, Note 2).

f) Rings. Whether each gives the other a ring, or whether one ring only is given and received, is determined by the couple in consultation with the minister.

g) The kiss is a part of most wedding ceremonies, normally immediately after the declaration. There was no provision made for the kiss in BCP, and it is also absent from APBA. Couples who wish to kiss should be gently reminded (usually at the rehearsal) to do so in a modest manner: there will be plenty of time for passion later. They can also be encouraged to interpret the act as 'sealing with a kiss' the promises they have just made.

h) Customs and symbols from other traditions may be incorporated into the service where it is appropriate to do so at the request of the couple concerned and in consultation with the minister. Examples of this may include the 'crowning' of the bridegroom and bride in the Orthodox tradition, the giving of the thaali in Tamil culture, and the scattering of green branches along the aisle in some Lutheran and Scandinavian traditions.

i) It is sometimes desired that more contemporary traditions such as lighting the 'unity candle', be part of the service. Where such symbolic acts are consistent with the nature of the wedding service as an act of Christian worship, this will be a matter of local custom and at the discretion of the minister concerned.

j) The 'announcement' or 'introduction' of the newly married couple, inserted in some ceremonies immediately prior to the recessional, is not provided for in APBA, but may be included in accordance with the wishes of the couple, taking note of what names and surname/s are to be used.

k) The prayer for the blessing of children (APBA, First Order, p. 652) is not identified as 'optional' since one aspect of the purposes for marriage in BCP is the procreation of children. However it is omitted where the couple are unable to have children (APBA p. 654, Note 9).

## M7.3 Movement and posture

Couples, and their attendants, are often anxious about many aspects of the wedding. These can include: the order of entry into the church, where to stand (which side?), when and where to sit (if applicable), who will hold the bride's flowers, who will have the rings, how the vows will be said and what actions should accompany them. These matters can be clearly explained, and practised, at the rehearsal.

Ministers will develop their own preferences and practices over the years for many of these matters, in accordance with the rubrics as set out in APBA, the nature of the worship space, and local custom. The rubrics require the congregation and the couple to stand at certain points, together with the joining of the man's and woman's hand/s at the point of the vows and the declaration. This can be explained and practised at the rehearsal. As APBA (p. 654, Note 7) advises, 'directions regarding posture, other than those noted in the rubrics' are at the discretion of the minister.

Practical considerations regarding movement and posture will include:

a) The congregation may need to be asked to stand as the ceremony begins (APBA p. 657, # 1).

b) APBA, following BCP, instructs that 'the couple, with the wedding party, stand before the minister in the presence of witnesses' (APBA p. 657, # 1), but is silent about how this happens. This will be a matter of local custom, the discretion of the minister, and/or the extent to which the couple wish to follow a particular tradition.

c) Whether the bride and bridegroom and/or the wedding party are seated at any point in the service (i.e. for the readings and sermon) and where, is at the discretion of the minister and according to local custom and practice. It can be helpful to check with the bridegroom and bride on their preference.

d) For the actual wedding (consent, vows, exchange of rings and declaration), the couple once again stand before the minister (APBA p. 660, # 9). Thought will need to be given in regards to how the public nature of the vows will be made clear in the context of the gathered witnesses, taking care that the bridegroom and bride can be seen and heard by as many as possible who are present. It is both liturgically and legally significant that the couple freely and audibly give their consent to their marriage, and exchange their vows, in the presence of the witnesses (the whole congregation).

e) At the point of the vows, the couple join hands in turn, and after speaking their respective vows, they should 'loose hands' (APBA pp. 649, 661), so that each action accompanied by the speaking of vows is deliberate and distinct. The minister will need to give some thought to, and provide some instruction, concerning how the couple will be asked to do this, and how they will say their vows—after the minister, by reading from a script, or from memory. The minister may have a preference, or may choose to discuss this with the couple.

f) Where rings are to be given by one or both partners to the marriage, the minister may take the ring and pronounce a blessing over it (APBA p. 661, # 12).

g) The ring is placed on the 'ring finger' of the other's hand (APBA p. 661, # 13). Some couples may need advice about which finger this is. The bride might ask whether she should wear the engagement ring also. There is no right or wrong practice, however some brides will wear the engagement ring on the other (right) hand during the ceremony and move this back to the left hand, with the newly received wedding ring, at the signing of the marriage certificates or after the ceremony.

h) At the declaration, the minister 'joins their hands' and addresses the congregation (APBA p. 662, # 14).

i) The couple kneel for the blessing in BCP, however may receive the blessing standing (APBA p. 662, # 15). If they are to kneel, a cushion or kneeler will need to be provided, or movement effected to an appropriate place, for this to occur.

j) The marriage certificates can be signed either after the blessing of the couple (APBA p. 654, Note 8 and p. 662, # 16) or 'at the conclusion of the service' (in the Second Order before the blessing and recessional—APBA p. 668, # 18). The certificates are normally signed in view of the congregation, possibly on the holy table, however local custom may prevail. How the couple will physically get to the place where the certificates are to be signed, and back, will require some thought and possible practice.

k) APBA is silent about how the couple leaves the church and this is, again, a matter of local custom, the discretion of the minister, and/or the extent to which the couple wish to follow a particular tradition.

### M7.4 Readings

There will always be at least one, and often more than one, reading from the Bible at a wedding in an Anglican Church, with a reading from the Gospel being always included when Holy Communion is to be part of the service (APBA p. 659, # 6). The reading/s will be chosen by the minister in consultation with the couple, and may be read by persons nominated by the couple with the consent of the minister. APBA (p. 675, Note 4) provides some selections, which it can be helpful to provide to the couple in printed form or have available for downloading on a website.

See further at 'Liturgical resources for marriage ministry'.

The sermon (or homily) will normally follow the reading/s. APBA First Order (p. 650, # 15, following BCP) suggests a sermon 'declaring the duties of husband and wife' is preached, whilst APBA Second Order (p. 659, # 7) describes this as 'an address appropriate to the occasion'. APBA First Order (p. 650, # 15), following BCP, advises that, 'if no sermon is preached, Ephesians 5.20–33 must be read'.

### M7.5 Other readings

The couple being married may request that a reading, which is not from the Bible, be read at their wedding ceremony. Sometimes this will be a poem or other passage that may have some special significance or meaning to them, but often it will be something they may have heard read at another wedding one or both may have attended, or perhaps heard read in the context of marriage in a movie or television program. Any policy developed as part of the parish's pastoral services policy concerning the use of readings from sources other than the Bible should be available to enquirers as part of the overall policy concerning marriage, or may be explained by the minister as part of the preparation.

The minister has discretion as to whether such a request will be agreed to, and at what point it ought to be read during the course of the service. Whatever is done, there is always at least one reading from the Bible at an Anglican wedding service, which should take prominence, and form the basis of the sermon.

M7.6   Music and hymns

Music is usually an important part of the wedding service and will require careful preparation along with other aspects of the liturgy, in close consultation with the couple concerned. Typically, music will be required, and desired, at the beginning of the service, especially if there is to be a procession, during the signing of the marriage certificates, and as the bridegroom and bride leave the church at the end of the ceremony. There may also be requests for music to accompany the gathering of the congregation for a period of time prior to the commencement of the service, and possibly at some other points of the service, for example, if there is to be a sung psalm or anthem, a musical or sung 'item', or music or anthems during the administration of Holy Communion. Music will also, of course, accompany the hymns, if any are to be part of the service.

In some contexts, the Director of Music, a Music minister or leader, and/or organist will also be involved in this process. Some practical considerations that commonly arise, many of which will need to be determined on a case-by-case basis as requests are made, include, but are not limited to:

a) The policy concerning the use of recorded music and, if allowed, the process for assessing suitability of the requested piece, who will operate the sound system on the day of the wedding, and in what format the recording should be supplied (see M7.7).

b) The policy concerning visiting musicians such as string quartets, a pianist, harpist, vocalist/s or music group. What facilities, if any, are provided, together with the arrangements for access and a rehearsal (if desired).

c) The process around, and fees associated with, arranging for a choir and/or vocalist/s.

d) The usual payment made to the person or persons who will provide the music (i.e. the organist or another musician).

APBA (p. 654, Note 7) advises that 'the placement of hymns or psalms' is determined by the minister, however some particular points are indicated in the rubrics to the Second Order at the beginning of the service, and at the point of the readings before or after the sermon. APBA (p. 675, Note 5) further provides suggestions for hymns appropriate to a wedding.

See further at 'Liturgical resources for marriage ministry'.

The Christian church is one of the few contexts for communal singing remaining in Australian social life. A key consideration in including one or more hymns as part of the wedding will be the extent to which the congregation will sing them, or otherwise. Well-known hymns sung to familiar tunes are often best, but in today's world, even these may be unfamiliar to many present.

### M7.7  'Secular' music

The couple being married may make a request for a particular song or piece of music to be played during the course of the wedding. Often this will be something that has special meaning or importance to them, and may be described as 'our song'. Sometimes the request may be that a singer or musician perform 'live' during the service, whilst more commonly the song or piece of music in question will be recorded and intended to be played at a certain point in the service.

The minister will have discretion concerning this, and should pay careful attention to the song or music requested, taking note of any lyrics, in determining whether the request is to be agreed to, and if so where it should occur in the course of the service. In some situations, it may be most appropriate that the requested song or music be played later, at the reception.

Recorded music (where included) presents a number of practical issues. The format will need to be checked (for example, CD or digital device) and tested on the sound system or other equipment, in the first instance to ensure it will play (not all equipment will play all possible formats), but also for quality and for sound, especially if the recording has been downloaded. Someone will need to be organised to play it at the appropriate time during the service. The minister should clearly delegate these tasks well before the service, to an assistant, sound desk operator, or verger if there is one, or if not to another person who may possibly be a family member or friend of the couple being married.

### M7.8    Holy Communion

BCP advised that 'it is convenient that the new-married persons should receive the Holy Communion at the time of their Marriage, or at the first opportunity after their Marriage'. APBA makes provision for Holy Communion to be part of the marriage service in both the First Order (p. 654, Note 1) and Second Order, which includes full liturgical resources together with a eucharistic preface specific to marriage (APBA pp. 669–672).

Receiving the sacrament of Holy Communion for the first time as husband and wife, as part of the wedding, can be important and of deep spiritual significance and meaning. It is true, however, that many weddings are celebrated in circumstances whereby one or both of the partners, and many of their family and friends, are not regular communicants of a Christian church, let alone an Anglican church. In such circumstances, including Holy Communion will need to be a matter of careful thought and dialogue between the couple and the minister.

Where Holy Communion is to be part of the service, the minister will need to ensure clear instructions are provided to the congregation (either verbally or through a printed order of service, or both) about who is being invited to receive the sacrament (with an emphasis on ecumenical hospitality), in what order (the couple and/or their attendants may receive first), and in what manner.

### M7.9    The congregation

At a wedding it is highly likely that there will be significant numbers of persons present who may not be accustomed to the 'culture' and practices of a church. This may require verbal instructions from the minister about when to sit and stand, the times during which photography or videography will not be appropriate, and other matters. Often this can be done as the congregation waits for the service to begin in the context of a welcome. Instructions can also be included in a printed order of service produced for the occasion.

## M8    Photography, videography and webcasting

The vast majority of weddings today will be accompanied by a photographer, whilst many ceremonies are also filmed, and an increasing number broadcast in real time, or by file upload, online. The key liturgical, and pragmatic, consideration for the minister will be preserving the 'sacredness' and solemnity of the occasion, in a context where the wedding is often seen as a photographic event and opportunity by congregants equipped with mobile phones and other devices. Further, the cost of photography, and videography, can be enormous, extending well beyond the fees associated with most other aspects of the wedding.

As part of the preparation, it can be important for the minister to offer guidance on this, encouraging the couple to see and understand the wedding as much more than a 'photo opportunity'. At times, it may be appropriate to remind the couple that any photographers and/or videographers are hired by them to work to their instructions.

Sometimes the minister and/or the couple will have particular requests that will need to be communicated to the congregation. This may take the form of instructions about the use (or non-use) of mobile phones (as cameras for taking digital photographs and video recording), or other devices or photographic equipment, and concerning the uploading of images to social media platforms. Such instructions should be given before the service begins and/or communicated via a printed order of service if one has been prepared. Often there will be adequate time for an announcement, and for the minister to extend a welcome to the congregation, whilst the congregation is seated inside the church waiting for the ceremony to begin.

Some further considerations and broad guidelines include:

a) There are no liturgical or theological reasons to prevent a wedding being recorded, filmed, photographed or webcast, but often very good pastoral reasons for doing so.

b) The policy that applies should be clearly communicated as part of an overall pastoral services policy (Appendix One).

c) It is important that the minister who will conduct the wedding meets with any professional person engaged by the couple to photograph, film and/or webcast the ceremony before the service begins. This provides an opportunity to set out where equipment such as lighting, stands, cameras and microphones can and can't be placed; at what points of the service (if any) photography and/

or flash photography is not to be used; where the photographer and/or videographer can and cannot go.

d) Issues around privacy may arise where the wedding is to be broadcast online in real time or uploaded later for viewing online. Most providers of such services will set up password protected sites for this purpose, enabling those who are separated from the wedding by distance, or unable to attend for other reasons, to log in and watch the service, either in real time or at a later, more convenient time. Obviously the necessary equipment, and an operator, will need to be in place. Where the church, or the place in which the wedding is to take place, is not equipped for this purpose, the onus will be on the couple to engage the necessary operator.

e) Posed photographs should not take place as part of the service. A professional photographer will be able to capture the moments as they unfold, and arrange to take any group or posed photographs desired after the ceremony.

Most couples will want to have a photographic, and often a filmed, record of their wedding service and, as noted, there are no liturgical or theological reasons to frustrate this. Difficulties can usually be avoided by treating the person or persons photographing, filming or webcasting the service as a fellow professionals, and engaging them in courteous conversation well prior to the commencement of the service, in a way that enables them to do their job and which also enables the minister to conduct the wedding, and importantly the couple to minister to each other, without being impeded or distracted by flash photography, lighting or sound equipment and so on.

## M9  The Blessing of a Civil Marriage

In many parts of the world it is common for the legal and the religious aspects of marriage, to be separate. Couples will normally be married legally by a civic official authorised to register their marriage, and then go to a place of Christian worship some time after the civil ceremony to receive the blessing of the church on their union. Occasionally the Christian rite precedes the civic registration. In Australia, following English practice, a wedding in an Anglican Church will combine both the legal and the religious aspects of marriage, conducted in the context of the one service or rite, with the minister acting as an 'authorised celebrant' both for the purposes of the religious rite and the civil law.

Sometimes the blessing of the Christian Church may be sought by a couple following a civil ceremony, for instance in a marriage registry office or town hall, or in situations where the wedding took place overseas or outside of a church for some reason. Where such requests are made, the priest who bears pastoral responsibility for the couple should take such steps as are appropriate, keeping in mind that any service used must clearly not be a wedding ceremony.

The Liturgy Commission of the Anglican Church of Australia provides a form of service for 'The Blessing of a Civil Marriage'. https://www.anglican.org.au/data/Blessing_of_a_Civil_Marriage.pdf

## M10 The Renewal of Marriage Vows

Many couples desire to renew the vows and promises made at their marriage, often on significant anniversaries, or for pastoral reasons, for instance, if the legal marriage was not celebrated in a public way for some reason. Offering an opportunity for this in the context of a Sunday service or another specially convened service for this purpose can potentially be a significant outreach activity for a parish.

The Liturgy Commission of the Anglican Church of Australia provides a form of 'Thanksgiving for Marriage'. https://www.anglican.org.au/data/Thanksgivings_for_Marriage.pdf

## M11  After the wedding

Weddings are very real opportunities to communicate the love and grace of God, to ignite and nurture faith, and to commend the Gospel.

Their wedding ceremony is one of the most significant occasions in a married couple's life. A couple being married in a Christian church will often form a connection with, and sense of belonging to, the church in which the wedding ceremony takes place. The minister who is privileged to solemnise the marriage may also be an important point of contact between the couple concerned and the life of the church. Parishes and other worshipping communities may develop a variety of ways and means to maintain their connection to couples married in the church. These can be as simple and effective as adding the couple (with their permission) to an email list or Facebook group, inviting them to special services celebrating marriages perhaps around St Valentine's Day, or other parish events and services such as the Christmas services.

Churches will often want to both commend marriage and provide support to those who are married. This can be done in multiple ways, from praying for couples who are to be married, to special services of thanksgiving for marriage such as those indicated above, to the provision of pastoral care and support to those who are newly married or who are experiencing marriage difficulties or breakdown.

### M11.1  Ministry to those experiencing marriage breakdown

This is an emotionally costly ministry, which may prove personally stressful to ministers involved: the possible need for those who minister to receive professional help should be recognised. It is also a specialist ministry, generally beyond the skills and responsibility of clergy, although they are responsible for ensuring that a couple is offered appropriate help (Lifeworks offer specialist counselling for those experiencing relational difficulties — https://lifeworks.com.au/services/couples).

The process by which a marriage—entered into with hope, love and the best intentions—becomes twisted and distorted, is complex. There are many factors, invariably involving the failure to live up to high ideals of marriage, whether directly involving the partners or not. But this is not always deliberate or blatant. Sometimes it may be unfaithfulness, sometimes growing indifference, sometimes violence (often well concealed, not least among 'respectable' people, including church-goers) that leads to growing apart.

Paradoxically, a congregation commonly finds it easier to care for a person in marital breakdown who has come to the church for help from 'outside', than to minister to someone 'inside'. The proper desire to uphold Christian ideals has to come to terms with reality: ideals are not law. Ministry to a person involved in a marriage crisis can be complicated by the defensiveness of other Christians in the face of marital breakdown in the church fellowship. There may be a spiritually threatening sense of powerlessness about being unable to help others. Some will feel compelled to take sides in order to care. Some may refuse to accept that abuse may have taken place, especially if another church member is involved. Others may feel that marital breakdown lets down the Gospel that the Church seeks to live, to the point where their attitudes are experienced as judgmental prejudice. Some married Christians may feel the stability of their own marriage challenged, particularly where frailties are not admitted to exist.

It is important to recognise that the emotional pain for a couple is usually greatest around the time of separation, rather than at the divorce itself, which finalises an existing reality. Separation commonly includes a sense of failure, and feelings of guilt—and may come as a surprise to the couple's family, friends and church members. The most helpful support will take these realities into account. The actual procedures of divorce may further exacerbate a person's isolation within the Christian community. There may be considerable anger, grief and frustration—none being easily accepted in a visible way in a congregation. The newly single person can be perceived as a threat to one's own marriage. Again, the failure of a marriage is a massive blow to the self-esteem of those involved. The Christian Gospel speaks powerfully to each of these situations, but much work and time is needed for it to be allowed to do its work.

Apart from sensitive personal care, and the offer of opportunities for penitence and forgiveness, two particular courses of action are sometimes sought by Christians who are going through relational breakdown that may end in divorce—a rite for 'Recognition of the End of a Marriage', and a rite for the 'Release from a Marriage now over'. These aim to help the person/s concerned have their new status acknowledged, and make a new start in their life. Further details of such rites, and practical assistance in planning them, can be sought from the bishop, and may also be found in the 2001 edition of A Pastoral Handbook for Anglicans (pp. 166–67).

## M12  Fees and charges

Wedding fees should be considered within the context of marriage as a ministry of the church, as an expression of the broader pastoral dimensions of the kingdom of God, and as a core function of the Christian church and the vocation of its ministers. At the same time, the parish or other entity that hosts and conducts the service will incur costs, and those involved deserve fair payment.

Holy Matrimony is celebrated today in the context of the modern wedding industry. The church may sometimes be seen in this light, as the provider of a service, especially where the wedding fees may be high. A careful balancing of the pastoral, evangelistic and liturgical aspects of marriage, with the need to fairly compensate the church itself together with the celebrant and others providing professional services, will need to be reached.

It is important that each parish, school or other ministry context develops a policy for marriage fees that is endorsed by the parish council or equivalent, and is readily available to all enquirers. In many places it is common for the marriage of a parishioner or a close family member to be 'by donation' rather than have the usual fees applied. Many also give the minister who has pastoral charge of the community discretion to reduce or waive fees. Such matters, together with the fees associated with marriage, should form part of the overall pastoral services policy (Appendix One).

The schedule of fees will normally cover:

a) The deposit payable to reserve the desired date, if one applies;
b) Any costs associated with the course of marriage preparation if this is provided directly (i.e. the cost of the Prepare/Enrich inventory);
c) The fee for the authorised celebrant, whether paid to the minister who conducts the wedding or allocated in another way;
d) Any fee or donation for the use of the church and the maintenance and upkeep of the building;
e) The fees paid to any musicians such as an organist or pianist, and any vocalists, choir members, or music teams engaged on a by-fee basis;
f) The fee paid to the verger, if applicable;
g) The fee paid to the bellringer/s, if applicable;
h) Any fee applied for the production of a printed order of service or other stationery;
i) The cost of the flowers, if applicable;
j) A fee for the use of a hall or other space afterwards, together with any catering arranged by the church or one of its groups or entities, if applicable;
k) In some situations, in particular where the service takes place somewhere other than the church, the fee for the authorised celebrant may be paid directly to the minister, unless the minister otherwise directs. If receiving fees directly, the minister must declare this as taxable income on his/her annual tax return.

## Liturgical resources for marriage ministry

Readings from the Old Testament (and apocrypha)

Genesis 1.26–31, Male and female God created them

Genesis 2.18–24, It is not good for a person to be alone

Genesis 24.48–51 & 58–67, Isaac and Rebekah

Ruth 1.1–18 (or selected verses), I will go where you go

Proverbs 3.3–6, The Lord will make straight your paths

Ecclesiastes 4.1–12, A three-fold cord cannot be easily broken

Song of Songs 2.8–14, My beloved is mine, and I am his

Song of Songs 4.1–7, How beautiful you are, my love

Song of songs 8.6–7, Set me as a seal upon your heart

Isaiah 55.10–13, You shall go out in joy

Tobit 8.4–8, Tobias and Sarah pray on their wedding night

Psalms

37.3–6, Commit your way to the Lord

67, God be gracious to us and bless us

121, I lift my eyes to the hills

127, Unless the Lord builds the house

128, Blessed is everyone who fears the Lord

138, I will give thanks to the Lord with my whole heart

Readings from the New Testament

Romans 12.9–18, Let love be genuine

1 Corinthians 12.31–13.13, The greatest is love

Ephesians 3.14–19, A prayer that Christ may dwell in your hearts through faith

Ephesians 4.1–6, Live a life worthy of your calling

Ephesians 5.21–33, Love as Christ loved his bride the Church

Philippians 4.4–9, Rejoice!

Colossians 3.12–17, Clothe yourself with love

1 John 3.18–24, Love one another

1 John 4.7–16, Let us love one another

Revelation 19.1 & 5–9, The marriage supper of the Lamb

**Readings from the Gospels**

Matthew 5.1–12, The Beatitudes

Matthew 7.24–29, Build your house on the rock

Matthew 22.35–40, The greatest commandment

Mark 10.6–8, What God has joined together, let no one separate

John 2.1–11, The wedding at Cana

John 15.9–17, Abide in my love

**Hymns from 'Together in Song'**

10. The Lord's my shepherd

5. All people that on earth do dwell

106. Now thank we all our God

129. Amazing grace

134. Praise my soul, the king of heaven

137. For the beauty of the earth

145. The king of love my shepherd is

152. Joyful, joyful we adore you

156. Morning has broken

217. Love divine, all loves excelling

398. Come down, O love divine

547. Be thou my vision

581. Happy the home that welcomes you, Lord Jesus

603. O perfect Love, all human thought transcending

607. Make me a channel of your peace

613. Lord of all hopefulness

645. As man and woman we were made

650. Brother, sister, let me serve you

664. Your love, O God, has called us here

699. A new commandment I give unto you

777. May the grace of Christ our Saviour

### Prayers

APBA p. 652, For the blessing of eternal life

APBA p. 652, For the blessing of children

APBA p. 652, For the blessing of mutual love and faithfulness

APBA p. 663, For faithfulness

APBA p. 663, For the joy of loving

APBA p. 663, For children

APBA p. 664, For an existing family

APBA p. 664, For grace to live well

APBA p. 664, For discipleship

APBA p. 665, For the families of the couple

APBA p. 665, For the healing of memory

APBA p. 665, For the joy of companionship

APBA p. 666, For all people

## Resources for marriage ministry

### Print

Body, Andrew. *Making the most of weddings*. London: Church House Publishing, 2007.

Foster, Greg. *Taking a wedding: A step-by-step guide for Church of England ministers*. Grove Pastoral Series 121. Cambridge : Grove Books, 2010.

Goldsworthy, Shirley. *I, you and us: Creating a loving, lasting marriage*. Melbourne: Acorn, 2009.

### Links—Liturgical

General Synod Liturgy Commission, Blessing of a Civil Marriage & Thanksgiving for Marriage
https://www.anglican.org.au/prayers

### Links—civil and legal

Attorney-General's Department, Australian Government (Guidelines for marriage celebrants)
https://www.ag.gov.au/FamiliesAndMarriage/Marriage/marriagecelebrants/Pages/Celebrant-resources.aspx#Guidelines

The Marriage Act 1961
https://www.legislation.gov.au/

Attorney-General's Department, Australian Government (marriage page)
https://www.ag.gov.au/FamiliesAndMarriage/Marriage/Pages/Getting-married.aspx

CanPrint Communications (to order marriage stationery)
http://canprint.com.au/

The Registry of Births, Deaths and Marriages Victoria
http://www.bdm.vic.gov.au/

Links—preparation

Lifeworks Victoria pre marriage preparation and relationship counselling and support services
http://www.lifeworks.com.au/shop/category/relationship-programs

Prepare-Enrich marriage preparation resources
http://www.prepare-enrich.com.au/

The Church of England, your church wedding
https://www.yourchurchwedding.org/

## Solemnisation of Matrimony Canon 1981

Canon 3, 1981

A canon concerning the solemnisation of matrimony
The General Synod prescribes as follows:
1. This canon may be cited as the 'Solemnisation of Matrimony Canon 1981'.
2. The canons numbered 62, 63, 100, 101, 102, 103 and 104 included in the Constitutions and Canons Ecclesiastical agreed upon by the Bishops and Clergy of the Province of Canterbury in the year of our Lord 1603 and known as the Canons of 1603, and any Canon amending or appended to the 62nd or the 102nd Canon, shall not have any operation or effect in this Church.

3. Matrimony shall not be solemnised according to the rites and ceremonies of this Church—
    a) unless the celebrant is a minister registered on the nomination of this Church as an authorised celebrant according to the law of the Commonwealth of Australia;
    b) unless at least one of the parties to be married has been baptised;
    c) except in a church or chapel of this Church or a church building licensed by the bishop of the diocese for the solemnisation of matrimony, unless the bishop of the diocese in the particular case gives express permission for the solemnisation of the marriage at some other specific place;
    d) where the persons to be married are within a prohibited relationship as declared by the law of this Church in force in the diocese concerned;
    e) where a party to be married is a minor, otherwise than in accordance with the laws of the Commonwealth of Australia relating to the consent of parents or guardians in the case of the marriage of such persons;
    f) except in the presence of not less than two witnesses; and
    g) where either or each of the parties to be married is a divorced person, except in accordance with the law of this Church as to the marriage of such persons in force in the diocese concerned.
4. Nothing in this canon shall affect the provisions of any ordinance of a diocese in force or having effect at the time when the diocese adopts this canon relating to the publication of Banns of Marriage and dispensation therewith.
5. The provisions of this canon affect the order and good government of this Church within a diocese and shall not come into force in any diocese unless and until the diocese by ordinance adopts it.

## Marriage of Divorced Persons Canon 1981

Canon 7, 1985 (passed provisionally as Canon 13(P), 1981)

A canon to regulate the practice and procedure of this church with respect to the marriage of divorced persons.

The General Synod prescribes as follows:

1. This canon may be cited as the 'Marriage of Divorced Persons Canon 1981'.
2. In this canon 'divorced person' means a person who was a party to a marriage that has been dissolved in accordance with law.
3. (1) The marriage of a divorced person shall not be solemnised according to the rites and ceremonies of this Church or by a minister of this Church during the life of the person's former spouse unless, upon application made by the proposed celebrant, the bishop of the diocese in which the marriage is to be solemnised has consented to the solemnisation of the marriage.

    (2) Where the consent of a bishop is given under sub-section (1), the bishop shall cause notice of the consent to be furnished in writing to the proposed celebrant.

    (3) The bishop of a diocese shall not consent to the solemnisation of a marriage pursuant to sub-section (1) unless either

    (a)  at least one of the persons proposed to be married ordinarily resides in his diocese, or

    (b)  the bishop of the diocese, in which one of the persons proposed to be married ordinarily resides, has given his consent to the solemnisation of the marriage.

4. Consent shall not be given by a bishop under this canon unless the bishop and the proposed celebrant are satisfied that the marriage of the divorced person would not contravene the teachings of Holy Scripture or the doctrines and principles of this Church.
5. (1) The bishop of a diocese may make regulations, not inconsistent

with ordinances (if any) made under sub-section (2) concerning the practice and procedure in relation to applications under this canon for his consent to the solemnisation of the marriage of a divorced person.

(2) The synod of a diocese may, by ordinance, regulate the practice and procedure in relation to applications under this canon for obtaining the consent of the bishop of the diocese to the solemnisation of the marriage of a divorced person.

6. A minister of this Church may refuse to solemnise the marriage of any divorced person during the life of the person's former spouse.
7. The provisions of this canon affect the order and good government of this Church within a diocese and shall not cvome into force in any diocese unless and until the diocese by ordinance adopts it.

# Chapter Four

## Funerals (F)

Jesus Christ, crucified and risen, is the Christian hope. In baptism Christians are buried with Christ, die to sin, and through the gift of the Spirit begin to experience the power of his risen life. Yet this does not obscure the reality that Christians share the sufferings of their Lord: we still face death, as do all mortals. We grieve, but not 'as those who have no hope' (I Thessalonians 4.13).

A Christian funeral marks the liturgical expression of Christian beliefs about death: thanksgiving to God for the life now ended, mixed with the reality of grief, alongside the sure hope in Christ of the resurrection of the body. In such a funeral, human loss and divine promise meet: the service itself, and all that leads towards and from it, should strengthen those present in faith and hope, supporting them not only in their immediate loss, but also enabling them to face the reality of their own mortality.

APBA (p. 711) sets out the context for funeral ministry in the Christian tradition both succinctly and presciently, in helpful words that are intended 'for the congregation'.

> Human beings have sensed the mystery of death, and the pain of grief, since time immemorial. Every society has developed rites to mark the passage from life through death, and to commemorate the dead. Today we do this through the funeral service, and the rites by which we lay a person's body to rest.
>
> The wounds of grief need time and care to heal. The funeral may help this process, by enabling us to acknowledge our loss,

give thanks for the life of the person who has died, make our last farewell, and begin to take up life once more.

Christians believe in God, the source and giver of life. God's Good News proclaims Jesus Christ to be our living Lord, who laid down his life for us. He knew death, yet triumphed over it, drawing its sting, and was raised by God to new life. Christians affirm the presence of the Spirit of Christ, who helps us in our weakness. Yet we, with all mortals, still face death. Those who put their trust in Christ share the sufferings of their Lord, even in the midst of God's love and care.

A Christian funeral proclaims the Christian hope in the face of death—Jesus Christ, whose resurrection is the promise of our own.

In most circumstances it is envisaged that requests for the provisions of Anglican funeral rites from parishioners and their immediate families, and from Anglicans living in the parish area, will be agreed to. Where it is not possible for a minster to do so, the bishop should be consulted, or another cleric engaged to meet the needs of the bereaved.

**F1 Funeral rites in the Christian tradition**

Human beings, made in the divine image, are named by God as 'earthlings' (ha'adam) from 'earth' ('adamah) (Genesis 5.2; cf. 1.26–27). Our mortal remains are 'of the earth, earthy' and are thus returned respectfully to the earth—'ashes to ashes, dust to dust'—in the hope of the resurrection of the body. There is, thus, a reverent realism about Christian attitudes to death, avoiding euphemisms that refuse to acknowledge reality, and rejecting attitudes that disrespect the body (for example, seeing it as a mere discarded shell).

The reverent burial of a body was the ancient Christian practice for the disposal of our mortal remains, following the practice of Judaism. With Jews, Christians hold that human beings are whole persons: body, soul, spirit, mind and heart are inseparable, and the manner of burial in the early centuries of the church illustrates this. The body was placed in niches in rock-cut tombs (kokkim), the bones then being buried or interred in ossuaries, often marked with prayers of hope.

### F1.1 Martyrs and the mass

The significance of martyrdom in the early churches led, as early as the second century, to martyrs' burial sites becoming places of worship (for example, Polycarp, d. 155). In the fourth century, relics of the martyrs began to be placed in church buildings as part of their consecration, and this became a feature of the medieval West. Such relics were thought to bring into the present something of the saint's participation in salvation: it was not seen as a morbid interest, but as helping worshippers to appreciate their hope in Christ of victory over death. Thus, the main focus of a funeral, up to the early Middle Ages, centred on resurrection. In time, however, the superstitious veneration of relics grew, and the notion of purgatory developed.

In the Church of England, before the Reformation, a funeral was generally set within the context of a 'requiem mass' offered on behalf of the person who had died so that their time in purgatory may be remitted, diminishing the sense of hope. This emphasis was continued through 'votive masses' and the provision of chapels and stipends to enable these to be continued in perpetuity. The English Reformers rejected both purgatory and relics: funerals became the 'Burial of the Dead', a brief, scripturally-based burial rite, focussed on the resurrection hope in Christ.

### F1.2 The Church of England in Australia

In the Church of England, until the mid-20th century, funerals thus revolved around the burial of a body in a churchyard, or in the church building itself, as the climax of a short rite of sentences, psalms and the reading of 1 Corinthians 15. Various pre-funeral customs continued to exist—for example, a vigil with the body, whether in the church or at home—but were not recognised in the church's ritual. The Book of Common Prayer (1662) service, and the prayers at the graveside, assume that the person concerned is a Christian, though care is taken not to presume anything about their status before God. (Note: coffins were not commonly used until the 19th century, hence the references in the Book of Common Prayer to 'the body'.)

In Australia, until recent times, countless non-Roman Catholic funerals —Anglican or otherwise—were taken using the objective, sparse service from BCP. By the 1970s, however, 'Burial of the Dead' (1662) was felt to be inadequate in many circumstances. The addition of hymns and a wider range of prayers, together with words of introduction and an address, became common ways by which the rite was filled out as necessary. The structure of such services, however, was not always clear, and it was still not common for a funeral to be set within the context of Holy Communion.

### F1.3 Cremation

A major change in Australian funeral practice, since World War II, has been the rapid growth of cremation, especially in metropolitan cities, to the extent that it is now the most frequent means of disposing of a body. Cremation evokes a different range of images from burial, and is associated with 'technology', the ashes having a much less personal association than a body. Although some Christian traditions have found difficulty with this form of disposal, the Anglican Church accepts cremation as a legitimate way of disposing of a dead person's mortal remains, since it is a form of accelerating the natural processes of decomposition.

Whatever the imagery, cremation entails a two-or three-stage funeral: the (public) service itself, possibly followed by a brief, often more private service at the crematorium, then a later (usually private) interment of ashes. Compared to a burial, this pattern tends to weight the service as more significant than the final disposal of the body. It may even lead to a 'two-stage' understanding of committal: one in which the person's life is commended to God, and a second in which their mortal remains are committed to the earth. This separation runs the danger of suggesting a 'life/body' distinction that is unscriptural. There may also be practical difficulties: some distance usually exists between the place of the funeral and the crematorium, and there will be a distance in time between the funeral and the interment. Such factors can have a 'disintegrating' effect, and increase the strain on those involved: sound liturgical and pastoral ministry will endeavour to alleviate this stress, and mediate God's wholeness.

### F1.4 Secularisation

There being no established church in Australia, the norm became state-sponsored graveyards, with separate areas for different faith traditions, rather than burial in a churchyard. As this nation has become more secular, dividing of graves according to denomination has largely disappeared, and most funerals have come to be held in funeral chapels or crematoria, rather than in church. A growing number of funerals are arranged and conducted by family and friends, as the 'celebration of the life' of the person who has died. This ethos goes along with the expectation of many today that friends and family should contribute to the service, wherever it is held, and whoever takes it.

Such changes in social context undergirded the revision of the BCP service in An Australian Prayer Book (1978), notably the provision for cremation. Continued reflection upon pastoral experience and theological issues, further shifts in society, and the work of others (especially the Roman Catholic and Uniting Churches) led to the publication of a trial service in 1993. This offered a much wider range of resources, and was readily adaptable: it formed the basis for the funeral services provided in A Prayer Book for Australia 1995.

## F2  Principles undergirding the funeral rites in APBA

The services provided in APBA seek to honour both human and gospel aspects of a Christian funeral. There are a wide variety of situations, new and old, in which funerals are conducted. As well as a general service, designed to be flexible to meet different needs and circumstances, APBA provides two services for particular cases, the 'Funeral of a Child', and 'Funeral of an Infant who has Died near the Time of Birth'.

When the body is to be cremated, a typical funeral service can be understood in three phases: the main service, a short rite at the crematorium, and the interment of the ashes some time later. Provision is made for each part in APBA, but their separation in time and place can make for a dislocated experience for mourners: the Committal of the body is therefore offered as an option within the funeral service, making a single full rite. Provision is also made for a funeral to be held in the context of Holy Communion, and a wide range of prayers for various situations are included.

Underlying all the services in APBA are a number of principles—theological, pastoral and liturgical. However the resources provided are adapted, the principles outlined below should be followed, so that sound and coherent ministry may be offered by all who minister in the name of Christ through this church.

### F2.1   Theological principles

Theologically, funeral ministry involves two inseparable truths. On the one hand, we believe in God—Father, Son and Holy Spirit—who is the source and giver of all life. We return thanks for the life that was given, and has now ended. In biblical terms, death marks the return of an 'earthling' ('adam) to 'earth' ('adamah). We are fellow-creatures with the rest of God's creation, committed as 'earth to earth, ashes to ashes, dust to dust'.

On the other hand, we proclaim Jesus Christ, the risen Lord who knew—and knows—death, yet has triumphed over it, drawing its sting (1 Corinthians 15.54-58). Those who die in Christ, the 'second Adam' whose resurrection was the 'first-fruits' of the 'new humanity', look to the resurrection of the whole person, as part of the 'new heaven and new earth' (cf. 1 Corinthians 15.20–23, 45–50). Returning to the earth thus marks the finality of a person's active participation in this creation, and identifies them with it, in expectation of resurrection.

Christian funeral ministry thus embodies elements of thanksgiving for God's gift of life, and faces our mortality in the light of the risen Lord Jesus, who shared every aspect of our human condition, and through his crucifixion and resurrection brought about its renovation. Christian faith holds the body in deep respect, as the vehicle of our Lord's incarnation and resurrection. Further, the Lord who overcame death is also the one before whom we are to give account; our high priest, advocate and judge who knows our every weakness (Hebrews 4.14–16; I John 2.1–6; I Corinthians 3.11–4.5), and the ultimate revelation of what it means to be human, of 'what God has prepared for us to become' (I John 3.2-3). A Christian funeral thus looks forward as well as back, calling us to live in the light of what is to come.

In Christian understanding death and dying are closely related to baptism, which speaks of our being buried with Christ, dying to sin and the old life, and being raised with Christ through the gift of the Spirit. Indeed, after the day of Pentecost the New Testament does not speak of Christians as having 'died', except in baptism (Romans 6.1–11). As regards physical death, they are 'asleep' (1 Corinthians 15.18; Mark 5.39; John 11.11): this way of speaking is not an evasion of death, which remains 'the last enemy' (1 Corinthians 15.26), but puts death in its place for believers. In the language of Revelation, Christians are not under the power of the 'second death', even though they may have been killed (Revelation 20.6). It was Jesus Christ who experienced the full pangs of death for us, who 'died'. Indeed, compared to this shocking truth, those who believe in him are not dead, but truly alive, though now 'asleep' (1 Thessalonians 4.13–14).

This great hope does not obscure the fact that Christians share the sufferings of their Lord. Believers still face death, as do all mortals. Death in human experience is complex, and each dying is as distinct as the person who dies is unique. Death can come as a merciful release, a sudden tragedy, a painful struggle, a gentle end of a long life. Each funeral thus needs particular preparation, and distinctive resources.

A Christian funeral seeks to blend these varying situations with the truths proclaimed in baptism. A Christian funeral points to the fulfilment of what baptism began in Christ. Through death we pass to life; our relationship with Christ, begun in faith, passes into sight. In traditional terms, a Christian funeral marks our transition from the 'Church militant here on earth' to the 'Church triumphant', our participation in the age to come. It therefore not only functions as a farewell, but also as a celebration of our fellowship in the communion of saints with the person who has died—or, better, who in Christ is now 'truly alive'. It is for this reason that provision is made for the Holy Communion to be celebrated: in such a Christian funeral, the proclamation of the death of Christ interacts wonderfully with the realities of human death, and offers the grace of God to those who mourn in a way which transcends words.

Two particular matters need fuller comment.

a) We pray in trust and hope, whatever the standing with God of the person who has died. A Christian funeral stops short of the language of absolute certainty, but also refrains from being so bland as to call in question God's gift of life, and the promise in Christ of resurrection. The Funeral Service in APBA is designed for Christian use, but is careful to avoid giving false hope, or to encourage hypocrisy about a person's relationship with God.

In the case of the Funeral of a Child or Infant, however, the theological tone is 'warmer' given Jesus' promise to children that the kingdom of heaven belongs to 'such as these' (Mark 10.14). This teaching is taken up in BCP, which states, 'It is certain by God's Word, that Children which are baptised, dying before they commit actual sin, are undoubtedly saved.'

b) 'Prayer for the dead' is a matter of some contention among Anglicans. It is important to realise that no Christian tradition holds that human intercession can change a person's ultimate standing with God beyond death. Care has therefore been taken in APBA to avoid any sense in which human action, even prayer, overrides the judgement of God.

On the other hand, the New Testament portrays those who are now 'truly alive' with Christ as continuing to worship God and offering prayers: we join with them in praise and intercession, as fellow members of the communion of saints (cf. Hebrews 12.1–2; Revelation 4.6–11; 5.8–14; 7.9–12). Further, all Christians pray for those who are dying, and the precise point at which prayer for them ceases is impossible to say. The attitude that prays in desperation for a dead person's salvation is as unhelpful as falling wholly silent before God about one dear to us who has just died. There is a proper Christian instinct to entrust into our Father's hands one whom we believe is in Christ's care, and this is reflected in the prayers of committal in APBA (p. 722, # 20).

### F2.2 Liturgical principles

In the light of these theological principles, the services in APBA are designed to be both earthy and Christ-centred, looking back to his death and resurrection, forward to our resurrection to vindication and new life, and calling us in the present to courage, repentance, and a renewed consciousness of God's grace and love. They aim to help mourners not only in their immediate loss, but also to face the reality of mortality and judgment, and look to the future in the hope of Christ. A Christian funeral is in the first place an act of corporate worship, part of the ongoing life of a congregation. Yet a liturgically sound funeral also includes a generous and honest commemoration of the person who has died, and ensures that an appropriate committal and reverent disposal of the mortal remains takes place.

One notable feature of APBA is the care given to offer a clear 'shape' to each service in the book. In the case of a funeral, neither the classic 'office' (Morning and Evening Prayer) nor the 'eucharistic' structures were used in BCP or AAPB, and neither readily fits a funeral. After some reflection, the concept of 'journey' was taken up, in the Christian sense of 'pilgrimage': setting out deliberately on a journey of discipleship towards a spiritual goal. Each funeral service in APBA is therefore shaped to enable the congregation, especially family, friends and ministers, to accompany the departed Christian on their final earthly journey, and then to take up their own.

There is, then, a definite sense of movement in the APBA funeral service. The body is brought in and received, marking the beginning of its final earthly journey. After an orientation and prayer for those present, the person's life story can be remembered by family and friends. The psalm links this with God's perspective on death; heard and elaborated on further in the scripture readings and sermon. These human and divine 'stories' come together in the prayers, as thanks is given for God's gift of the person's life, and prayers are offered for those who mourn, strengthened by the Holy Communion where this is celebrated. The Farewell (and Committal, when used here) marks the turning point, where journeys part: the body leaves us, and we are then blessed and sent out to take up the journey of life without the person who has died.

This 'pilgrimage' shape is grounded in theological convictions about God's gift of life, of Christ's saving incarnation, and the hope of resurrection, intertwined with human struggles with death. Whatever local variations are made, this shape should be respected, so that the services in APBA may be treated with integrity. When this is done, the human and gospel dimensions of funeral rites will be kept together, as a unified witness to the grace of God which alone is able to meet our needs. Further, the service will be seen more clearly to mark the completion of a Christian's baptism: the walk begun there in faith passes into sight, to know Christ's presence 'face to face'. The last stages of the service should thus bear the sense not only of farewell—which is both real and significant—but also of our being embraced in the communion of saints.

From a practical point of view, a clear sense of structure will enable effective preparation of the service, and also give a sense of where adaptation is desirable. Further, as the service unfolds, a clear sense of 'where we are going' also allows for the spontaneous or unexpected. Especially in 'Funeral of an Infant', APBA encourages ministers to adapt the service as appropriate to the situation.

### F2.3 Pastoral principles

Pastorally, in funeral ministry, Christians have particular opportunities to exercise unconditional caring. In doing so, we are called to proclaim with integrity the Christian gospel, and seek to meet the needs of the bereaved for genuine help, whether their faith be firm, frail or apparently absent. Death is sometimes welcome, but always brings loss, and grief needs to be acknowledged. Yet mourners' responses to their loss vary: funeral liturgy must take this into account. Nevertheless, a Christian funeral has its primary focus upon God, and God's loving purposes, not solely upon the needs of those present.

Funeral ministry can be of great assistance in helping people work through some of the stages of grief. But different people will do this at a different pace and in differing ways, depending on such factors as their relationship with the dead person, whether the death was sudden or expected, and the like. Someone who was present during the final days of life will be at a different stage from people who come from interstate after an unexpected death, for example. Ministers should be alert to see that the funeral, including preparation and follow-up, assists the grieving process as is appropriate for the various people concerned.

Those ministered to pastorally may include the family, friends, people paying their respects, funeral staff—and the minister, whose own actions and attitudes may speak most strongly of the ministry of Christ to the bereaved. The effectiveness of such ministry is closely related to a minister's own facing of death and dying. It needs to be recognised that the grief process is costly: both minister(s) and participants in funeral liturgy will in all likelihood find themselves under stress. With this in mind, the traditional custom of wearing robes takes on pastoral significance. Robes allow the minister to stand a little apart from mourners, reflecting the steadiness of God's love 'amid the changes and chances of this fleeting world'—a key part of the ministry of Christ to us in times of stress.

Ministry that is unreal can be disastrous: it can hinder people from coming to know God's love and grace, disturb relationships with funeral directors, and make follow-up pastoral care difficult. Unreality about suffering or the inexplicable circumstances of death is one danger; its converse is failure to recognise the relief at death's coming which may be present in some circumstances, or destructive feelings about unresolved relationships between the deceased person and their friends or relations.

Ministers bear particular responsibility to ensure that proper commemoration, appropriate committal and reverent disposal of the earthly remains of a person in their pastoral charge, takes place.

## F3  Ministry with the Dying

Death is a part of life, and a certainty for everyone. Clergy should be willing and able to teach the congregation committed to their care in pastorally sensitive and effective ways about the reality of human mortality, the need to be 'right with God' and to make adequate preparations in the event of one's death.

Ideally, ministry with a person approaching death will have been ongoing for some period of time before he or she dies. As part of this, the person should be encouraged to set their affairs in order, and where necessary seek reconciliation of strained relationships. This is more likely where the dying person is, or has been, a parishioner. In many other situations, the minister's first point of contact with the person approaching death, and sometimes their family and friends, will be at the point of offering prayers and possibly administering the anointing for the dying person.

APBA (pp. 696–706) provides resources for ministry to a person approaching death that include an act of faith or commitment, scripture readings, prayers, anointing, commendation and blessing. These are set out in sections that may or may not be used, as appropriate to the person and their circumstances, and at the minister's discretion. As the note in APBA (p. 706, Note 1) advises, 'the dying person should be encouraged to set their earthly affairs in order with generosity, to forgive any whom they have offended, to confess their sins, and so receive assurance of God's forgiveness, love and care'. In some circumstances it will be pastorally appropriate for 'Reconciliation of a Penitent' (APBA pp. 774–778) to be used.

On the provision of these services, see Chapter 5, sections O2 and O3.

Discussion between the dying person and family and friends, about the funeral, can be helpful—its setting, form, prayers, hymns, readings and so on—and ensuring the dying person's requests are known when the time for preparation of the service comes. It needs to be remembered, however, that the person concerned will not be present (at least in an earthly sense) for the service: if too many details are tied down, family and friends can feel unable to make their own contributions.

## F4  Preparation

Preparation is an essential part of every funeral service, whether the service is to be a small family-only gathering or a large public occasion. The complexities of the occasion, the relational dynamics, and sense of loss and grief among the mourners will bear no relation to the number of persons present. Each funeral marks the end of an individual life that will require, and sometimes demand, a unique response. Although often very similar in form, no two services are ever entirely the same.

ABPA (p. 771, Note 1) assumes that the family and friends of the deceased will be involved in the preparation of the funeral service and participate in appropriate ways on the day of the service as pall bearers, by placing symbols on or near the coffin, giving the eulogy and/or having an input into its composition, and by requesting particular readings, prayers or hymns.

Although it is not possible to address every eventuality, the following provide some general guidelines that will apply to many situations.

Note: It can be very helpful to have a funeral ministry checklist at hand, to note the arrangements as they are finalised, together with the principal liturgical detail. For a sample, see F16.

a) The first contact with the minister will often come from the funeral director, who may have already met with those arranging the funeral. The funeral director, or the person who makes first contact, will normally provide preliminary details about the deceased and their situation, contact details for the person arranging the funeral, and may want to check on the availability of the church and minister for a preferred time and day.

b) In some situations, especially where there is a dispute or some uncertainty as to who has authority to make the arrangements, it can be important for the minister to be aware that one of the duties of the executor of the will of a deceased person is to arrange for a funeral, hence the executor of the will of the deceased is the person who should be dealt with directly in such situations.

c) Time frames are often short, emotions are running high, and many of those arranging the funeral will be experiencing considerable stress and anxiety, mixed in with their grief and bereavement. Ensuring enquiries are responded to quickly and efficiently, both to the funeral director and the family concerned, is an important aspect of pastoral care in the context of funeral ministry.

d) At an early opportunity the minister will normally meet with the family of the deceased and/or the other person or persons responsible for arranging the funeral. This is an opportunity to listen to the mourners describe the life of the deceased, especially where the deceased is unknown to the minister, and to clarify details regarding the time, place and nature of the service. This may be the only meeting, although there are likely to be subsequent phone calls and email correspondence, with both the funeral arrangers and other parties concerned.

e) It is important to check and to clarify names. Some persons can be known by names other than those that appear on their personal documentation, and which might have been provided to the funeral director by a hospital or other organisation. Taking care to get the name, and pronunciation, right, can be very important. A mis-pronounced name will jar and grate on a congregation. A wrong name is pastorally disastrous and will seriously erode the minister's credibility.

f) In addition to the form of the liturgy, it may be helpful to explain how the service proceeds, and to consider matters such as how the immediate family and/or chief mourners will arrive (do they need to come in through the front door where they are likely to encounter members of the congregation, or is there a side entrance available to them?), where they will be seated, and what they will do at the end (follow the coffin out of the church, or if a memorial service without a coffin, should the minster escort them out the church?) These considerations may seem unimportant or of lesser importance, but can sometimes be very significant to the mourners concerned.

g) It is unlikely all the details of the service will be confirmed and finalised at the first meeting, but they obviously need to be before the service. It can be very helpful to have a template of the funeral service in Word format that can be used as a guide to the service and worked on in consultation with those arranging the funeral. Often this can be achieved through email exchange.

h) Providing access to recommended readings, psalms, music and hymns can also be very helpful to those arranging the funeral. These can be in printed or digital form, the latter providing the opportunity for the selections to be cut and pasted into a template.

i) Experience has shown that it may be helpful to ask whether there is something that those organising the service do not wish to have done or said at the funeral.

Whatever is planned, the family's wishes are to be taken into careful consideration.

A situation may, however, arise whereby the minister concerned cannot agree to a particular request. This will be rare and exceptional, and call for a carefully sensitive, pastoral response. It is not possible, for instance, for a civil celebrant to lead a funeral service in a parish hall let alone a place consecrated for divine worship, nor for a minister to omit all references to 'God' and 'Jesus' from the liturgy (such requests have been made). In situations of special difficulty of this nature, the minister may need to seek the counsel of the bishop.

Whatever the circumstances, and whether the death was long expected or sudden, the family and friends of the deceased person will almost always be grateful to know they are being held in prayer, both by the minister in person, and the congregation. It may be helpful to the family of the deceased to be included in congregational prayers at the next opportunity; importantly, after asking permission from them for this to occur and only if permission is given for their names to be used. Even if the family concerned are not churchgoers and are unknown to the community, this will be one simple way of bringing them into the prayerful parameters of the Christian community concerned.

### F4.1  When children are involved

Children may well be present at any funeral, but particular sensitivity needs to be shown when one or more children are family members or friends of the person who has died. In relating to children who have lost someone close to them, care needs to be taken to avoid trite ideas, paternalistic or unrealistic attitudes. Since children tend to think in concrete ways, they may carry unfounded fears and worries about death and dying. Statements such as 'Grandpa did not die because of something you did' or 'we won't meet Aunt Jane again, but we believe that she is in God's care' may be helpful.

Making abstract concepts concrete is the challenge here, but is well worth the effort. For example, some have found that having children release balloons as a sign of 'letting go' can be helpful to everyone present. Children appreciate receiving a symbol that reminds them of their friend—a photo to keep in a special place, or a plant for the garden, for example—or a sign of Christ's victory over death such as an Easter egg or butterfly.

When the family is first visited, the minister should meet with any children involved, so that when they come to the funeral the children have some knowledge of the person conducting it. It will often be appropriate for the minister to talk with and listen to the children, and offer prayer with them. Where children wish to view or touch the body, the minister should not discourage them.

Children should be present and take their part in the funeral. Well-meaning adults wishing to 'shelter' children from death may be reflecting their own fears: facing the reality of the loss of someone close to us is a key part of the grieving process. A Christian funeral offers to all present resources that touch us at the deepest level: children may get more out of the service than adults realise. Children may participate at a funeral by lighting candles, placing flowers or other symbols, or sharing in a reading, as appropriate. Such involvement should be planned with the family, especially the child's parents, and may entail some rehearsal (ideally involving family members).

The service 'Funeral for a Child', which has been shaped keeping in mind the likelihood of significant numbers of children being present, offers resources that may be of assistance when children are present at other funerals.

### F4.2 When the Coroner is involved

Under Victorian law (and similar such legislation in other states and territories) some deaths must be reported to the coroner. These are known as 'reportable deaths' and include most accidental deaths, suicides, and homicides, among other circumstances.

When a death is reported to the coroner, an investigation is conducted to determine the identity of the deceased, the circumstances surrounding the death, and the actual cause of death. This may involve medical procedures such as a post-mortem examination, for which the body of the deceased will be in the possession of the coroner.

There will usually be a longer than normal delay in time between death occurring and the funeral service, and sometimes a degree of uncertainty as to when a funeral can take place, in such circumstances. The funeral director responsible will liaise with the coroner's court, however the court will also communicate directly with the family if desired.

The funeral will not be delayed by the time it takes for the coroner to conduct the whole of the investigation, but only for the period of time during which the body of the deceased is in the possession of the coroner's court to enable any post-mortem procedures to be conducted.

There are further details at the coroner's court website http://www.coronerscourt.vic.gov.au/home/

## F5   Contextual matters

A wide range of possibilities exists regarding requests for funeral ministry. It is quite likely that families will have seen and experienced a variety of different types of ways of conducting a funeral, and may come with requests that a minister may not easily accommodate or find easy to agree to. These should be fully discussed with the funeral director and with those arranging the funeral.

### F5.1   The type of service

The main possibilities for an Anglican funeral service include, but are not limited to:

a) A funeral service in the church with the committal taking place during the course of the same service;
b) A funeral service in a funeral director's facility, a cemetery, crematorium or memorial park, with the committal taking place during the course of the same service;
c) A funeral service in the church with the committal taking place at another location (the crematorium or graveside) after the service;
d) A funeral service that is to be held entirely at the graveside, with the committal taking place during the course of the same service;
e) Anglican rites have always included forms for burial at sea and this continues to be the case in APBA (p. 732, # 27). A naval chaplain will be a valuable resource to consult in such instances;
f) In some instances, families may ask a minister to lead a funeral in another place such as a home, an outdoor venue, a hall, function centre or other public facility. Conducting services at other

locations is at the discretion of the minister concerned and will normally be undertaken for good pastoral reasons and where there is a meaningful connection to the life of the church, its community and/or the minister concerned.

Particular theological and liturgical issues arise where requests might seem to be displacing the deceased from the community or context with which they had been associated in life—for instance, requests for the funeral of a lifelong churchgoer to be held entirely in a crematorium. Some requests might seem to be an attempt to deny the reality of death—such as a memorial service with no prior or subsequent committal. On other occasions, a family may feel their grief is such that a 'private' service (normally including the committal) attended only by the immediate family and possibly some select friends should take place, followed by a 'public' memorial service. These possibilities are addressed in section F5.2.

### F5.2 Memorial Services

The cultural emphasis on the funeral as a 'celebration of life' together with a general trend in society toward denying the reality of death, or seeing the deceased as somehow continuing to live on in the hearts, minds and memories of the family and friends, has led to a marked rise in requests for funeral services at which the body of the deceased is not present. These are, generally, described as Memorial Services.

Clearly the absence of the body greatly diminishes the sense of movement and pilgrimage, and serves to deny, or at least diminish, the reality of death. It also precludes the pronouncement of the Committal, in which the deceased is commended to Almighty God and which may be considered the pivotal and essential element of the Christian funeral service, and the point to which the whole of the preceding liturgy—the eulogies, readings, sermon and prayers—has been progressing and finds its culmination.

A variety of requests might be received in relation to such services, including, but not limited to:

a) A 'public' Memorial Service that is preceded by, at a separate time, a 'private' or 'family only' Committal service with the body of the deceased present;

b) A 'public' Memorial Service that is followed by, at a separate time, a 'private' or 'family only' Committal service with the body of the deceased present;

c) A 'public' Memorial Service that is not preceded or followed by any Committal service;

d) A 'public' Memorial Service that is followed by, at a separate and often much later time, the interment of the ashes of the deceased in a memorial garden or other place dedicated for this purpose.

Clearly, for the reasons outlined above, such services are not considered normative in APBA, which acknowledges them only in a brief note (p. 772, Note 10), advising that 'these forms of funeral service may be used for a Memorial service the Committal being omitted'. It is anticipated, then, that a minster should carefully and sensitively set out the reasons why a Memorial Service is not to be preferred, when presented with such a request. The reality is, however, that often the decision may have already been made, and sometimes the deceased has already been cremated.

Where the service is to be a Memorial Service at which the body is not present, the same planning, liturgical shape, and elements of the APBA funeral service will normally still be present, except for those that require the presence of the body.

A practical matter requiring some attention in the context of a Memorial Service arises in situations where the funeral director may not attend. This may leave unresolved matters such as who will welcome the congregation and hand out any printed orders of service, who will oversee the signing of any memorial book, and who will play any recorded music or supervise the set up and operation of any audio-visual display or associated equipment necessary.

Careful thought will also need to be given as to how the service will end. Where there is not a coffin to escort, the congregation, and the chief mourners, may need a clear cue as to when they are to leave the church, and who they are to follow (the minster, the crucifer?) if anyone.

### F5.3 Cremation before the funeral

The custom of cremating the body before the funeral should take place only for significant pastoral reasons, and where the funeral is to be conducted in a church building.

Where cremation does take place prior to the funeral, the minister who is to conduct the funeral may attend the cremation, and use such prayers as are deemed suitable. Since this act is a preparation for the funeral, family and other mourners should be discouraged from being in attendance. The ashes are to be returned to the church building as soon as possible after the cremation, preferably within a day or two.

The funeral will normally then take place with the ashes present. Some thought, therefore, needs to be given to the placing of the ashes during the funeral. They must be treated with respect, but not made to appear as an object of devotion: a dignified simplicity serves here best. Symbols that are appropriate for placing on or next to a coffin can make a small ashes container appear to be set up as a 'shrine'. It is therefore recommended that the ashes' container be set on a small table in clear view of the congregation, with any symbols of the person and his or her life arranged nearby but not immediately adjacent. The paschal or Easter candle will normally be placed near the ashes.

The ashes should be carried to the Memorial Garden for the Committal as the conclusion of the funeral rite, and interred immediately, unless there are strong pastoral reasons for delaying this until later.

### F5.4 A vigil or viewing

An opportunity to 'be with' the deceased in a quiet place before the service, or for a vigil or viewing, may sometimes be requested. If circumstances permit and it is physically possible, the chief mourners may have a period of time alone with the deceased prior to the service commencing, perhaps in a side chapel or other place, or in some circumstances and where desired, overnight. This can be facilitated by the funeral director. In some cultures, this will be important and expected.

Whatever has taken place previously, the coffin will normally be securely closed before the funeral service begins, unless there are cultural reasons and expectations for the coffin to remain open throughout the funeral service. Advice from cultural community leaders might need to be sought as to the appropriate conducting of a funeral sensitive to cultural norms.

### F5.5   The location

The venue will often be determined by the type of service—see F5.1 and F5.2. The most appropriate location for a Christian funeral service is a place consecrated for divine worship. Practicalities and pragmatics, the wishes of the deceased and/or the family of the deceased and, in some situations, the intervention of the funeral director, often mean that a minister is asked to conduct a service at another location. There may be more than one location; typically when the committal is to take place at the graveside or crematorium after a service in the church.

If unknown, the minister will need to become familiar with the layout of the venue prior to the service, for instance, by arriving early on the day of the service. It will be important to determine where the coffin will be placed, where the speaking will take place, where the minister will stand at the point of the committal if there is to be one, and how the service will end. It can be important to have ensured that there are reserved seats for the chief mourners, if necessary, and that the ushers know where things are and what to do, as well as planning for any other logistical matters that may arise depending on the location and the nature of the occasion.

APBA provides some guidelines for situations in which a funeral and/or the committal takes place in a crematorium chapel (p. 771, Note 7) or in a home (p. 772, Note 9).

### F5.6 The time

The time of the service/s will normally be determined in consultation with the funeral director. The arrangements will need to suit the funeral director, the church, chapel or other venue in which the funeral is to be held, and the place where the committal is to occur, if at another location. The funeral director will normally make all of these arrangements. The time must also, of course, suit the minister, who is not 'on call' for the funeral director and will have many other responsibilities.

The exception to this will be where the service is a Memorial Service at which the body is not present. In such circumstances the funeral director may not attend, or have any input into the service, or the arrangements, at all.

Requests for funeral ministry may often involve more than one service in different locations at different times. There are no canonical, liturgical or theological reasons governing the time of a funeral service, however the practicalities are such that most services at the funeral director's chapel or a crematorium will, generally, commence between 10am and 4pm during weekdays.

### F5.7 The minister

The minister has overall responsibility for all aspects of the conduct of the service, not the funeral director, and will need to agree to all of the arrangements regarding the time and location, authorise the final form of the liturgy, and may also need to take charge of some of the logistical and pragmatic matters that may arise where the funeral is to be in the church. Most funeral directors are experienced professionals, and will understand and appreciate the role of the minister and have an awareness of their own role in relation to that of the church and the clergy.

The officiant will normally be an ordained person who has pastoral charge or care within the church or chapel, or the parish area, in which the main service associated with the funeral takes place. This may be a deacon or an authorised lay minister (APBA p. 771, Note 3).

Often the association between the deceased and his/her family and friends and the minister concerned will arise out of an existing or prior relationship. The emotive nature of funeral ministry means that requests for a particular minister to lead the service, or participate, should be met sensitively, and hospitality extended to colleagues, both Anglican and ecumenical, insofar as it is possible to do so.

### F5.8 Funeral directors

Most funeral directors see their work as a caring ministry, and offer considerable professional expertise in assisting people through the grieving processes. Funeral staff, who have a taxing task, can become facile about death and may need ministry themselves. The ideal is where local clergy and funeral directors know one another and work in a cooperative partnership. Personal contact with the local funeral directors is part of Christian ministry. When new to a parish, clergy should visit the local funeral directors to introduce themselves, and listen to what the funeral director believes is important in ministry to mourners. In this way a working relationship may eventuate, and mutual respect and understanding grow.

Where clergy gain a poor reputation with a funeral director, this affects far more than personal reputation. Whether we realise it or not, clergy are seen to represent the parish in the wider community, and poor attitudes damage the relationships that parishioners have with others in their community.

Funeral staff rightly expects high standards—ethical, financial and professional—of Christian ministers. Yet—tragically, for the sake of the gospel—they are not infrequently disappointed. What funeral directors dislike most are ministers who are late or rushed, or show insincerity or hypocrisy in their attitudes. Other complaints are made about clergy who are hard to contact, do not return phone messages or email, are inflexible in relation to family needs, or woodenly impersonal in the way they take a service. This ought not to be. Funeral directors today have the choice of using civil celebrants as well as Christian ministers. They cannot be expected automatically to refer people to parish clergy: if a service taken by a Christian minister proved to be unsatisfactory, then people would not use that funeral director again. A funeral director will generally only refer people to a Christian minister in whom he or she has confidence, whatever the parish relationships involved may be.

Ideally, if the deceased is a practising Anglican, the parish priest will be the first person whom the family contacts after a person dies; but more commonly they will have made contact with the funeral director, who has responsibility for taking possession of the deceased person's body and will then seek to arrange the time and place for the funeral. In normal circumstances, it is to be hoped that the funeral director will have sufficient confidence in the parish priest as to make immediate contact when they learn of the death of an Anglican. If the priest is unavailable, the funeral director should have a list of his or her preferred nominees, supplied by the parish priest. Even so, funeral staff sometimes makes arrangements with the family, which, from a minister's perspective, is less than helpful. This makes the fostering of good relationships between the clergy and funeral directors all the more important.

## F5.9   Recording and webcasting

It is standard practise at most memorial parks, cemeteries and crematoria for a service within the chapel facilities to be filmed with a DVD or other storage device then given to the family after the funeral. On some occasions, those planning the funeral may request this of a funeral service in a church. There may be good pastoral reasons for this, for instance, if a close family member is unable to attend. The funeral director will normally be able to provide advice to the family about engaging the necessary professional services.

A funeral service may be webcast for similar reasons, either professionally or in other ways such as through a mourner, who is present, utilising a device such as a phone or tablet. Issues around privacy may arise, but will generally be beyond the control of the minister and the church where the funeral takes place, unless the webcast is being provided by the church or under its auspices. Most professional providers of such services will set up password protected sites for this purpose, enabling those who are separated by distance or unable to attend for other reasons to log in and watch the service, either in real time or at a later, more convenient time.

## F6   Liturgical principles and practice

The Christian funeral rite is essentially Christological, finding its centre in the person of Jesus Christ, who lived and died, as all human beings must, and who rose from the grave, with the promise that those who trust and believe in him might also share in a resurrection like his. This is the Christian hope. Hence the sentence appointed to be read at every funeral service by APBA (p. 712, # 7) is John 11.25—'I am the resurrection and the life, says the Lord, Those who believe in me, even though they die, yet will they live.'

A funeral service conducted under Anglican auspices and according to Anglican rites is always first and foremost an act of Christian worship.

Required sections of the liturgy are carefully worded so as to be silent about the current state or condition of the deceased. The purpose of the service is to give thanks to God for the life of the deceased and to commit him or her into the keeping of God, who alone judges our thoughts and deeds.

### F6.1  Liturgical considerations

Some liturgical considerations include, but are not limited to:

a) The liturgical colour is at the minister's discretion or determined by local custom. BCP assumed the minister would be vested in surplice and preaching scarf (choir dress). White or gold, the colours worn on Easter day, pointing to the resurrection of Christ and his victory over death and dying, are also appropriate. In some places the custom is to wear violet or purple.

b) The coffin (if present) should normally be closed before the service begins (but may be open prior to the service commencing, if requested) and be placed in view of the congregation.

c) The lighted Easter or paschal candle may be placed near or behind the coffin, symbolising the light of Christ and the new life gained through baptism (APBA p. 709, # 4).

d) The coffin may be sprinkled with water symbolising baptism (APBA p. 709, # 4).

e) A pall may cover the coffin (APBA p. 708, # 3).

f) Flowers or similar natural objects may be placed near the coffin (APBA p. 708, # 3).

g) Symbols of the person's life may be placed on or near the coffin (APBA p. 708, # 3). This may form part of the service or occur before the service begins.

h) The preface included in APBA (p. 771) and titled 'for the congregation' is not intended to be read out as part of the service, but may be included in a printed or digital order of service for the congregation to read as they wait for the service to begin.

Many of those arranging a funeral today will want the service to be 'a celebration' of the life of the deceased. The Anglican funeral rites allow for the appropriate thanksgiving, to God—the giver of all life, and for the deceased and all that he or she achieved in life. This can embrace and encompass most aspects of what is often meant by 'celebrating' a life, in particular, at the point of the eulogy. The reality of death and the pain of grief should not, however, be denied, neither should the Christian hope in the resurrection of Christ be 'watered down'.

## F6.2 The liturgical 'shape'

As noted in F2.2, the APBA funeral rite, as is the case for that in BCP, does not correspond neatly to either the 'office shape' familiar from morning and evening prayer, or the 'eucharistic shape', but is best thought of in the sense of movement or pilgrimage. The funeral rites in APBA are shaped by the concept that the deceased person makes, in the funeral service, a final journey away from those who have known and loved him or her in life. This is powerfully symbolised by the final procession of the coffin out of the church, after which the mourners gather to witness the hearse leave, before resuming their own earthly journey. The deceased leaves those who mourn for him or her—they do not leave the deceased. The sense of movement is evident as the service progresses:

a) The body is accompanied into the church or other place where the service will take place (APBA p. 708—see F6.3);

b) The Gathering—including the sentences from scripture, gathering prayer, eulogy or eulogies—focus around the story of the deceased (APBA pp. 712–715);

c) The psalm marks the turning point toward the story of God, explicated in The Ministry of the Word, including the readings and sermon (APBA pp. 716–718);

d) The Prayers concluding with the Lord's Prayer (APBA pp. 719–721);

e) The possibility of including the sacrament of Holy Communion in the service is provided for (APBA p. 721, # 17);
f) Both human and divine journeys come together in The Farewell (APBA p. 722) and, where included, The Committal (APBA p. 723);
g) The journey of the congregation into their living without the deceased friend is marked in the Blessing and Dismissal, culminating with the procession out of the church (APBA p. 724).

Given the range of services possible and the complexities that arise, together with the rise of cremation as the preferred means for the disposal of the body, the APBA funeral service can, with due thought and planning, accommodate a committal occurring at a different time and place and, in the case of cremation, makes provision also for the subsequent interment of ashes.

### F6.3 Reception of the body

The minister is responsible for ensuring the body of the deceased is received and accompanied into the venue where the service takes place. APBA (p. 708) provides some liturgical resources for the reception of the body. Often the minister will do this alone, but not necessarily—in English custom all the mourners meet and accompany the coffin (and thereby the deceased) into the Church.

### F6.4 Participation of family and friends

As APBA (p. 771, # 1) advises, 'family and friends may participate in many ways'. These include, but are not limited to:
a) The placing of Christian symbols. APBA (p. 709) provides a form for the placing of memorabilia such as a candle, water, bible or cross on or near the coffin, either with or without accompanying words. The symbols may be used 'at any appropriate point' in the service. If it is desired that symbols other than those indicated be used, they must be 'consistent with the Christian faith' (APBA p. 771, # 2);

b) Lighting candles; Giving a eulogy or tribute;
c) Acting as a greeter, welcomer or usher;
d) Giving a reading;
e) Participating in the leading of the prayers;
f) Participating in the music or singing;
g) Acting as pall bearers (the funeral director will arrange for and supervise this);
h) At the graveside—casting earth on to the coffin, placing flowers in or near the grave.

It is often possible to involve the family and friends of the deceased in the service to the extent to which they wish to participate. On other occasions, those arranging the service may ask the minister to take responsibility for and lead almost all aspects of the service. The nature of the participation of family and friends in the service will normally be a significant focus of dialogue in the preparation stage.

## F6.5   Eulogies and tributes

In most situations it is likely that one or more persons will wish to speak about the deceased at the point of the eulogy or eulogies. Often the family and friends of the deceased will have already made preparations for this to occur, sometimes at the express wishes of the deceased person. APBA (p. 714, # 9) makes provision for 'a member of the family or a friend' to speak about the dead person. There are several possibilities for the eulogies, including, but not limited to:

a) One family member or friend may speak on behalf of all by delivering 'the eulogy';
b) More than one person my deliver a eulogy, covering a different aspect of the deceased person's life—for example, a family member, a friend, a colleague;
c) The minister may read a eulogy prepared by others who are

unable to, or do not wish to, deliver it themselves on the day of the funeral;

d) The minister may prepare and deliver the eulogy.

It can sometimes be appropriate to distinguish between eulogies and tributes. Such occasions might occur when one or more mourners (often close family members) may wish to offer a short reading such as a poem, or perhaps share a single anecdote, in honour of the deceased. These are properly tributes, and would normally follow the eulogy or eulogies.

In all situations it is important to take time during the preparation to thoroughly discuss the eulogy with those arranging the service. Experience shows the following points can be helpful and important to clarify with, and to provide appropriate direction to, those arranging the funeral.

a) The total time allocated to the all of the eulogies should be clarified; 15–20 minutes in the context of a one-hour service is normally sufficient. Most will not want the service to be overly long and in some instances (for example, at a funeral chapel or crematorium) the time limits must be observed. The one place where the minister does not have control over the content of the service will be the eulogy and this is, consequently, the place where the overall length of the service will be determined.

b) Where there is one speaker, it can be helpful for that person to gain input from a variety of others.

c) Where there is more than one speaker, the speakers should complement each other and not go over the same ground. This can be achieved by asking those who are to speak to compare notes with each other.

d) That the eulogies are written out in full is often helpful. Many people are not used to public speaking and will often underestimate the time required to read out a speech. A useful guide in this respect is that it will take most people speaking at normal pace about 10 minutes to read out a 1,000-word speech. If the eulogy is written out in full it will be easy to check the word length. A eulogy written out in full will also have the advantage of helping the person who delivers it, especially if affected emotionally on the day of the funeral. If the deliverer is unable to continue, it can then be read out by another person on their behalf at very short notice (in many cases, the minister).

e) That, if possible, the minister be provided with a copy of the eulogies in advance of the service by email, which is often helpful to the minister in shaping the sermon and prayers, as well as providing an opportunity to check for potentially over-long speeches.

The person/s giving the eulogy or eulogies will often be anxious and emotional on the day of the service. It can help to ensure they are shown beforehand where they will speak from, how to operate the microphone if necessary (many people not used to speaking in public will fail to speak into the microphone and not be heard), what the cue is for them to come forward (will there be a verbal prompt?) The eulogist should be provided with a reserved seat near the place they will speak from.

## F6.6   Audio-visual displays

It is increasingly common for there to be a request that an audio-visual display be part of the service. Usually this will comprise images of the deceased throughout the stages of their life, set to music. This is now standard practise in many funeral directors' facilities and at cemeteries, memorial parks and crematoria chapels, which will usually have the necessary equipment and the staff to operate it during the course of the service. Whilst many places of worship will also have the necessary equipment and be well set up for this, not all will be. It may be necessary to seek advice from the funeral director, who will normally be well used to handling requests of this nature and will be able to refer to a professional person who provides the service, and who will bring and operate the necessary equipment on the day of the service.

The minister will have discretion as to whether or not such a request is to be granted, especially at a service conducted inside a place of worship. The pastoral sensitivities involved, which can often be very emotive with such a display sometimes being considered an essential and expected part of the service, will need to be balanced with preserving the integrity of the service as a Christian rite. Most of the time this can be achieved. The audio-visual display will often supplement the eulogies in a way that can be helpful and meaningful to the congregation, whilst providing, in the context of the liturgy, a 'bridge' from the eulogies to the psalm, readings from the bible, and sermon.

Difficulties may arise where the display may be overly long, or where the accompanying music or song, or images, may be inappropriate to a service inside a church. In such situations a resolution may be that the audio-visual display takes place at a wake or gathering after the service. This can sometimes be desirable regardless of the content, for instance, if the necessary screen cannot be placed where the congregation can easily see it during the course of the service, or where it may be desired that the mourners have time and space to watch the display at their leisure and be free to comment on it.

#### F6.7    Psalms and Readings

APBA (p. 715, # 10) requires that 'one or more psalms is said or sung' and provides the text and responses for three (Psalms 23, 90, 121). The minister will determine whether the psalm should be sung by the whole congregation, said by the whole congregation, whether a responsorial form will be used, or whether the psalm is read by a single reader (all four options are often possible, for instance, in the case of Psalm 23).

At the point of the 'Ministry of the Word', APBA (p. 716, # 11) requires that 'one or more of the following readings is read, or some other suitable passages from Scripture'. The suggested readings, the texts of which are included in APBA (pp. 716–717) are Romans 6.3–9,

1 Corinthians 15.50b–58, and John 14.1–6. These passages of scripture are chosen to reflect the three main emphases in the funeral:

1. The link between our baptism into Christ and our death (Romans 6.3–9);
2. The resurrection of Christ (1 Corinthians 15.50b–58);
3. Jesus' promise, as 'the way, the truth and the life', to prepare a place for us (John 14.1–6).

Eleven further 'suitable passages' are suggested (APBA p. 717). It can be very helpful to make a selection of scripture readings available to those arranging the funeral, for instance, through a website or printed booklet.

See further at section F.14—Liturgical resources for funeral ministry.

It is at the minister's discretion to what extent the family and friends will be invited to select the readings, and who may read them, although it is customary for family and/or friends to give a reading as may be appropriate to the circumstances. Where the service is to include Holy Communion, a reading from the Gospels is included.

## F6.8 Other readings

Those arranging a funeral may desire to include readings from places other than the Christian scriptures. This can be a pastorally sensitive matter, especially in situations where the reading is the particular request of the deceased or of a close family member, or intended to be read by one of the mourners as a tribute in place of a eulogy.

Many non-biblical readings will not be objectionable or problematic, and some are entirely consistent with Christian truth (such as a passage from the writings of a saint). Others may be less so, and some may be considered inconsistent with, or contrary to, the Christian tradition. The pastoral needs of the mourners and of those planning and participating in the service will need to be held in balance with the integrity of the funeral service as a Christian rite.

The minister will have discretion in determining what can, and cannot be read. In all cases, there will be at least one reading from the Christian scriptures, which should take prominence and form the basis of the sermon.

### F6.9   The sermon

The sermon, or homily, will normally follow the reading or readings as indicated by APBA. The length, style and content is determined by the minister, however APBA (p. 771, Note 5) stipulates that the sermon should contain at least some of the following:

   a) Proclamation of the Christian hope—Christ crucified and risen;
   b) Acknowledgement of the reality of suffering, and that God in Christ has embraced it;
   c) Sensitive concern for the bereaved;
   d) Thanksgiving to God for the life of the deceased;
   e) Some reminder of our own coming death and judgment.

The words used in a funeral need to be direct and accessible to those present, both in the sermon, and throughout. 'Religious' words and technical theological language, even words that carry great meaning to long-term Christians, may not only fail to connect with others, but put people off. Falling back on words with which the minister is comfortable can also be a sign that he or she has not sufficiently come to terms with the pastoral situation of the funeral. It is usually better to say less well, than to use many words that may convey merely a religious veneer. This is especially true when speaking of the deceased person—anything said that is false or inauthentic, however well meant, will rankle with the congregation long after the funeral and is likely to alienate them during it.

The 'hard' situations will call for particular care and preparation, for instance, where the tragedy of the death is especially evident. Here it is important to acknowledge our agony and puzzlement, yet in the context of trust in the God who took on death in Jesus, and stands alongside us in our struggles. 'Quick fix' solutions, or an overly confident resurrection sermon, are not only unhelpful, but dangerous, encouraging avoidance of reality.

Those who have come to a funeral do not want to be harangued, but do, normally (or perhaps should, given their presence in a Christian church), expect to hear God's perspective on death and dying, and be helped to work through grief with dignity. The most effective form of evangelistic witness in this context is pastoral care, liturgical leadership, and well-prepared preaching, which proclaims God's life-giving love in Christ. One element in this ministry is helping all present (including the minister) to acknowledge our accountability to God for the way we live, but it is as unhelpful to focus exclusively on this truth as it is to ignore it.

### F6.10 The prayers

The shape of the prayers is set out in APBA (pp. 719–721) and some additional prayers for a variety of situations are also provided (pp. 765–770). Whilst the minister who is the officiant will normally lead and offer the prayers, it may be appropriate for a family member or friend, or an assistant cleric or another minister (whether Anglican or from another Christian tradition) who may be known to the family or the deceased, to be involved at this point.

APBA (p. 772, Note 11) provides for the possibility that the form of the Lord's Prayer printed on p. xi (the 'traditional version') may be used instead of the contemporary language translation provided for in the text of the service. This can sometimes be a pastorally important matter, and is at the discretion of the minister.

See further at section F.14—Liturgical resources for funeral ministry.

### F6.11 Music and hymns

The emotive qualities of music mean that the selection of music, hymns and any items or solos will assume considerable importance for those arranging the service. Some form of music will normally be a part of the funeral service, although as APBA (p. 771, Note 7d) advises, especially in the context of a funeral chapel or crematorium, 'inappropriate background music should be avoided'. Music may be desired at certain points of the service including, but not limited to:

a) As the congregation gathers prior to the service;
b) In accompaniment of any hymns, songs and choruses;
c) In accompaniment of any sung psalms, anthems, choral pieces or items and solos;
d) As a 'reflection', whereby a selected piece of music or song follows the eulogy or eulogies;
e) As part of any audio-visual display included in the service;
f) During the administration of Holy Communion (if included);
g) At the conclusion of the service—it can be important to explain to those arranging the funeral that the selection of the music or song at this point will often be very significant, as it will accompany the procession of the coffin out of the church and be the last thing heard in the context of the final 'journey' of the deceased.

In some contexts, the Director of Music, a music minister, or organist will be involved, often to a great extent, in the preparation of the service and with the selection of the music and hymns. In other places the minister will perform these tasks alone.

Some practical considerations that commonly arise, many of which will need to be determined on a case-by-case basis, include, but are not limited to:

a) The policy concerning the use of recorded worship and, if allowed, the process for assessing suitability of the requested piece, who will

operate the sound system at the service, and in what format the recording should be supplied (see F7.12);
b) The policy concerning visiting musicians and/or singers and what facilities, if any, are provided, together with the arrangements for access and a rehearsal (if desired);
c) The process around, and fees associated with, arranging for a choir and/or vocalist/s.

APBA provides for hymns at various points in the funeral service. The key consideration will be the extent to which the congregation will sing any hymns selected, or otherwise. Well-known hymns sung to familiar tunes are usually best, but in today's post-Christian world even these may be unfamiliar to many present. The Christian church is one of the few contexts for communal singing remaining in Australian social life. The decision to include one or more hymns will be influenced by these factors and may also be influenced by the ability of the minister, or another person (a soloist or choir member) to lead the singing, or by the presence of a choir.

See further at section F.14—Liturgical resources for funeral ministry.

### F7.12 'Secular' music

A request may be made for a song or piece of music that has some special meaning or importance to the deceased, or to those arranging the service. Sometimes the request may be that a soloist, duet, choir, or a musician or group of musicians, perform this 'live' during the service. Commonly, however, the song or music in question will be a recording, which is to be played at a certain point in the service.

The minister will have discretion in this, and should pay careful attention to the song or music requested, taking note of any lyrics, to determine whether the request is to be agreed to and, if so, where it should occur in the course of the service. In some situations, it may be most appropriate that the requested song or music be played later, at the wake or post-service gathering.

This will often be an emotive area. In the context of grief, especially new and raw grief, what might seem a small matter to one party, can assume a significance and importance to another party, well beyond that anticipated. It is usually best to err on the side of grace and pastoral accommodation, unless the integrity of the service, or Christian truth, is being called into question.

Recorded music presents a number of practical issues in a place of worship depending on the facilities present. The format will need to be checked (CD, digital device?) and tested on the sound system or other equipment, in the first instance to ensure it will play (not all equipment will play all possible formats), but also for quality and for sound, especially if the recording has been downloaded. Someone will need to be arranged to play it at the appropriate time during the service. The minister should clearly delegate these tasks, possibly to a funeral director, or a verger if there is one, or another person, well before the service commences.

### F6.13 Holy Communion on the day of a funeral

It can be appropriate, and of great spiritual benefit and significance, to include the sacrament of Holy Communion in the funeral service, especially, for instance, if the deceased person was an active member of a Christian community. APBA (pp. 725–729) provides for this. Where Holy Communion is to be part of the service, the minister will need to ensure clear instructions are provided to the congregation (either verbally or through a printed order of service, or both) about who present is able to receive the sacrament (with an emphasis on ecumenical hospitality).

### F6.14 The Farewell and Committal

The Farewell begins the concluding act of the service and should be undertaken carefully and deliberately, observing silence, where appropriate, to enable the mourners to gather their thoughts and focus their remembrance. The Committal immediately follows unless it is to take place in another location.

Wherever the Committal is to be said, the congregation should be asked to stand. As the rubric in APBA (p. 723, # 21) requires, the minister says the committal 'facing the coffin'. Depending on the type of service —see F5.1—this may occur in the church, at a chapel or crematorium, or at the graveside. It may be appropriate, at the discretion of the minister, to use one of the commendations provided for ministry with the dying (APBA p. 703).

In all situations, the committal should be audibly clear to the congregation, and may be accompanied by symbolic acts or gestures (such as the sprinkling of dust onto the coffin at the graveside). The versicle printed in bold for congregational use at the end of the prayer (APBA p. 723) may be said on behalf of all by the minister where it is not practical for the congregation to join in saying these words.

### F6.15 Masonic and RSL rites

The inclusion of Masonic and/or RSL rites may be requested where the deceased was a Freemason or returned serviceman or servicewoman. This will be a matter of local custom and at the discretion of the minister. Such rites should be clearly distinguished from the Christian service. This is best achieved when they occur in a place other than the church, typically in the crematorium or at the graveside. The circumstances of the service, and the pastoral imperatives present, will sometimes require a different approach, but, whatever is done and where, the integrity of the Christian rites should not be distorted in any way, and the Christian funeral service should not be seen to include and embrace other rites and ceremonies.

## F7   Special circumstances

Particular pastoral needs and careful preparation will arise in circumstances where the deceased was a child or infant. Pastoral care after the service will also assume special importance. As APBA (p. 753) notes, 'every death involves loss, shock and grief, but especially that of a child'. For this reason APBA provides a separate liturgy for the funeral of a child, and a further liturgy for the funeral of an infant.

### F7.1  The funeral of a child

APBA (pp. 739–751) provides a liturgy intended for use where the service is for a child, modelled on the principal funeral service but utilising different readings and prayers. As the notes to the service advise, if the child concerned was a baby under one year of age the funeral service for an infant may be more appropriate, and if the child concerned was in or near the teenage years the principal funeral service 'suitably adapted' may be more fitting.

The structure of this service is based on the funeral service, but takes into account the reality that many children may be present. The main differences are the 'warmer' theological statements about the standing of the deceased child with God, the choice of scripture sentences and passages, and more direct language.

It is assumed that the Committal is included in the service, rather than taken separately, so that children present are not left in a state of suspension about the final farewell of their friend. However, a second stage rite, 'At the Graveside or Crematorium' is provided where this is needed.

### F7.2 The funeral of an infant who has died near the time of birth

APBA (pp. 753–764) provides a liturgy for use at the funeral of an infant who has died near the time of birth. As indicated in the notes to the service (p. 753), 'the theological emphasis which underlies the service has as a major component the conviction that God is ultimately involved in and through the pain of grief. The words and actions of Jesus in receiving young infants as members of the kingdom of God are highly significant in this context.' Symbol and action also take on heightened importance.

The service as a whole is intended to be flexible and to be supplemented with appropriate periods of silence, actions, symbols and gestures.

It is the experience of those who have been involved in this ministry that preparation, immediate pastoral care, and follow-up can take considerable time and spiritual energy. Where the infant has died in hospital, parish clergy and hospital chaplains will normally work together as colleagues in pastoral ministry.

The structure of the service is similar to the funeral service, but there is no provision for a eulogy, and a wider range of prayers is provided. The theological tone is wholly positive about the infant's standing with God, and the language is quite intimate in parts.

**F7.3 Stillborn infants**

A stillborn infant may be considered theologically as one who has never left God's care, but pastorally as the death of a child or infant.

When an infant is stillborn, parents' reactions can vary considerably: in particular, the mother has lived with the growing child in her body, while others (including the father) have had a real, but less intimate relationship with the infant. Some parents may want to put the death behind them, perhaps not even wanting to know the child's gender, though this is generally seen as highly undesirable for the long-term welfare of the parents. Others will be overwhelmed with grief at the loss of a longed-for child.

Whatever the situation, 'did we cause the death?' is a question raised in many parents' minds. Reactions may change as time goes on, and an initial 'putting behind' attitude turns to a desire to remember the child. And the complex situations that can arise from in-vitro fertilisation blur the picture even further.

Hospitals take considerable care with the welfare of the grieving parents. Current practice is for them to arrange for the burial or cremation of stillborn infants, including (at least once each month) a service for these children with families and friends. Hospitals usually ask to see the mother for a physical check-up six weeks after the birth, and offer counselling as well.

Whilst theologically, a stillborn infant may be considered as one who has never left God's care, pastorally it is not inappropriate to consider the still-born infant as a child who has died—from the mother's point of view this is very much the case. Ministry to the families of stillborn infants needs to be sensitive to the particular situation concerned.

The following suggestions are therefore quite tentative.

a) Where a minister is contacted following a stillbirth, it is expected that an immediate response will be made, preferably by personal visit, or by contacting another minister where this is not possible.

b) The first contact with the parents is likely to be in hospital. Appropriate prayers can be offered, including those that may assist in extreme grief. Often such ministry will be undertaken by a hospital chaplain: this is an area in which close co-operation between those ministering to a family is essential, including any Pastoral Care department in the hospital. Parish clergy who have a pastoral relationship with the family should be contacted by the chaplain as soon as possible; conversely, parish clergy should look to hospital chaplains for specialist counsel.

c) It is important that, wherever possible, a distinct liturgical act takes place in which the parents can remember the child, grieve at their loss, and begin the process of resuming life once more. It has been found helpful to hold such services at the site of burial or interment: some cemeteries give fee reductions for stillborn infants' burial.

d) The naming of the stillborn infant calls for special attention. Pastoral workers in the field recommend that this be done, to assist parents in ongoing family relationships. They recommend strongly against using the name planned for the stillborn infant for a child born later, since this may lead to the living child having unhelpful expectations placed upon him or her.

e) Particular difficulties exist where family members ask for baptism where a child has already died. All Christian traditions affirm that baptism concerns the exercise of faith by living persons. Where such a request is made, it should be carefully and sensitively explained that baptism is unnecessary, since, as Jesus taught, 'to such as these (young children) belongs the kingdom of heaven'. When an infant has died, it remains only to commend her or him into God's loving care. A naming and blessing (possibly with the sprinkling of water on the parents and child, or anointing with oil) may be used for this, and often can be incorporated into the funeral.

f) The longer term care of the bereaved is vital. As a person or family picks up the threads of life again they need genuine Christian care. The processes of grief can take some time. Practical and pastoral follow-up ministry should be shared where possible amongst suitable members of the congregation.

## F7.4 Suicide

The Anglican funeral rite in APBA is silent about the condition of the deceased person or the circumstances of their death. Optional prayers are provided for instances where the death has been by suicide (APBA p. 769, # 15–16). The role of the minister in these circumstances is to provide pastoral care and support for the family and friends who gather. It is not the role of the minister to be judgemental in any way about the decision made by the deceased, nor to consider the standing of the deceased to be any different to any other deceased person. The focus should clearly be on the living, and support and care for them.

## F8 The interment of ashes

Where a body has been cremated, the funeral necessarily involves two (or three) stages: the funeral with the committal of the body at the end of this service—or in a separate brief rite at the crematorium—and the final disposal of the mortal remains, through interment of the ashes. This last stage is not uncommonly overlooked, but from a Christian perspective it is the essential conclusion of the funeral. For these reasons, where the body has been cremated the funeral service will usually be completed by the interment of the ashes of the deceased. APBA (pp. 735–737) provides a brief liturgy for this, which may be used as a stand-alone service or immediately following an earlier service such as a regular Sunday service.

There is no difference in principle between the interment of a body or of its ashes: both are to be treated with equal regard. Where a body is buried, however, the only possibility is its lowering into the grave. In the case of a cremation, the ashes can be disposed of in a variety of ways, not all of which commend themselves to Christians: this matter calls for some theological and pastoral sensitivity. The general principle to be observed in the interment of ashes is that cremation is an acceleration of the natural process of decomposition—'earth to earth, ashes to ashes, dust to dust'.

Many parish churches have established memorial gardens for this purpose, however there are other possibilities such as interment in an established cemetery, or the sprinkling of the ashes at sea. The ashes of the deceased are normally available for collection shortly after the cremation, and may be provided to the safekeeping of the church in which the interment is to take place. Unless prevented by some circumstance, the minister who officiated at the funeral service should also officiate at the interment of ashes.

Where the ashes are interred in a memorial garden or other similar place:
a) A necessary practical task prior to the interment is to open the lid to the plastic container in which the ashes are normally supplied.

This requires a tool such as a chisel or other instrument, and should be done out of sight of the family;

b) The ashes are transferred from the plastic container in which they are supplied to an urn or similar vessel (owned by, and kept in, the church) from which they can be readily poured out (burial of the ashes in the container does not return the deceased to 'the earth');

c) The place of interment will need to be prepared in the garden. A hole in the soil dug to a depth and width slightly larger than that of the container will normally suffice;

d) The minister should take care when pouring the ashes into the soil that they are not dispersed by wind. This can be achieved by pouring directly into the prepared hole from near ground level, especially on windy days.

Where ashes are scattered at sea or in another place, careful consideration should be given to the wind speed and direction.

## F9  Memorial gardens

Many parish churches have Memorial Gardens, or Gardens of Remembrance, in which cremated remains are interred. These gardens are a witness to the Christian belief in the resurrection of our Lord Jesus Christ, and to our assurance that we will share in his resurrection to eternal life. A memorial garden located in the grounds of a parish is manifestly different to a cemetery or memorial park, or other such facility for the interment of ashes, wherein the ashes of a deceased person are normally interred in a container or other receptacle and marked by a plaque, for a set period of time. At the end of that period of time, the ashes so interred may remain upon payment of a further lease, or in the absence of any further payment, and if the descendants cannot be contacted, they are buried permanently.

Ashes interred in a church memorial garden are interred directly into the soil. The interment is permanent and the actual place of interment is not to be marked or identified in any way. The principle is that the whole garden is the place of remembrance.

Niches, 'columbarian' walls, or arrangements that preclude the return of the mortal remains to the earth, are not authorised under Anglican auspices in this diocese. Existing facilities having a faculty may continue to be used until full, by special permission, but no additional niches are to be constructed. Where the use of an existing niche is allowed, and the amount of ashes exceeds the available space, surplus ashes are to be interred, preferably in a nearby Memorial Garden.

A memorial garden involves the church concerned in significant long-term responsibilities. A memorial garden may only be established by faculty, after application by the vicar and churchwardens, following consultation with the Archdeacon. The garden should normally be adjacent to, and abut, a permanent wall of the church building; will need to be free of underground piping; and in a place where it is unlikely to be disturbed for maintenance or other reasons. The site should be of modest proportions, clearly designated, and expected to be free from other use for the foreseeable future. Memorial gardens are to be maintained in good condition out of respect for those whose remains are interred there, and provision made for family members and friends to freely have unhindered access.

A separate memorial book containing the names of those whose ashes are interred, and when, is to be kept in the church building in an accessible place. The churchwardens will normally bear responsibility for the tending and safeguarding of a memorial garden, however these tasks can be delegated to one or more parishioners, as a significant expression of their own ministry.

A memorial garden will normally only be moved when a church building is closed and/or ceases to be a place of worship. In such a case, all earth to a depth of about half a metre is to be removed to another memorial garden, and a written indication of where the ashes are now interred is to be made in the appropriate Registers.

## F10  Fees and charges

Ministry to the bereaved and the provision of Christian rites of passage marking the death of a person should be considered within the context of the overall pastoral ministry of the church, and as an historic and ongoing aspect of Anglican ministry. At the same time, the parish, or other entity providing funeral ministry, will incur costs, and those involved deserve fair payment. It is important each parish, or other ministry context, develop a policy for fees associated with funeral ministry that is endorsed by the parish council or equivalent body, and that this policy be readily available to both funeral directors and to those arranging a funeral. In many places it is common for the funeral of a parishioner or a close family member to be 'by donation' rather than have the usual fees applied. Many also give the minister who has pastoral charge of the community discretion to reduce or waive fees.

The schedule of fees will normally cover:

a) The officiant's fee, whether paid to the minister who conducts the service directly or to the parish or other entity;
b) Any fee or donation for the use of the church and the maintenance and upkeep of the building;
c) The fees paid to any musicians such as an organist or pianist, and any vocalists, choir members, or worship leaders engaged on a by fee basis;
d) The fee paid to the verger, if applicable;
e) Any fee applied for the production of a printed order of service or other stationary;
f) The cost of the flowers if applicable;
g) A fee for the use of a hall or other space afterwards, together with any catering arranged by the church or one of its groups or entities, if applicable.

In some situations, in particular where the service takes place entirely at a funeral chapel or crematorium, the officiant's fee may be paid directly to the minister, unless the minister otherwise directs. If receiving fees directly, the minister must declare this as taxable income on their annual tax return.

See Appendix One and Appendix Two for a sample parish policy for pastoral service and the diocesan policy regarding surplice fees.

A minister may occasionally be asked to conduct a funeral service for a person who has no known family or resources (pauper's funeral). In such instances, the minister should be willing to conduct the service without expecting any fee or payment.

## F11  Registers

In each parish, school chapel or worship community there should be:
a) A Register of funerals or burials in which the details of each funeral service are recorded, whether the service took place in the church or other place of worship, or in another place (normally memorial services are also included in this Register);
b) A separate Register for the interment of ashes, giving the details of the names of all those whose ashes are interred in the memorial garden, together with the date of the interment.

Where the funeral or memorial service takes place in the church, the details should also be recorded in the service Register.

## F12  After the funeral

The provision of Christian ministry to the bereaved is an expression of the love and care of God and a theological statement about the victory of Christ over death and dying. The death of a loved one is often the catalyst for a person discovering or rediscovering faith, and reconnecting with a Christian community. Continued ministry to the bereaved after the funeral service can have both pastoral and evangelistic effects, although it should never be the case that funerals are used opportunistically or in a way that might give the perception that the circumstances of the bereaved are being exploited.

In most instances, some form of contact should be made with the principal mourner/s in the weeks after the funeral service by the minister who officiated, or by another representative of the parish or congregation concerned as may be appropriate. Continued contact, as appropriate and often by card or other printed communication on the anniversary of death, for instance, can also be a greatly appreciated ministry, assuring the family and friends that their loved one continues to be remembered, and that those who mourn continue to be held in prayer by the Christian community concerned.

Some particular times of year lend themselves to remembrance of those who have died and to which the families of those whose funerals the parish has hosted, together with any members of the community who might find the service helpful, may be invited to attend.

a) All Souls' Day, on 2 November, is an occasion on which all those whose funerals have taken place under the auspices of the parish or other community concerned may be remembered, often in the context of the Holy Communion using the Thanksgiving Prayer from the funeral service.

b) Services of remembrance in the lead up to Christmas may also be offered—as they are by some funeral directors, aged care facilities and hospitals—as a way of providing a time and place for those who continue to mourn the loss of a loved one, providing an opportunity for remembrance as the Christmas season approaches.

At such services the names of those remembered will normally be read out at some point, and there will often be an opportunity for an act of remembrance such as lighting a candle or placing flowers. The particular focus of services of this nature means that they are often best observed outside the usual pattern of Sunday worship.

## F13 Times of tragedy and crisis

Places of worship may often become a focal point in their communities, for both individual prayer and corporate services, following a tragedy or crisis affecting large numbers of people such as those services held in the wake of the September 11 attacks on the United States of America, the Bali bombing, and Black Saturday bushfires. Such services may often be ecumenical and take place in large community facilities.

In many circumstances, where a tragedy may affect a distinct community such as multiple deaths in an accident, another localised catastrophic event, or in some cases the death of a single person, the parish church or school chapel and its clergy may become the focal point for communal grief, and a service organised under its auspices pastorally desired.

In many cases, the appropriate response will be a service offered to the entire community affected, which may be ecumenical and/or interfaith in nature. In other situations, the tragedy or crisis may call for a liturgical response the following Sunday in the context of the usual regime of the community's worship. Often there will be a subsequent service, especially on significant anniversaries such as the first year and the tenth year following the event.

Services conducted in such circumstances will often take on the form of a funeral or memorial service, and some of the same liturgical resources and traditions will be useful and applicable. The nature of the ministry offered to those who attend will often be closely akin to that offered to the family and friends in the context of a funeral, only amplified by the common grief of whole communities in many cases.

## F14 Liturgical resources for funeral ministry

### Readings from the Old Testament (and apocrypha)

Ruth 1.1–18 (or selected verses), I will go where you go

2 Samuel 1.1, 17 & 23–27, David's lament for Jonathan

2 Samuel 12.16–23, The death of David's son

Ecclesiastes 3.1–8, A time for everything

Isaiah 11.6–9, The wolf shall live with the lamb (APBA p. 742)

Lamentations 3.17–26, The steadfast love of the Lord never ceases (APBA p. 742)

Sirach 2.1–9, Trust in the Lord

Wisdom of Solomon 3.1–9, The destiny of the righteous

### Psalms

23, The Lord's my shepherd (APBA p. 714)

42, As a deer longs for water (APBA p. 755)

46, God is our refuge and strength

71, To you Lord have I come for shelter

90, Teach us to rightly number our days (APBA p. 714)

103, God's mercy endures for ever (APBA p. 741)

121, My help comes from the Lord (APBA p. 715)

130, Out of the depths (APBA p. 741)

139: 12–14 &16, Before I was born you knew me (APBA p. 755)

### Readings from the New Testament

Romans 6.3–9, Baptism is into the death of Christ (APBA p. 716)

Romans 8.31–38, Nothing can separate us from the love of God (APBA p. 756)

Romans 14.7–12, Christ is the Lord of the living and the dead

1 Corinthians 12.31–13.13, The Greatest is love

1 Corinthians 15.50b–58, We will all be changed (APBA p. 716)

2 Corinthians 4.16–5.10, Living by faith

Ephesians 3.14–19, That you may know the love of Christ (APBA p. 756)

Philippians 3.10–16 & 20–21, Our citizenship is in heaven

1 Thessalonians 4.13–18, The dead in Christ will rise first

2 Timothy 4.6–8, I have fought the good fight

1 Peter 1.3–9, A Living hope

1 John 3.1–3, We are children of God

Revelation 7.9–17, The great multitude in

Revelation 21: 1–7, The new heaven and the new earth (APBA p. 743)

### Readings from the Gospels

Matthew 5.1–12, The Beatitudes

Matthew 18.1–5 & Mark 10.13–16, Let the little children come to me (APBA pp. 744, 757)

Luke 12.22–31, Do not worry

John 6.35–40, I am the bread of life

John 11.17–27, The raising of Lazarus

John 12.23–27, The seed must die in order to bear fruit

John 14.1–6, In my father's house (APBA p. 717)

John 20.11–18, Mary encounters the risen Jesus

### Hymns from 'Together in Song'

10. The Lord's my Shepherd

47. Our God our help in ages past

59. All People that on Earth do Dwell

93. Praise the Lord, you Heavens Adore Him

100. All Creatures of our God and King

106. Now Thank we all our God

111. Praise to the Lord, the Almighty
112. Through all the Changing Scenes of Life
123. Be Still my Soul
129. Amazing Grace
134. Praise my soul, the King of Heaven
137. For the Beauty of the Earth
143. Immortal, Invisible, God only Wise
145. The King of love my Shepherd is
153. God is Love
154. Great is your Faithfulness
155. How Great Thou Art
202. I know that my Redeemer Lives
222. Rock of Ages
315. Mine eyes have seen the glory of the coming of the Lord
367. The Strife is Past, the Battle Done
380. Yours be the Glory
458. The Day you gave us
561. Who would true valour see
569. Guide me, O Thou Great Redeemer
580. Lead us, Heavenly Father, Lead us
585. I Heard the voice of Jesus say
586. Abide with me
590. What a Friend we have in Jesus
595. O Jesus, I have promised
602. O love that wilt not let me go
607. Make me a Channel of your Peace

### Additional prayers

APBA p. 703, Commendations

APBA pp. 745–746, At the funeral of a child

APBA pp. 758–762, At the funeral of an infant

APBA p. 765, Thanksgiving for the victory of Christ

APBA p. 766, Thanksgiving and commemoration

APBA p. 767, For those who mourn

APBA p. 768, For a married person

APBA p. 768, After release from suffering

APBA p. 768, For a child who dies before being baptised

APBA p. 768, After a sudden death

APBA p. 769, After a suicide

APBA p. 769, Prayers of struggle

APBA p. 691, j – A prayer in doubt and tested faith

APBA p. 692, k – Prayer for those suffering severe illness

APBA p. 481, Collects for Ash Wednesday

APBA p. 519, Prayer of the Week for Easter 7

APBA pp. 621–622, Collects for All Saints

APBA p. 633, Collect for All Souls

APBA p. 642, Collects for a Saint

## Resources for funeral ministry

### In print

Lewis, C.S. *A Grief Observed*. London: Faber & Faber, 1961.

Lloyd, Trevor. *Dying and death step by step: A funerals flowchart*. Grove worship series 160. Cambridge: Grove books, 2000.

McCarthy, Flor. *Funeral liturgies*. Dublin: Dominican publications, 1994.

Norén, Carol M. *In times of crisis and sorrow: a minister's resource manual*. San Francisco: Jossey-Bass, 2001.

Smith, Margaret. *Facing death together: parish funerals*. Chicago: Liturgy training publications, 1998.

Thorp, Helen. *Establishing a Bereavement Ministry Team*. Grove pastoral series 113. Cambridge: Grove books, 2008.

Watson, Nick. *Sorrow and hope: preaching at funerals*. Grove pastoral series 86. Cambridge: Grove books, 2001.

Links

Victorian Council of Churches, guidelines for ecumenical worship services
http://www.vcc.org.au/images/Worshipping_Ecumenically.pdf

The Church of England, life events - funerals
http://www.cofe.anglican.org/lifeevents/funerals

## A sample funeral ministry checklist

| THE DECEASED | | |
|---|---|---|
| Surname: | Christian Names: | |
| Name to be used during the service: | | |
| Date of Birth: | Date of Death & Age: | |
| Home address : | | |
| Place of Death (if different) | | |
| Any involvement in the parish? | | |
| **NEXT OF KIN (OR PERSON RESPONSIBLE FOR THE ARRANGEMENTS)** | | |
| Name: | | |

| | |
|---|---|
| Address: | |
| Phone No: | |
| Email: | |
| Relationship to the deceased: | |
| **FUNERAL DIRECTOR** | |
| Company: | |
| Arranger: | |
| Phone No: | |
| E Mail: | |

| **SERVICE/S DETAILS** | | |
|---|---|---|
| Type: (please indicate which) | Funeral | Memorial Service |
| Time and Date: | | |
| Location: | | |
| Officiant/s: | | |
| Subsequent or Prior Service? | None | |
| | Burial | Cremation |
| Time and Date: | | |
| Location: | | |
| Officiant/s: | | |
| Organist required? | YES / NO | |
| Verger required? | YES / NO | |
| Any instructions about Flowers? | | |
| Parish to print the service booklets? | YES / NO | |
| If Yes, number required: | | |
| Service to be recorded? | YES / NO | |
| Service to be streamed online? | YES / NO | |
| **MEMORIAL GARDEN** | | |
| Are the ashes to be interred in our Memorial Garden? | YES / NO / UNDECIDED | |

| LITURGICAL DETAILS | | |
|---|---|---|
| Eulogies | | |
| Reading 1. | | |
| Read by | | |
| Reading 2. | | |
| Read by | | |
| Psalm | | |
| Music | | |
| Hymn 1. | | |
| Hymn 2. | | |
| Hymn 3. | | |
| **NOTES** | | |
| | | |
| | | |
| | | |
| | | |

# Chapter Five

## Other pastoral services and occasions (O)

Whilst the provision of services of Christian initiation, marriage, and funerals will normally comprise the vast majority of the pastoral services in most settings, these do not exhaust the pastoral ministries of the Christian Church, nor the liturgical expressions thereof. The reach and embrace of pastoral ministry is vast.

Included in this section are, firstly, the services in APBA that are pastoral in nature, but which are not generally included in the category of 'pastoral services' alongside Christian initiation, weddings and funerals. This is followed by the General Synod Liturgy Commission resources that relate to the pastorally sensitive matter of sexual misconduct and abuse by clergy and church workers, and then by further resources addressing some 'occasional' requests that are again pastoral in nature.

### O1  Ministry with the Sick

As APBA (p. 678) notes, 'Sickness is a reality of human life.' Any illness, but in particular life changing and life threatening illnesses, may be an occasion for the one afflicted to turn to the Christian faith and its ministers for comfort, support and hope. The minister bears, in such situations, a 'particular responsibility' to be sensitive to each situation and to 'accept the responsibilities placed on them as ambassadors of Christ to those in need' (APBA p. 678). The title of the service is carefully chosen—it is not ministry to the sick, but ministry with the sick. As APBA (p. 678) explains, 'of first importance in this ministry is the relationship between those in need and those who care for them. It is a mutual relationship, in which vulnerable people minister to one another in and through the grace of Christ.'

### O1.1   The visitation of the sick

The liturgy provided includes preparation and prayers, options for the anointing and laying on of hands, and the administration of Holy Communion, together with a treasury of further prayers for a variety of situations (APBA pp. 678–693). In addition to the readings provided in the order of service itself, which are taken from Isaiah 40.28–31 ('those who wait for the Lord will renew their strength'), Hebrews 4.14–16 ('we have a great high priest, able to sympathise with us in our weaknesses'), and John 15.7–11 ('abide in me'), a number of other suitable readings are suggested (APBA p. 693, Note 1). It is anticipated that the minister may select other passages at his or her discretion, and might also offer ex tempore prayer at one or more points.

The service in APBA is a direct descendent of the BCP rite for 'the Visitation of the Sick', reflecting the fact that ministry to those suffering illness and infirmity has always been a part of Anglican pastoral ministry. Whilst Cramer's first Book of Common Prayer (1549) did include anointing in the context of the 'Visitation of the Sick,' the custom was not preserved in subsequent Prayer Books and only revived in Anglicanism during the course of the nineteenth and twentieth centuries. This was, no doubt, at least partially due to the association of the practice with the Roman Catholic sacrament of extreme unction. Whilst the 'anointing' of the sick person is now included with associated prayer and the laying on of hands if desired (APBA p. 683), it is important to note that the warrant for this is not traditional, but biblical—James 5.14–16 ('Are any among you sick? They should call for the elders of the church and have them pray over them, anointing them with oil in the name of the Lord'). The anointing, and associated prayer in 'Ministry with the Sick' (APBA p. 683, # 9) is for healing and a restoration to wholeness. This is to be distinguished from the anointing provided for in 'Ministry with the Dying' (APBA p. 700, # 8)—see further at O2.1.

As the late Owen Dowling noted in his commentary on the APBA liturgy for 'Ministry with the Sick', the material provided is intended 'to be a resource to be drawn upon, rather than an order to be followed strictly or sequentially.'[51] The key question pastorally will be how to respond to this person, at this moment, in this time of infirmity? Selected use of the liturgical resources provided for in APBA will form part of the response, as may readings from the bible, whether those suggested in APBA or others, together with ex tempore prayer appropriate to the sick person's circumstances. In some circumstances it may be appropriate that 'Reconciliation of a Penitent' (APBA p. 774) be used in whole or part with the sick person—see further at O3. In circumstances where the sick person is nearing the end of life, the liturgy for 'Ministry with the Dying' (APBA p. 696) should be used instead—see further at O2.

### O1.2 Holy Communion with the sick

A form for 'Communion with the Sick' was included in BCP (1662) and is incorporated in APBA into 'Ministry with the Sick' (APBA pp. 685–688). It is anticipated that others such as family and friends, will be present on such occasions, however the possibility that the minister and the sick person may be the only communicants is also recognised (APBA p. 693, Note 2). A beautifully worded preface, specific to the occasion ('He took upon himself our human nature, shared our joy and our tears, bore all our sickness, and carried all our sorrows') is provided in the Thanksgiving Prayer, however any authorised form may be used (APBA p. 693, Note 3). It should be noted that it is assumed the communicant will be suffering illness or infirmity, not an inability for some other reason to attend church, and the prayers and other resources reflect this.

---

51 'Ministry with the Sick,' in *A Prayer Book for Australia: A practical commentary* (ed. Gillian Varcoe; Alexandria, NSW: E J Dwyer, 1997), p. 117.

It will usually be necessary to have an excerpt of the service prepared for use by the minister, the sick person, and any others present, setting out the structure of the liturgy and including the prayers said together. It is good pastoral practice to have pre-prepared orders of service, together with a home communion set, bible, candles, and the oil of healing (if desired) in a convenient place ready for use.

Particular issues arise concerning the administration of Holy Communion to a sick person. The Thanksgiving Prayer may need to be truncated in situations where the nature of the illness requires it. APBA (p. 693, Note 3) gives instructions as to what can and cannot be omitted in such situations. In some circumstances, for instance, where the sick person is physically unable to take a cup or when their posture may prevent it, the minister may consider it necessary or best that communion be given by intinction (the bread is dipped into wine and administered in both kinds together). In some situations, the sick person may be unable to receive the bread and wine but instead engage in spiritual communion. APBA (p. 693, Note 4) provides helpful advice for this situation.

The service provided for in APBA does not include communion from the reserved sacrament (whereby bread and wine already consecrated, usually during the course of a Sunday or other service, are administered to the sick person). By its nature, such ministry does not require the presence of a priest and might be administered by a deacon or authorised layperson, in accordance with local custom and practise.

## 02   Ministry with the Dying

The rite for the 'Visitation of the Sick' in BCP included prayers for the dying. APBA departs from this by providing for two separate services, one for 'Ministry with the Sick' and a distinct liturgy for 'Ministry with the Dying'. The liturgical material provided for in APBA (pp. 696–705) is, like that of 'Ministry with the Sick', intended as a resource for selection and adaptation as appropriate to the circumstances.

A number of pastoral issues will arise in the course of ministry with a dying person, which may include and embrace not just the dying person, but also, potentially, their spouse and immediate family, close friends and, in some situations, medical or clinical staff who have been caring for them. There will be a sense of grief and sadness, and displays of emotion can usually be expected. It is important the minister is able to remain in control and to take appropriate charge of the situation whilst others present may be 'falling apart'.

Particular sensitivities will arise where the person concerned is not known to the minister and when the person's commitment to Christian faith and the church is not known or appears slight. A range of possibilities, including an 'act of faith' (APBA p. 697) and confession and absolution (APBA p 699) are provided for. In some circumstances it may be appropriate that 'Reconciliation of a Penitent' (APBA p. 774) be used, in whole or in part, prior to the material in 'Ministry with the Dying'. Often time will be short, sometimes critically so, and the minister will need to make quick decisions about what to use and not use as confronted with the circumstances. A pause for prayer, however brief, seeking the guidance of the Holy Spirit and asking for wisdom to speak the 'right words' as an act of preparation, will usually be an important part of the whole of the ministry offered.

It may appear that the dying person is not conscious, or is drifting in and out of consciousness. The ability to speak or communicate in other ways may have been lost. Sometimes the attending medical staff may provide advice about these matters. It is always advisable to speak audibly and directly to the dying person by name, and for the minister to identify him or her self. Even if only the minister and the dying person are present, prayers should be said aloud. Where family and friends are present, there will be a concurrent ministry to them also. Familiar words such as the Lord's Prayer and the 23rd psalm, can be especially important.

In addition to readings from the bible and prayers, the liturgical resources in APBA offer a number of other possibilities that may be used as appropriate. The 'act of faith' (APBA p. 697) invites the dying person to express their trust in God and provides a number of options as to the form of the words used, leaving open also the possibility that other 'similar words' might be preferred. Confession and absolution (APBA p. 699) is included with the conditional note in the rubrics, 'If the dying person is moved to make a special confession of sins'. It would not be appropriate for the minister to assume that such a confession must be made—indeed, in some cases the dying person will not be capable of making a confession. On the other hand, as the note in APBA (p. 706, Note 1) advises, 'the dying person should be encouraged to set their earthly affairs in order with generosity, to forgive any whom they have offended, to confess their sins, and so receive assurance of God's forgiveness, love and care'. Finally, a number of beautifully worded prayers of commendation may be said (APBA p. 703), again at the discretion of the minister. These are also sometimes suitable to include in a funeral service at the point of the Farewell.

### O2.1 The anointing

The form of the anointing provided in 'Ministry with the Dying' (APBA p. 700) is distinct from that in 'Ministry with the Sick' and, again, is only used 'if desired'. The form of the words point to the purpose:

> May he forgive you your sins
> and release you from suffering.
> May he deliver you from all evil
> preserve you in all goodness
> and bring you to everlasting life.

The sign of the cross may accompany the anointing, as the explanatory note in APBA (p. 706, Note 2) advises, this 'recalling our baptism into Christ'. The oil used for anointing the dying person may be that blessed by the bishop, usually during Holy Week, if readily available.

Whilst the anointing will be used in situations where it is apparent—or where the medical or other advice provided is—that death is imminent, it is possible that the person commended to God may recover. Sometimes the minister may be placed in a situation where it is unclear whether the appropriate prayer is for a return to physical health, what hope there is of such a return, or whether the pastoral imperative is to assist the person, and their family and friends, to prepare for death. It is always appropriate to commit a person to the care and keeping of God, whether the ultimate outcome is the healing and wholeness that comes through a good death in the faith of Christ, or a healing resulting in the continuance of earthly life.

**A note on assisted dying**

In November 2017 the Victorian Parliament passed the *Voluntary Assisted Dying Act 2017*. The passage of this Bill made Victoria the first state in Australia to legalise voluntary assisted dying. From mid-2019 Victorians who meet the strict eligibility criteria set out in the Act will be able to request access to voluntary assisted dying, if suffering from a terminal illness and approaching the end of their life. Consequently, Anglican ministers in Victoria may receive a request for ministry with a dying person who will end their life under the provisions of the state's assisted dying legislation. Those called upon to provide ministry in this situation may well share the ethical and theological concerns about the legislation that continue to be expressed by people of faith. Notwithstanding the gravity and importance of such concerns, the pastoral imperative will be to commend the dying person to God. Anglican ministers should respond to a request for ministry in these circumstances in the same way as they would for any dying person; or, if unable to, should advise the bishop and ask that another minister do so.

## 03   Reconciliation of a Penitent

The service for the 'Reconciliation of a Penitent' (APBA pp. 774–777) gathers up the biblical concepts of conversion, repentance and forgiveness, and castes them into a liturgical form for use by 'a priest' (only, as the rubric instructs) with an individual penitent. The explanatory note at APBA p. 774 sets out the biblical foundations, and its soteriological function and parameters, using clear and helpful language. It also notes that individual reconciliation is a valid part of the Anglican tradition, being allowed for in BCP at the point of the exhortations to Holy Communion and in the context of the rite for the 'Visitation of the Sick.' It is important to note that 'Reconciliation of a Penitent' is a private rite between a priest and individual penitent, to be distinguished from the public confession of sins and absolution that will take place at a service of Holy Communion and at other times.

For some Anglicans, including some clergy, the practise of individual confession may be a normative part of their spiritual discipline. There may be a priest whom they see at regular intervals for this purpose (traditionally described as their 'confessor'). Other Anglicans will never have been involved in this ministry. Ministers may choose to offer individual reconciliation for a number of reasons. In some communities, and among some clergy, the custom is to offer the ministry at particular times of the church year and especially during the penitential seasons of Lent and Advent, or it may be offered as part of a spiritual retreat. As *Faithfulness in Service* (4.27) advises, 'this service should normally be in a public place at advertised times or by arrangement.' Where the penitent is a child, the minister should only hear the confession in circumstances where there is an open space available and a clear line of sight to another adult.

The ministry of reconciliation may also be the appropriate response to a particular pastoral situation and/or the particular request of the penitent person. As APBA (p. 778, Note 1) notes, it is 'especially appropriate during illness' but is not, by any means, restricted to such times.

It is important to be aware that, in most civil legislation providing exemptions for clergy hearing confessions, the 'seal of the confessional' (see O3.2) will only apply in situations where an authorised liturgy of the church is used and in which it is clearly apparent to both the priest and the penitent that confession and absolution, in the context of reconciliation, is occurring. This can be marked by moving to a private space and the priest putting on a stole.

> *religious confession* means a confession made by a person to a member of the clergy in the member's professional capacity according to the ritual of the church or religious denomination concerned.[52]

As noted in the quotation from the Commonwealth 'uniform' Evidence Act ('uniform; because is it substantially replicated by most of the states and territories), an authorised liturgy such as that provided for in APBA must be used as a matter of both church and civil law. On some occasions, it may not be immediately clear or apparent that a pastoral 'encounter' or conversation is becoming a confession of sins for which the penitent may seek absolution. *Faithfulness in Service* offers helpful clarity: 'there is a distinction between disclosures made in ordinary pastoral situations and disclosures made as a confession, as provided in the applicable pastoral service in the Church's authorised liturgies' (4.27).

The liturgy provided for in APBA has the same flexibility and portability as the services for Ministry with the Sick and Ministry with the Dying, with the material capable of being selected and used, or not used, at the priest's discretion, and as may be appropriate to the circumstances. The actual confession of sins (APBA p. 776) may follow the form provided or be in the penitent's own words, although the absolution is prescribed ('the priest pronounces this Absolution'—APBA p. 776, # 7). The place in which the rite is conducted is left open. It may be a suitable space within a church, at the bedside in a clinical setting, or in a home. Whatever the locale, privacy will need to be assured.

---

52   This is the definition provided by the *Evidence Act 1995* (Cth) s 127(4).

## 03.1 Penance and absolution

It is important to note that true penitence requires both recognition of the need for forgiveness and amendment of life. It is not the case that every confession of sin is to be immediately followed by the pronouncement of absolution. The important rubric at APBA p. 776, # 5 advises that 'the priest may offer guidance, counsel and encouragement' following the penitent's confession. Sometimes it may be pastorally and spiritually appropriate or necessary for the penitent to perform some action, traditionally referred to as penance, prior to being absolved.

This may involve, for example, action required to remedy some wrong insofar as it is possible to do so, to forgive or to ask forgiveness of another person, or to report a crime committed to the appropriate authorities, both civil and ecclesial. In such situations, the absolution will normally be withheld, and may take place at a later time, after any act of penance required has been carried out.

The advice of the Australian bishops to clergy hearing a confession in circumstances whereby true contrition will require reporting to an appropriate authority, is that an assurance of God's forgiveness should not be offered at the time of hearing the confession. The bishops suggest wording such as the following be used:

> I am unable to offer the assurance of God's forgiveness until your contrition is shown by your reporting of this abuse to the appropriate authorities. It is best, if you do this, that I accompany you.
> If you are unwilling to report your behaviour, I will do so.

Absolution should only be pronounced when it is certain the matter has been reported to the appropriate authority or authorities (which may include both civil authorities such as the police, and church authorities such as a director of professional standards).

The ministry of reconciliation requires considerable pastoral acumen and awareness, and ideally, experience in such situations. Priests who may not have received any specific training or instruction in the area, or who may be undertaking the ministry for the first time, or for the first time in some years, should seek the counsel and advice of the bishop, or of a fellow priest with experience in hearing confessions.

O3.2 The 'seal of the confessional'

Questions may arise around what is often called the 'seal of the confessional,' especially in relation to both the civil law and canonical (or church) law. This can be an area of some uncertainty and complexity, giving rise to anxiety for ministers who are to hear confessions, especially in situations where it is known, or suspected, that the confession may involve the disclosure of a crime and/or some form of grave misconduct or abuse.

Canon law

The 'Canon concerning confessions 1989' contained a statement relating to what is often called 'the seal of the confessional.'

> If any person confess his or her secret and hidden sins to an ordained minister for the unburdening of conscience and to receive spiritual consolation and ease of mind, such minister shall not at any time reveal or make known any crime or offence or sin so confessed and committed to trust and secrecy by that person without the consent of that person.

This served to make the 'seal of the confessional' absolute, in common with practice in other Christian traditions.

It has not always been the case, however, that there was no possible exception to the absolute confidentiality of the confessional in Anglican formularies. The proviso to Canon 113 of the Code of 1603 permitted a single exception in circumstances where the sins confessed were such that 'by the laws of this realm' the life of the priest hearing them might be in danger 'for concealing the same.'[53] For example, a Church

---

53   Even if the exemption was never invoked, the historical fact is it exists.

of England minister who heard a confession of treason at the time this proviso was in force will not have been required to keep that confession confidential on the grounds that it may be a capital crime to do so, thus endangering the priest's own life. This single exception points to two important elements of the Anglican understanding of the confessional:

   a) it affirms in principle that confidentiality is extremely important and normative, and;
   b) it establishes, nonetheless, that an exception to the principle of confidentiality could be made under extraordinary and exceptional circumstances.

At this point, the Anglican understanding of the confessional is recognisably different from that of other Christian traditions, such as the Roman Catholic, in which the so-called 'seal of the confessional' is always absolute and allows no possible exceptions.

Following an extensive report by the Doctrine Commission, which considered in detail the matters summarised above, the 2017 session of the General Synod proposed two new canons containing amendments to the 1989 Canon concerning confessions, both of which were adopted by the 2017 General Synod and sent on to the individual dioceses for adoption. The two forms in which the canons were proposed reflects a diversity of theological and liturgical views on the nature of confession and absolution across the national church, and anticipates that, whilst all dioceses are likely to support a single, narrow exemption in relation to child sexual abuse, reflective of the proviso in the 1603 Canons, not all would be supportive of extending this more broadly to 'vulnerable persons.' The two canons promoted, and adopted, by the 2017 session of General Synod were:

A Bill for the Canon Concerning Confessions (Revision) Canon 2017 that amends the principal Canon to create an exception to the otherwise absolute requirement of confidentiality in relation to a 'grave offence,' and which defines a grave offence to mean 'child abuse' as defined in the National Register Canon 2007.

A Bill for the Canon Concerning Confessions (Vulnerable Persons) Canon 2017, which expands the definition of 'grave offence' to include abuse of a vulnerable person, and expands the exceptions to confidentiality to include non-criminal conduct that the priest hearing the confession might reasonably believe to put a vulnerable person at risk of significant harm.

The October 2017 session of the Synod of the Diocese of Melbourne adopted the 'Canon Concerning Confessions (Revision) Canon 2017' and it has been assented to by the Archbishop.[54] In effect, the Canon makes mandatory the advice of the Australian bishops referred to above (that an assurance of forgiveness is withheld until reporting to the appropriate authority), in situations where the confession concerns child abuse.

It is anticipated that one or both of these two General Synod canons will be considered by diocesan synods across the Anglican Church of Australia in the years immediately following the 2017 session of General Synod. All clergy, both within the Diocese of Melbourne and beyond it, should therefore make themselves aware of what status these two canons have in their diocese, especially if intending to offer the ministry of Reconciliation and/or if this ministry is requested of them. Because the General Synod resolved that both Canons should not be 'special bills', they are in force in the diocese in which they are duly passed by the diocesan Synod immediately upon gaining the assent of the diocesan bishop, and do not need to return to a subsequent session of General Synod for any further ratification.

### Civil law

The situation in relation to the civil law varies across the different jurisdictions of the Commonwealth, with the six states and two territories each having their own legislation in relation to any exemption at law provided

---

54   The 'Canon Concerning Confessions (Vulnerable Persons) Canon 2017' was not considered by the 2017 session of the Melbourne diocesan Synod.

to priests hearing confessions. In some places the existing legislation is being actively reviewed in the light of the Royal Commission into institutional responses to child sexual abuse, which completed its public hearings, and handed down its recommendations, during the course of 2017.

As the legal situation varies across Australia, clergy will need to become aware of the civil law that applies in their context, as it relates to the 'seal of the confessional'. Even so, the better, and more theologically- and spiritually-aware approach, is to be guided by the 'moral law' rather than to rely on the provisions of any civil law. As noted above, the canon adopted at the 2017 session of the Melbourne diocesan Synod removes the 'seal of the confessional' in instances where the confession concerns a 'grave offence' involving child abuse, unless that grave offence has been reported to the police and, if the person is a church worker or a member of the clergy, to the Director of Professional Standards or other relevant Church authority. This applies regardless of any protections or exemptions available in the civil law. For priests of the Anglican Church of Australia, canon law takes precedence in such situations, as does the moral duty to protect the vulnerable and abused, ahead of the spiritual comfort and rights of the abuser.

Even where canon law does not apply, the moral duty to report a crime as an appropriate act of penance will normally result in the withholding of absolution, even if the nature of the crime being confessed lies outside of the exceptions provided for in the canon law in force. In circumstances where the absolute confidentiality of the confessional will still apply, the priest will rely on the penitent to make the offence known, possibly at pain of withholding absolution until such time as this occurs.

The penitent should always be made aware of the priest's obligations before the confession is made.

In most cases you should tell someone who is to give you confidential information of the limits to confidentiality and the arrangements for supervision or obtaining advice. This should be done before the disclosure of the confidential information, such as at the beginning of an interview (*Faithfulness in Service* 4.25).

This can be achieved by the priest as part of the introductory rite to any confession, making it clear to the penitent that, in some circumstances, absolution may be withheld pending an appropriate act of contrition and penance, which may include reporting of a crime to one or both of the civil or church authorities; and, that in some further circumstances (which the priest can then define according to the canons in force in that diocese), the priest will be obliged to make a report to the relevant authorities and the 'seal of the confessional' will not apply, unless the matter has been, or until such time as the matter is reported to the relevant civil and/or church authority.

## 04   Abuse and misconduct

The Christian Church as a whole, including the Anglican Church of Australia, has been greatly affected by the harrowing testimony of survivors, and other revelations, arising out of the Royal Commission into Institutional Responses to Child Sexual Abuse, and deeply shamed by the recent and historic failures of the church to protect the vulnerable. The Liturgical Commission (General Synod) has developed resources to assist the pastoral response of the church and church workers in situations where the disclosure of misconduct impacts on the whole community.

### 04.1   A Litany following sexual abuse

A litany, intended for use in communal contexts, has been developed by the Liturgical Commission for situations where a community is seeking to come to terms with the disclosure of sexual misconduct or abuse, and is available on the General Synod website.
https://www.anglican.org.au/data/Litany_following_sexual_abuse.pdf

The explanatory note sets out the purpose of the litany: 'Following the disclosure of sexual misconduct or abuse by a church worker, not only the individual offended against, but also the communities of the survivor and the offender have pastoral needs which may call for appropriate liturgical resources. For example, in the early stages of the community's journey, feelings of hurt, anger, and shock must be recognised and given expression. The community's dependence on God for present help and future healing needs to be affirmed. This litany is intended for use at this stage. It is for the church community rather than for an individual.'

## 04.2 A prayer for healing after sexual misconduct

The Liturgical Commission have provided a further prayer for healing following sexual misconduct or abuse by a church worker that is specific to 'thanksgiving for support and healing already received by the survivor of misconduct or abuse, and on the survivor's continuing trust in God'. The liturgy is not intended for use at large, public occasions, but by a smaller group limited to those invited to be present by the survivor. https://www.anglican.org.au/data/Prayer_for_healing_after_sexual_misconduct.pdf

Detailed introductory notes preface the service. These should be carefully consulted, and followed, by the person or persons (who may be ordained or lay) responsible for planning the service in conjunction with the survivor.

## 04.3 The prayer for a companion to a person who has been abused

Recognising the significant spiritual strain placed on those who are accompanying, and pastorally supporting, a person who has been abused, the Liturgical Commission have provided two prayers for pastoral carers in this situation.

https://www.anglican.org.au/data/Prayer_of_a_companion_to_a_person_who_has_been_abused.pdf

## 05   The Blessing of a Home

The custom of blessing a home is an ancient one to be warmly encouraged. It is widely practised in Roman Catholic, Orthodox and Lutheran traditions, as well as among many Anglican and other Christian communities. The Episcopal Church (United States) provides a liturgy for the 'Celebration of a home' in its Book of Occasional Services 1994 (New York: Church House Publishing, 1995) with antiphons, psalms and prayers for each room of the house, culminating with a general blessing for the home. A Zealand Prayer Book (p. 762) also contains a liturgy for blessing a home.

The custom of Epiphany-tide house blessings finds its source in the visit of the magi to the home of the child Jesus—'On entering the house, they saw the child with Mary his mother; and they knelt down and paid him homage. Then, opening their treasure-chests, they offered him gifts of gold, frankincense, and myrrh' (Matthew 2.11). The Epiphany blessing may sometimes be performed by the residents themselves, and accompanied by 'chalking the door' or lintel of the door with the relevant year, and sometimes accompanying symbols, depending on local custom.

When a minister is called upon to conduct the blessing of home, a range of ritual acts may accompany the prayers and invocations of God's blessing on the home and its residents. These may include ritual sprinkling with holy water (asperges), lighting and carrying a candle, and incense. The blessing may take the form of prayers said in each room of the house as desired by the residents, or be as simple as an ex tempore prayer said by the minister in one place.

Requests for this ministry from those who are not normally members of a worshipping community may be made for a variety of reasons and sometimes because it is felt something may not be 'right' about the house. It is prudent for the minister to establish as much information as possible in advance of attending an unknown situation, and to always bring a second person with them in such circumstances.

## O6 Exorcism

The tradition of the early church, which continues to be observed to the present day, requires that any requests or possible needs for the ministry of exorcism should always be referred to the bishop for advice and direction about the appropriate pastoral response.

## Canon Concerning Confessions (Revision) Canon 2017

A Canon concerning confessions.

Whereas every confession to an ordained minister is heard in the context of the desire of the penitent to be reconciled to God, to the fellowship of the church, and to those who have been harmed by the penitent's sin:

The General Synod prescribes as follows—

1. This canon may be cited as 'Canon concerning confessions 1989'.
2. Subject to section 2A, if any person confess his or her secret and hidden sins to an ordained minister for the unburdening of conscience and to receive spiritual consolation and ease of mind, such minister shall not at any time reveal or make known any crime or offence or sin so confessed and committed to trust and secrecy by that person without the consent of that person.

2A. (1) In this section—

**abuse** means sexual assault, sexual exploitation or physical abuse; child means a person under the age of 18 years;

**child abuse** has the same meaning as in the National Register Canon 2007;

**Church authority** has the same meaning as in the National Register Canon 2007;

**church worker** has the same meaning as in the National Register Canon 2007;

**clergy** has the same meaning as in the National Register Canon 2007;

**Director of Professional Standards** has the same meaning as in the National Register Canon 2007;

**grave offence** means conduct that amounts to a criminal offence against the laws of the Commonwealth, a State or Territory, or another country which is equivalent to a criminal offence of the Commonwealth, a State or Territory involving child abuse;

**ordained minister** has the same meaning as clergy;

**penitent** means a person who makes a confession to an ordained minister;

**police** means the Australian Federal Police or the police service of a State or Territory of Australia;

(2) Subject to subsection (3), where a penitent confesses to an ordained minister that he or she has or may have committed a grave offence, that ordained minister is obliged to keep confidential the grave offence so confessed if he or she is reasonably satisfied that the penitent has reported the grave offence to the police and, if the person is a church worker or a member of the clergy, to the Director of Professional Standards or other relevant Church authority.

(3) An ordained minister to whom a penitent has confessed that he or she has or may have committed a grave offence may, for the purpose of obtaining advice as to whether that conduct constitutes a grave offence, reveal the nature of

that confession to a person nominated by the bishop of the diocese for the purpose of giving that advice.

(4) It is a defence to a charge of breach of discipline or any offence brought against an ordained minister, arising from his or her disclosure to any person of conduct confessed by a penitent that did not constitute a grave offence, that the ordained minister believed in good faith and on reasonable grounds that the conduct may have constituted a grave offence. The proviso to canon numbered 113 of the Canons of 1603, and any other law of this Church concerning the making of confessions to an ordained minister, in so far as the same may have any force, shall have no operation or effect in this Church.

4. The provisions of this canon affect the order and good government of this Church within a diocese and shall not come into force in a diocese unless and until the diocese adopts this canon by ordinance of the synod of the diocese.

## General resources online

The Anglican Church of Australia
   https://www.anglican.org.au/

Faithfulness in Service as adopted by General Synod
   https://www.anglican.org.au/prevention

The Liturgy Commission—General Synod
   https://www.anglican.org.au/liturgy-worship

The Doctrine Commission—General Synod
   https://www.anglican.org.au/doctrine-theology

The Constitution and Canons of the Anglican Church of Australia
   http://www.anglican.org.au/governance/Pages/canons_of_general_synod.aspx

The Anglican Diocese of Melbourne
  http://www.melbourneanglican.org.au/Pages/Anglican-Diocese-of-Melbourne.aspx

The Bishop Perry Institute for Ministry and Mission
  https://bishopperryinstitute.org.au/

Common Worship—The Church of England
  https://www.churchofengland.org/prayer-worship/worship/texts.aspx

The Anglican Communion
  http://www.anglicancommunion.org/identity/about.aspx

# Appendix One

## A sample parish policy for pastoral services

It is recommended that parishes, authorised congregations and other worship communities develop a policy for pastoral services, worked out in accordance with the principles outlined in this Handbook. Such a policy, owned and agreed to by the parish council, can assist in guiding those involved in receiving requests for, and conducting, pastoral services, and ensure a consistency of approach, especially in circumstances where significant numbers of pastoral services are experienced.

The sample policy provided here is intended as a template that can be adapted to suit the custom, approach and decisions reached at local level. Whilst some options are given, not every situation or eventuality, nor every possibility, is covered. The sample policy is intended as a starting point.

Pastoral services policy
For the parish of (name of parish)
Adopted by the Parish Council on (date)

Preamble

Pastoral ministry is an integral part of the whole ministry of the people of God. In a parish setting, pastoral ministry is the responsibility of both the clergy and laity working as a team to effectively reach out to, nurture, and care for those who seek the pastoral services of the church. To facilitate effective pastoral ministry, and to guide those seeking pastoral services in our context, and those conducting them, the parish council have adopted the following policy.

1. Definitions

1.1   The term 'pastoral services' here relates to the preparation and conduct of the pastoral offices contained in A Prayer Book for Australia 1995. These are, principally, the services of Christian initiation (in particular baptisms and confirmations), weddings and funerals.

1.2   In this context 'pastoral services' are distinct from 'pastoral ministry', which encompasses much more than the preparation and conduct of services.

1.3   Usually requests for services such as a baptism, wedding or funeral will come to the clergy or be directed to the clergy, and the service conducted by the vicar // or assistant curate // assistant clergy.

1.4   The preparation and conduct of pastoral services are, however, the shared responsibility of the parish as a whole, and of the clergy, churchwardens, and parish council in particular. For a large number of people today, the initial or only contact they will ever have with a church community is through the exercising of one of the pastoral services. It is essential then, that our response commend the Gospel and our parish community to all who come to us.

## 2. Baptism and Confirmation

2.1  All requests for Holy Baptism and/or Confirmation in the parish will be directed, in the first instance, to the vicar // the parish office.

2.2  Preparation is conducted by the vicar or the vicar's delegate.

2.3  The Service

   i. Baptisms will be conducted at a time and place determined by the vicar in consultation with those bringing the person for baptism. This will normally be during the course of a regular Sunday service.

   ii. In some exceptional circumstances, a baptism may take place outside of a service of worship, for instance, if an emergency baptism. In such situations, the parent/s and/or godparents of a child baptised will be required to attend a service of worship on a Sunday at which time the certificates will be presented and the 'Welcome' liturgy conducted.

2.4  Fees

The gospel sacraments of Holy Baptism and Holy Communion should never be subject to fees, and any freewill offerings in connection with them will go into parish funds.

## 3. Weddings

3.1 All requests for weddings in the parish are directed, in the first instance, to the vicar.

3.2 Preparation is conducted by the vicar or the vicar's delegate // the couple are referred to Lifeworks for preparation // another approach.

3.3 Fees.

   i. Church Fee ($)
   This provides for the use of the church for the rehearsal and the wedding ceremony, the provision of flowers inside the church, and the preparation and lodging of all necessary forms and certificates

   ii. 'Authorised Celebrant' Fee ($), to be paid directly to the cleric who conducts the service // paid into parish funds.

   iii. Organist Fee ($), paid directly to the organist and/or other musician or musicians.

   iv. The vicar, in conversation with a couple preparing for marriage, may choose to waive the 'authorised celebrant' and/or church fee for pastoral reasons, and where one or both of the persons being married are regular members of the congregation, or closely related to a regular member of the congregation.

3.4 Flowers
Flowers will be provided by the parish and will be the floral arrangements normally present in the church on Sundays. Those

normally rostered on to arrange flowers will be contacted and advised of the time and date of the wedding to assist in their preparation and may call on others more experienced to help them. The couple concerned may indicate preferences for the type and colour of the flowers. Any additional floral arrangements desired (such as floral arrangements on the end of the pews) will be at the expense of, and organised by, the couple being married.

3.5 Requests for the conduct of weddings by clergy from outside of the parish

From time to time requests are made for persons other than the parish clergy to conduct weddings. The following policy reflects generally accepted clerical etiquette.

i. Normally the vicar // or assistant curate // associate clergy will conduct all weddings within the parish. Other options should not be offered and only canvassed if specifically raised by the enquirer.

ii. In some circumstances, the vicar may invite another cleric holding the Archbishop's license to assist in the wedding ceremony and/or conduct the service, where a genuine pastoral reason for doing so exists.

iii. Ministers ordained in Christian traditions other than the Anglican Church are unable to conduct pastoral services in an Anglican Church, however may be invited by the vicar to participate if requested to do so.

## 4. Funerals

4.1     Pastoral responsibility of the parish

The exercise of funeral ministry occurs at a time of personal loss for the family and friends of the deceased who are involved in the preparation and conduct of the service. It will be essential for a parish policy, and for all involved with the conduct and planning of the service, to maintain a genuine concern and compassion for the bereaved that properly reflects the nature of Gospel ministry, and to pray for them in private and, if appropriate, in the public intercessions.

4.2     Requests for the conduct of funerals in the parish will be directed to the vicar // parish office, or if the vicar is unavailable, the assistant curate.

4.3     Preparation for the service will be conducted by the cleric who will preside in consultation with the family and friends of the deceased.

4.4     Fees.

    i. Fees payable to the parish are applied by the Funeral Director (not by the parish) and included within the total cost of the funeral.

    ii. Where the funeral service is that of a member of the parish, or a close relative of a member of the parish, no parish related fees will be applied // the church fee will be waived.

4.5.     Flowers

Flowers will be those provided by the parish for Sunday services unless other arrangements are made.

4.6    Requests for the conduct of funerals by clergy from outside of the parish

Any requests for persons other than the parish clergy to conduct a funeral will be directed to the vicar. The sensitive nature of funeral ministry demands that such requests be treated flexibly and with appropriate discretion and compassion for the needs of the bereaved. The vicar will respond on a case-by-case basis.

4.7    Masonic and RSL services

The parish has no objection to including the Masonic and/or RSL rites at the point of the committal, if this is the express wish of the family of the deceased // the parish does not allow for the inclusion of Masonic and/or RSL rites in the church building at any point in the funeral service // another policy as agreed to.

4.8    The Interment of Ashes in the Memorial Garden (if applicable). The cremated ashes of those whose funerals have taken place in the church and/or a worship centre in the parish; or whose funerals were conducted by one of the clergy of the parish / may be interred in the memorial garden at the request of the family or executor of the deceased person. Optional—(Requests for the interment of ashes in the parish memorial garden of other deceased persons may be made to the vicar and will be at the vicar's discretion / in consultation with the churchwardens)

# Appendix Two

## Pastoral Offices and Surplice Fees policy

This policy for the payment of surplice fees was agreed to by the Senior Staff of the Diocese of Melbourne in December 2014, and replaces any and all previous policies on this matter, whether implied or expressed.

**Background**

1. **Definitions**

In this paper the term 'pastoral offices' refers to weddings and funerals (and memorial services). 'Surplice fees' means the fees paid to the clergyperson by the recipients of these Offices as distinct from other charges that may be made for the use of church facilities or the employment of additional people.

2. **History**

We inherited from the Church of England the notion that when a priest is inducted to a living he is entitled both to his stipend and all surplice fees for pastoral offices conducted in the parish, no matter by whom they are conducted.

In England that situation no longer applies. Stipends are paid centrally, and surplice fees (when retained by the priest) are deducted from the amount paid from the central source, or else they are remitted to the central paying body which then pays the normal stipend to the priest.

3. Diversity

There is great diversity in the Anglican Church of Australia with respect to surplice fees. The number of pastoral offices conducted varies greatly from parish to parish. Some incumbents retain surplice fees as a part of their personal income; some pay them into parish funds; some use them as discretionary funds, retaining control over them but not treating them as personal income. Some disclose to churchwardens and vestries how they handle surplice fees. There is also diversity with respect to non-parochial clergy, particularly with funerals. Some clergy virtually act as 'chaplains' to funeral directors and gain considerable income thereby.

4. What are the issues?

a. It can be tempting to see pastoral offices primarily as a source of income rather than ministry to people for the sake of the kingdom of God.

b. There can be an imbalance in the time devoted to pastoral offices and that given to other aspects of ministry.

c. There can be considerable inequalities of income among the clergy, which may bear no relation to quantity of work or effectiveness of ministry.

d. Concentration on a 'funeral chaplaincy' ministry may be a genuine and needed form of ministry, but it may not be fair for a parish (particularly a poor and struggling one) to be asked to pay a full stipend to a priest who has a large income from that ministry which makes severe inroads into his or her time for parish ministry.

e. On the other hand, if clergy work hard and effectively at pastoral offices without financial recognition of their labours, they may be tempted to neglect this important part of Christian ministry.

5. **Principles**

   a. The pastoral offices are to be administered with reverence and care, so that they are in every case a faithful expression of the gospel of Christ.

   b. They are to be seen as pastoral and evangelistic opportunities, with careful preparation, instruction and follow-up.

   c. They are an integral part of a priest's ministry, neither being neglected nor taking so much time that other important aspects of the ministry are neglected.

   d. The mode of conducting them should be such as to make them genuinely personal to the individuals and families concerned.

   e. Arrangements with respect to offerings and fees for pastoral offices should be such as on the one hand to reflect their character as means of grace and on the other hand to acknowledge the cost to the priest and the church.

   f. The gospel sacraments of baptism and Holy Communion should never be subject to fees, and any freewill offerings in connection with them should go into parish funds.

   g. Surplice fees should be clearly distinguished from charges relating to the use of church facilities or the employment of other people, for example, musicians, verger, cleaners.

h. A priest is always free to dispense with surplice fees in particular cases.

## Policy

Because of the great variety of circumstances it is not practicable to lay down a rigid rule for the application of surplice fees.

However the following guidelines apply:

1. Any arrangement about Surplice Fees should be discussed with and agreed to by the Wardens.

2. Full-time Stipendiary Clergy should direct surplice fees to either regular Parish income or a parish discretionary fund.*

3. Part-Time Stipendiary, Non-Stipendiary and Retired Clergy may retain the Surplice Fee as income.

4. If agreed with the Wardens, Surplice Fees (or a portion thereof) to be retained by the Cleric must pass through the Parish accounts and be acknowledged on the Master Remuneration Form.

*Parish Discretionary Funds may be used for any purpose a parish sees fit (for example, helping the poor, new ministry initiatives, theological students, study aids, conferences), and would require two signatories. Note: In particular cases, where the number of pastoral offices is unusually large, this may lead to appropriate arrangements, for example, the employment of additional staff funded (at least in part) by the fees, or the allocation of part of the fees to the priest's stipend (for example, where a 'funeral chaplaincy' occupies a large part of the priest's time). These are matters that should be discussed, and some understanding reached with the Churchwardens, at the time of appointment.

## Taxation

Naturally, clergy are bound to ensure that all their financial arrangements meet the requirements of taxation law. If surplice fees are retained by the priest, they must be declared as part of taxable income.

## Recommended Fees

The Diocesan recommendation for surplice fees for a Wedding or a Funeral is between $250 and $300.

Other fees: Parishes may charge other fees for other aspects of the Pastoral Services. Some Parishes only charge to recoup actual costs, viewing the church as a community facility that is available for all. However if fees are charged, the following is a suggestion:

| | |
|---|---|
| Church Use | $100–$300 |
| Verger | $100–$150 |
| Organist | $250–300+ GST |
| | (recommended by the Society of Organists) |
| Flowers | At cost |
| Printing | At cost |

It is best if these fees are itemised by the Funeral Director for a funeral, or by the Church for a wedding.

It is recommended that fees may be waived for members of the Parish for Pastoral offices. Remember that waiving a fee for a Funeral Director, may not necessarily be refunded to the family concerned, especially when the funeral has been pre-paid. An alternative (for example, returning the fee direct to the family, assisting them with some other cost, or clearly letting them know how it will be spent) may be the preferred course of action.

**Ratified—4 December 2014**

www.ingramcontent.com/pod-product-compliance
Lightning Source LLC
Chambersburg PA
CBHW020106020526
44112CB00033B/1019